W9-AFV-043

ROSA MEXICANO

BY JOSEFINA HOWARD
WITH LILA LOMELI

TRANSLATED BY ESTHER ALLEN

VIKING

VIKING
Published by the Penguin Group
Penguin Putnam Inc., 375 Hudson Street, New York, New York 10014, U.S.A.
Penguin Books Ltd, 27 Wrights Lane, London W8 5TZ, England
Penguin Books Australia Ltd, Ringwood, Victoria, Australia
Penguin Books Canada Ltd, 10 Alcorn Avenue, Toronto, Ontario, Canada M4V 3B2
Penguin Books (N.Z.) Ltd, 182–190 Wairau Road, Auckland 10, New Zealand
Penguin India, 210 Chiranjiv Tower, 43 Nehru Place, New Delhi 11009, India

Penguin Books Ltd, Registered Offices: Harmondsworth, Middlesex, England

First published in 1998 by Viking Penguin, a member of Penguin Putnam Inc.

10 9 8 7 6 5 4 3 2 1

Translation by Esther Allen

Grateful acknowledgment is made for permission to use the following copyrighted works:
"Leave-taking" from *Collected Poems* by Federico García Lorca, translated by Christopher Maurer. Translation copyright © 1991 by Christopher Maurer. Reprinted by permission of Farrar, Straus & Giroux, Inc.
Cartoon by Barney Tobey. © 1978 from The New Yorker Collection. All rights reserved.
"Breve diccionario de los chiles y otros picantes" from *El chile y otros picantes* by Arturo Lomeli Escalante, published by Colección Biblioteca del Consumidor. By permission of the author.

ISBN 0-670-87947-9

CIP data available

This book is printed on acid-free paper.

Printed in the United States of America
Set in Bodoni Old Face

DESIGNED BY JAYE ZIMET

TO RUPERTO CANTOR, MY HEAD CHEF,

WHO FOR EIGHTEEN YEARS HAS SUPPORTED ME

IN MY OBSESSION TO BRING MEXICAN FOOD

TO WHERE IT BELONGS

—J.H.

ACKNOWLEDGMENTS

To my son Anthony, with love.

I have so many people to thank I don't know where to start. But let me begin with my three partners because, after all, without them there would be no Rosa Mexicano. I thank them for their patience with my tenacity. Thank you, Dan Hickey, Doug Grible, and Nicos Pharasles. Next, Leonard Lopate and Theresa Thompson for their constant sharing and exchanging of ideas and opinions. And to Gloria Lajous for the same reasons. Thanks to the staff of Aeroméxico for helping me plan many, many trips and to the great pilots who helped take away my fear of flying. And special thanks to Canirac (Mexican Association of Restaurants) and Roberto Gonzales for recognizing my efforts to acquaint people with Mexican cuisine. Thanks also to the Mexican Consulate and the Mexican Cultural Institute for their support, and to the Mexico City Museum of Anthropology for letting me photograph the Tlatelolco market.

The first time I was on Martha Stewart's television program, I received a call from the restaurant: "Come over quickly, we're having Martha Stewart madness." There was a line halfway around the block. You can imagine what that does for business. Thank you, Martha.

And of course to Laura Esquivel, who grasped so well the way I feel that I was moved to tears by what she wrote. To Lila Lomeli, my friend, collaborator, and partner in this venture, and to Arturo Lomeli, her husband, for lending Lila to me and for his wonderful chile dictionary. To Esther Allen for her excellent translation.

To Barbara and Justin Kerr for reading and correcting the anthropological facts, and Charles Goirand for the beautiful furniture at the restaurant. To Amelia Durand, Myra Dalland, and Rory Rodner for their constant support and encouragement. To Michele Gilardi for testing and writing the recipes.

And now the best of all. To the staff at Rosa Mexicano who have followed my vision with love and dedication. My gratitude to them for helping me have the type of restaurant where the kitchen and the dining room don't fight.

And of course without whose effort this book would not be, to Dawn Drzal, Barbara Grossman, Patti Kelly, Theodora Rosenbaum, Roseanne Serra, Jariya Wanapun, Jaye Zimet, and all of the people who helped me at Viking.

For all the customers of Rosa Mexicano and, above all, the people of Mexico.

CONTENTS

INTRODUCTION

In addition to being good friends, Josefina Howard and I share a nationality. You might wonder how such a thing can be, since Josefina is not Mexican and I am, but that doesn't matter in the least. You are what you eat, who you eat it with, and how you eat it. Nationality isn't determined by where you are born, but by the tastes and smells that stay with you from childhood. Nationality has to do with land—not some petty idea of territorial borders and boundaries, but something deeper. It has to do with the foods the land bestows on us, their chemistry, and their effects on our bodies. The biological compounds in foods we eat penetrate our cells and impregnate them with their innermost flavors. They slip into the deepest corners of our unconscious, there where the events of the past make their nests and curl up forever in our memories.

Is it true that only someone who was born in Mexico and grew up eating tortillas can be Mexican? No, of course not. There are certain exceptional beings who are capable of arriving in an unknown city and, like children, letting themselves be suckled by cultures that are not theirs from birth. Josefina is such a being. Her vocation for universality allowed her to open herself up to the world of smells and flavors of a Mexico she made her own, and Mexico reciprocated by adopting her as its own legitimate daughter.

The fraternity of the hearth is one of the strongest bonds. When you walk into a place and immediately recognize the fragrances wafting from a pot of beans, some freshly made tortillas, or even just a simple guacamole, you know you are on a tiny patch of Mexican soil. This was my experience the first time I visited Josefina's restaurant, Rosa Mexicano. I was immediately transported back to Mexico, to food cooked with passion, food Josefina has dedicated her life to praising and celebrating. Like any self-respecting Mexican woman, Josefina left Mexico carrying her little trove of chiles and homemade tortillas for her nostalgia to feed on. And not only that; driven by her desire to share our cuisine's wealth of flavors with others, she was brave enough to start a restaurant in the very heart of Manhattan. At Rosa Mexicano, you can regale yourself with dishes that run the gamut from sophisticated to simple, from traditional to innovative.

In this book, Josefina not only shares her recipes and her past with us in the most delicious way; she also invites us along on a joyful journey through the infinite possibilities and combinations offered by Mexican culinary culture.

Josefina has a lesson for us, a lesson of solidarity and understanding among peoples. Only this solidarity can allow us to share hearths, meals, joys, and sorrows–the joys of festive gatherings and daily life, and the sorrows of life's most difficult and painful moments: death and loss. With this solidarity, we can ultimately make the whole world sit down at the table with us and share what makes us human and what gives us a homeland and a nationality, an unending legacy of past flavors and smells: the nationality of food, which is both a nationality and a universal heritage. So, beloved friends, let's clink our shots of tequila together and drink to Mexican food, to Rosa Mexicano, and to Josefina, the Mexican.

–Laura Esquivel

PROLOGUE

The guests at my restaurant, Rosa Mexicano, have often come over to the booth where I have spent most evenings for the past fifteen years to congratulate and thank me for the good food they enjoyed. Sometimes, though, I wonder if they realize that in addition to serving them wonderful food I also want to offer them an educational experience. When you've lived in Mexico you can learn a lot about people and their ways of doing and looking at things. One of the things that fascinated me most about Mexico was the food. And I'm far from being the only person to have experienced that fascination.

Toward the second half of the nineteenth century, there were a number of elegant French restaurants and bakeries in Mexico City, owned and operated by skilled European chefs and bakers. Two of them were particularly outstanding—one, the restaurant known as the Casa Deverdum and the other run by the family of the Widow Genin. The chefs of both establishments expressed their enthusiasm for Mexican cookery in no uncertain terms.

Alfred L. Deverdum published a Mexican cookbook in his native France in 1921. Some years later, he also wrote several articles in praise of Mexican food for a Mexican weekly called *El Gastrónomo* and for an important newspaper that is still published today, *El Universal.* The Genin family's eldest son, Auguste, offspring of a Belgian father and a French mother, wrote the prologue to Monsieur Deverdum's book. Here are a few lines that he wrote in tribute to Mexican cooking:

> *All men eat, but only the French know how to eat. In this respect, Mexicans are very French. Indeed, Mexico is among the few countries whose national dishes stand out for their high degree of flavor, their particular use of condiments and their sophistication. The French eat snails and the Chinese eat swallows' nests; I don't think a snail has a better appearance than a maguey worm. . . . When a poll, as they call it nowadays, was conducted a few years ago on world gastronomy, it was found that outside of France, Mexico was one of the three countries on the globe where there exists a culinary tradition worthy of adding something to* De Re Coquinaria, *the famous collection of recipes from the third century A.D. ascribed to Apicius.*

In telling the story that follows, which is part of my life, I would like to pay homage to the greatness of Mexican cooking and the thousands of individuals through the centuries who have created, developed, and loved it, not only for how good it tastes but also for all the extraordinary cultural significance that it embodies. In Mexico I've found pure, unique, and extraordinary flavors that represent, for me, the last frontier of the palate: a cuisine full of possibilities and surprises that has inspired in me an undying passion.

The Mexican food with which I started this romance was part of a culture that is now on the point of vanishing. In Mexico, too, flavors have changed to make cooking more convenient with less physical effort. For centuries, sauces were ground up in a *molcajete,* a stone mortar in which ingredients were crushed with a pestle called a *tejolote* and mixed in their own juices. For many years now home cooks and professionals have been using blenders, which, since they chop rather than crush, produce quite a different consistency. Technology has replaced the human hand in other cases as well, most notably for the corn dough known as *masa* and the tortillas that are made from it. Life is easier for millions of Mexican women because the corn for masa is ground by machines and tortillas are mass-produced. Of course, the taste and texture are not the same.

It's taken quite a while to decide to write this book, but I think the moment has finally come to clear up some mistaken ideas and prejudices about Mexican cooking, and to talk about some of the things I've experienced in a country that often seems so far away—though it's only separated from us by a line on the map. In recent years, a public that is increasingly eager to enjoy fine Mexican cooking has emerged in the United States. Still, there are some people who, for reasons I have a hard time accepting, continue to scorn and ignore it. Once, I was invited to the opening of a show by a very well-known painter in a New York gallery. When I arrived, the host introduced me to a group of people. At the moment, the profession of chef is quite chic and socially acceptable in New York society, and even more so if you happen to be the owner or co-owner of a restaurant. The people around me were extremely friendly and sugar-sweet. The first question they asked was, "Where is your restaurant?"

"At First Avenue and Fifty-eighth Street," I answered, trying not to name the elegant neighborhood where Rosa Mexicano is located. "Oh, Sutton

Place. How nice!" someone said. Then came the inevitable question, "What kind of food do you serve?" I got ready for the response I knew was coming. "Mexican food," I answered. The reaction was exactly as I had feared: an empty space opened up around me. Some of them even turned their backs. This was just one of many occasions when I wasn't given the chance to say anything more about the kind of food I cook—fine, authentic Mexican food.

Lack of information is a large part of the problem. Many food writers barely mention the great contributions made by the New World to the eating habits of the entire globe. They forget to add that among the Aztecs, who had one of the most highly developed indigenous cultures of Mesoamerica, unusual and fascinating flavors were created and combined to produce an extraordinary cuisine. The fast-food and canned-food industries have also done their part to reinforce the knowledge barrier. The "Mexican" products they make and sell use only a few inexpensive ingredients, and don't come close to reflecting the breadth and variety of Mexican cooking. For example, when many people hear the word *enchilada,* they think of a tortilla filled with chicken and covered with a fiery hot sauce. But in true Mexican cuisine, a soft tortilla can be filled with crab or duck and served with a delicate green sauce made from pumpkin seeds and spices, a dish that is worlds away from the Tex-Mex experience. While there has been a general lack of information and mistaken ideas have been disseminated to the United States public, I must acknowledge the important work of Josefina Velázquez de León, Elizabeth Lambert Ortiz, Diana Kennedy, and, in recent years, a group of Mexican women who have promoted Mexican food by emphasizing its visual appeal.

In order to work with Mexican ingredients, you must return to the ancestral experience and culinary knowledge of the peoples who formed the Aztec empire, which influenced the entire region known as Mesoamerica. Their foods were prepared with specific herbs that were used not only for their taste but also as digestive aids, in precise combinations with different chiles, mushrooms, vegetables, and meats. The cooks of those times wisely understood that food was meant to be a pleasure in the mouth and a comfort for the stomach.

The words *spicy* and *hot* have somehow become inextricably linked to Mexican cuisine. Many people think that they know Mexican food and won't believe that any dish that doesn't scorch the mouth is "real" Mexican food. They think the chiles in every dish should leave them gasping, and if the food they are served doesn't use chiles to that degree, they claim it must be condescending to U.S. tastes. In fact, the variety of Mexican dishes is such that I can assure you without exaggeration that you could try a different dish every day of the year without ever eating anything that included chiles. Like most cross-cultural confusions, the idea that Mexican food scorches the mouth is not entirely without a basis in reality. There are some Mexicans who dearly love to eat fiery hot food. Soon after I first moved to Mexico City, I was invited to a restaurant by a nice Mexican executive. I watched as he ate a chile; pearls of sweat formed on his bald pate. "It's because we Mexicans love to suffer!" he explained.

Chiles are always a challenge. Often I've been served a dish with the promise that it wasn't very hot and then found it to be painfully so. At other times, a dish that was supposed to be ultraspicy didn't bother me at all. I've come to the conclusion that the degree of spiciness in a given food is a fairly subjective matter. Just as I enjoy a brisk chill wind but can't bear the heat of summer, the spiciness of chiles has to do with individual sensibilities and habits. What doesn't bother some people at all can be devastating to others. The hotness of a given chile is also variable; one chile can turn out to be hotter than another even though the two were harvested from the same field or plant. When I'm asked if a dish is spicy, I always tell people how one apple can be sweeter than another that grew on the same tree. And, of course, it has to be taken into account that hot chile can become addictive and therefore is not only a passing sensation.

Another misperception of Mexican food has to do with frying. I've sometimes heard people on television shows in the United States refer to a "greasy taco." In fact, fat is used in moderation in the best Mexican cooking. As everyone knows, fat adds flavor. But in Mexican cooking, the flavors come primarily from herbs and pureed sauces that include vegetables, grains, nuts, seeds, and toasted spices. Moreover, as every good cook knows, if food is fried correctly it doesn't become greasy. Fine Mexican food is neither hot nor greasy. Over the course of almost five centuries, Iberian and French influences have melded with the Mesoamerican base to produce a distinct yet subtle cuisine, one in which the use of spices is wonderfully balanced. Some dishes include several spices, but always in restrained quantities, and in classic Mexican recipes the spices are blended in such a way that one doesn't dominate the others. Mexican cuisine provides a perfectly healthy and digestible diet. It has its own special techniques, limitless flavors and colors, and endless possibilities for new taste combinations.

I've been shocked and saddened by the way timeless Mexican recipes are sometimes interpreted. Some cooks try to enhance them by adding what they believe to be a higher class of ingredients. But this intrusion disrupts the perfection and balance of recipes perfected over many generations. The addition of ingredients that don't blend in devalues and falsifies the intelligence of the original dish. With regard to such tampering, I remember the comment of a French friend who was having dinner with me one night: "The intention is there, but the chef has not thought about the reality of the dish; the flavors are confused." We started separating out the different ingredients that had been cooked and combined in the dish we were eating, and we counted thirteen! But does anyone really want to eat duck smothered in chipotle barbecue sauce and served with *achiote, quesillo,* avocado, and green tomatillo sauce, over black beans cooked with orange, with a puree of mango and habanero chiles on top? Some chefs have used the word *tamale* to describe what is really just a garnish on a plate; they put strange combinations like grilled scallops with vanilla sauce on a corn husk and call it a tamale!

I have approached this extraordinary cuisine little by little, through a series of experiences and surprises. First I had to understand how its characteristic flavors and colors are obtained, as well as the forms that give the dishes their visual expression. I've studied the history of the ingredients, how they were discovered and how they have developed. This quest has taken me to fields and libraries here and in Mexico and has led me to many discoveries. At every visit to a town or tiny hamlet, to villages and marketplaces, I come upon ingenious new ways to prepare and present a complicated regional *mole* or a single cook's innovative technique for making *buñuelos* or tacos. Mexican cuisine is flexible and extremely open to new influences, which is part of what makes it unique and continuously evolving.

I would venture to say that among the world's culinary traditions, the one that still remains to be explored (along with Chinese cuisine, which has yet to be fully discovered, but whose flavors most people have experienced) is fine Mexican cuisine. Many people have never tasted it at all! Experts estimate that Chinese cuisine includes at least eight thousand different dishes. The cuisine of Mexico has between three and four thousand different recipes, and uses more than a hundred different types of chiles, roots, and herbs, along with a whole gamut of varieties of corn. This is not to deny the contribution of the great cuisine of France, which is distinguished by its refined culinary techniques, most of which were introduced into Mexican cuisine during the reign of Maximilian in the mid-nineteenth century. I agree with the European chefs who say that the best food is eaten in the homes of families who have educated their palates for generations, as is the case in Mexico today.

The people of the United States, for their part, have demonstrated an adventurous spirit in their quest for new flavors. Even fast food has, over time, incorporated flavors from many different regions of the world, including Mexico. The resulting dishes are rudimentary and often vulgar or completely unauthentic, but, in some way, fast food has brought the public to the verge of new flavors and sensations. In the case of Mexican food, this initial awareness has stimulated people's interest and curiosity. But at the same time it has been an obstacle in the path toward knowledge and real understanding. This also happened with Italian cooking. By now it is familiar to everyone, but it began to grow popular with dishes like spaghetti and meatballs, minestrone soup, and veal Parmesan, a far cry from today's sophisticated offerings. Forty years ago, pizza could be hard to find. Today, it has become a practically indispensable part of the U.S. diet, and at the other end of the spectrum there seems to be a fine Italian restaurant on most street corners. And think of Chinese food; for many years the only Chinese dish known here was a strictly local invention, chop suey. When a foreign culinary tradition is presented to the U.S. public, it often happens that a single ingredient is overemphasized. In the case of Thai food, too much use is often made of lemongrass, and people don't have a chance to get to know all the mixtures of aromas that Thai cooking has to offer.

A traditional cuisine is born in its own land, but it is always influenced by neighboring countries and historical events: wars, migrations, invasions, famines. Someone from Ireland or Poland may have trouble accepting it, but the potatoes that are such a fundamental part of their daily diet originated in Peru. Likewise, a person from Thailand or India may not want to believe that chiles originated in America. Meanwhile, Mexicans are startled by the idea that the pomegranates they use in their *chiles en nogada* and *sangritas* originally came from the Middle East. And cilantro, an indispensable ingredient in many Mexican dishes, is an extremely ancient herb that reached Mesoamerica by a route that is not fully understood. From generation to generation, ingredients from around the world come to form part of the regional cuisine of a given place. Long before the globalization of the world's cultures that we spend so much time talking about today, people from all parts of the planet were brought together by their taste buds. A knowledge of ingredients, their origins, and the way they are used can help to narrow the distance between different peoples and their cultures.

Everyday life can sometimes be lacking in excitement, and the varied sensations of the palate produced by the art of fine cooking can be a consolation. Cooking is an ephemeral art, one which requires technique and an in-depth acquaintance with ingredients and their uses. Like sculptors or painters, chefs must know the materials with which they express themselves since, unlike that of any other artists, their work is destined for the senses of taste and smell. It is also essential to know a great deal about the traditions of a given cuisine in order to build on them when innovating. It's clear that as we approach a new millennium, more and more people are discovering that the ephemeral and generous art of cooking well can be a relaxing adventure that begins with the purchase of ingredients, continues with their preparation, and culminates when the dish is finally eaten. I have written this book for those people, along with anyone who happens to be curious about our neighboring country. But my primary aim is to praise the cuisine of Mexico, which is something I can't help doing!

REMEMBRANCES OF KITCHENS PAST

Doña Josefa Fernández de Alvarez-Quiñones was owner and mistress of the grandest house in the town of San Martín de Lodón in the Spanish province of Asturias. Widowed at a very early age, austere, her imposing figure draped in flowing black wool, she ruled her estate and her staff with an iron hand. Images of a huge stone house, framed by mountains and rivers, fill my mind. Its interior was a long succession of beautiful details, from the doors to the heavy silk damask portieres that divided the rooms and conserved the heat from the fireplaces, to the ornaments of all types and periods that were perfectly arranged. In that house there was indeed a place for everything, and everything was indeed in its place. For all her devout rigidity, my grandmother, Doña Josefa, lived in a world of sensations that she strove to pass on to me, or perhaps it was all I could accept from her.

Her mansion had existed for almost five hundred years and lacked various modern conveniences, but it had plenty of bedrooms, enormous salons, a vast dining room, and an atmosphere in which its owner's character was palpable. My father, Eduardo, her only son, moved to Madrid. Despite his training as an engineer at the University of Bilbao, and against his mother's wishes, he devoted himself to literature, journalism, and the theater. What was more, he married Josefina Beceiro Ortiz (known professionally as Lina Ortiz), a lovely young soprano whom my grandmother had deemed "not of his class." Doña Josefa wasn't happy with my parents' lifestyle, but she couldn't hide her joy when I, her only grandchild, came to spend summers and Christmases with her. My legs dangling from the edge of the seat, I rode the train by myself for long hours, passing through León and Puerto Pajares, until I rushed into my grandmother's arms in the station at Oviedo, the capital of Asturias. From there, her chauffeur drove us to her estate. While I was there, my grandmother assigned a young member of the household to follow my every footstep and instruct me in the proper way of carrying out tasks and maintaining the order that reigned everywhere. I could do anything I was curious about, but I had to do it correctly.

My grandmother's kitchen was the liveliest place in that huge house; it bulged at the seams with every good thing the region had to offer: various types of butter; thick, foamy milk; cheeses; the apples known as *reinetas* that are used in making a traditional hard cider; pears; wild strawberries; and several varieties of cherries. The nearby rivers yielded trout, eels, and salmon; from the nearby coast of the Bay of Biscay came the tang of the sea in clams, sardines, glass eels (known in Spanish as *angulas*), crabs, and glossy, fat fish. At that giant hearth, traditional foods from the region and from across Spain were prepared, as well as dishes from France, Hungary, Russia, and other countries. A whole world of flavors seemed to dwell in that ancient kitchen, where water was kept in enormous copper caldrons that hung from the high ceiling, the floor was made of heavy white-pine planks, always gleaming, and the iron stove was heated with wood and flanked by two vast covered copper tanks that provided us with hot water. The brick oven was wedged in a corner next to the stove so as not to cut off the view through the vast windows overlooking the vegetable garden and the rosebushes, which my grandmother attended to with such care and devotion that she once astonished me with a rose that was black, intensely black, with undertones of the deepest red—the result of one of her grafts.

In my grandmother's beautiful garden, I set up a pretend kitchen of my own. Next to a wall was an area planted with calla lilies, whose enormous leaves gave me a private space where I made meals. I finely chopped the white petals of the lilies and imagined they were onions; their firm, yellow pistils were like ears of corn. I had to stop myself from tasting the dishes I made—they might have poisoned me. Corn was a familiar item—there is a lot of corn in Asturias—but in those days it was used as fodder for cattle. Only the poorest peasants had found a way of eating it, in a dish called *fariñas* (once known as *cuecho*) made with a cornmeal similar to polenta. They ate their fariñas throughout the day: in the morning, with milk and sugar; in the afternoon, fried with chorizo sausage; and at night the same way as in the morning. They also made a kind of baked corn bread called *boroña,* which was sometimes stuffed with fried onion and chorizo and called *boroña preñada* (which in English would mean "pregnant corn bread"). One of my adventures in the Asturian countryside was going to eat a boroña that had just emerged from someone's oven in the village. That was the best time to eat a boroña, which didn't keep very long; by the next day it was inedible.

At my grandmother's house, the formal dining room was only for important visitors; usually we ate in the kitchen. From her seat at the head of a long table, my grandmother supervised the bustling staff while gazing out at the rosebushes, the vegetable garden, and the mountains covered with chestnut trees, our family's property and legacy. I learned, under my grandmother's strict supervision, how to choose wines from the cellar and the proper way to wash dishes (something I still enjoy doing). I gathered chestnuts from the trees and learned how to extract the nut from its shell. Men would beat the chestnut trees with long, flexible poles of hazelwood, and the spiny fruits, which looked like burrs, would fall. Carrying wooden pincers and baskets, we ran to pick them up. Through a slit in the spiny outer shell, we extracted the chestnut. It made an impression on me that I will never forget.

My vacations in my grandmother's house were a delightful sequence of adventures and experiences that live on in me, in my way of being, feeling, and working. Life in Madrid, on the other hand, was very different. My parents led the lives of artists. They traveled continuously; my father had new artists to promote, my mother had concerts to give, or they needed to see journalists, writers, and editors. I was born in Cuba, during one of their trips abroad. Maps have always fascinated me. From my earliest years, I excelled at cartography, primarily because I was always aware of having been born on a small, faraway island in the Caribbean.

An only child, I was the companion on my parents' journeys, excursions, and gatherings and, of course, their meals, which my mother prepared with such care and excellent results. Lina Ortiz took me with her to Barcelona and introduced me to the world of theatrical performers. My first trip on an airplane was with my father, who took me with him to visit a small island off the west coast of Africa, near the equator, then called Fernando Po, but now known as Bioko. Eduardo and Lina's marriage was very progressive for their time. My mother developed her voice and pursued her career. My father worked with publishing houses in Europe and America and I traveled with him, with her, or with both of them. Those trips occasionally took me to New York City, and my childhood memories of certain streets and Central Park sometimes reappear before my eyes as I walk across the city today.

Our life flowed like the rivers that run down the slopes of Asturias, sometimes tranquil, sometimes rushing violently. Summer came with the yellow of chamomile blossoms, winter was harsh and flavored with hazelnuts and chestnuts; everything came in its time and, hopelessly, irremediably, the Spanish Civil War came, too. It happened while we were in San Martín. My father was working in Oviedo, and before he left he warned my mother, "If you see anything out of the ordinary happening, get to a seaport!" When we started to see trucks loaded with armed men, we knew the time had come to flee. All along the endless, twisting road, wherever life had been, now there was death. For the first time I saw corpses, rubble. In the newly planted fields, once filled with singing voices, the sound of stifled sobbing wrung our hearts. Silence hung over everything; the birds had stopped singing and the wind had stopped whistling.

We reached the port town of Gijón, and there, little by little, without realizing it, we grew accustomed to the sound of alarms and bombardments. Scarcity was not something we had ever experienced before, but we had a capacity to adapt to our circumstances that astonishes us in retrospect; the things we went through then are only stories we tell now. There's the story of the days and evenings we spent with needles in our hands, picking out the tiny worms that had infested the dried peas we got with coupons from our ration book. There's the story of the shoes made from strips of leather that arrived on a boat from Mexico. The whole town lined up to get a pair. Soon a continual squeaking filled the streets; the Mexican huaraches on our feet made a noise that was audible everywhere. There was no newspaper, but when something needed to be announced, the information was printed on sheets of paper that were pasted up at street corners. One such sheet told us how to solve the problem of the shoes; linseed oil that would stop the sandals from squeaking was distributed from an abandoned oil factory. The leaflet also gave information on casualties and troop movements, and printed stories like the one about the bombs that never went off: there was a message of solidarity from the Italian workers who made the bombs, and who had refused to charge them with explosives when they learned the bombs were to be dropped on our town.

Franco's Spain was not the place for my father's liberal ideas, especially not since he expressed them in writing. It was not the place for my traditional, devout grandmother either. Franco's side killed my father; the opposition, my grandmother. The Spanish Civil War left my mother and me orphaned. We lost not only the people who were closest to us but a way of life, a homeland, the chestnuts, the grand house, the artistic circles, the parties. . . . We left Gijón on a fishing boat packed with refugees, to cross the rough waters of the gulf and reach southwestern France. For two years we lived in Cibure, a small town on the French coast next to the well-known resort of Saint-Jean-de-Luz.

Running from war along the highways and byways of France we came to know how good people can be. I cannot say precisely where I ate it, but I will never forget the plate of slender haricots verts with small new potatoes, sautéed in olive oil and seasoned only with paprika that a kind lady prepared for us. My taste buds also remember the incredible café au lait that I savored along with a roll during our stay of three or four days in a small boardinghouse in Paris. The war was hot on our heels, and we walked or rode in automobiles or carts, south to north and north to south. We had to get out of Europe. One thing was in our favor: I was born in Cuba. My mother went to a Cuban consulate and my birth certificate was declared valid. We were able to board one of the last boats that left Cherbourg for Havana.

My father had worked with a New York publishing house and there was a bank account in his name there; that money enabled us to leave Havana and move to New York, to an apartment in Murray Hill where we could begin to live a real life again, having escaped at last from the refugee's existence so many Europeans were condemned to during that time. In New York I observed firsthand the democracy my father had spoken of and dreamed of. I can still hear many of the things he used to say. He often recited to me an early poem by the great Spanish poet Federico García Lorca, and the lines are like a small pearl:

If I die,
leave the balcony open.

The boy is eating oranges.
(From my balcony I can see him.)

The reaper is reaping the wheat.
(From my balcony I can hear him.)

If I die,
leave the balcony open!

NEW YORK, NEW YORK

My mother's career as a soprano was cut short in our new life, but she didn't leave the performing arts behind entirely. Every Wednesday, I listened to her interviewing important people from Mexico and Latin America on CBS Radio. We couldn't give up on good food, though New York's supermarkets yielded only the most industrialized products; all the women were working in factories and hardly anyone cooked at home anymore. Everything came in cans: meat, vegetables, beans. Cereals were in cardboard boxes and bread in plastic bags. But in those days, as now, New York City offered alternatives and we pursued them in our quest to recapture Spain. On Arthur Avenue, an Italian neighborhood in the Bronx, we bought calamari, eels, and vegetables, everything fresh. The next stop was Brooklyn, where a store on Atlantic Avenue run by a family from the Middle East furnished us with olive oil and olives. Casa Moneo, on Fourteenth Street in Manhattan, was a veritable institution for all the Spanish exiles living in New York, the best place for satisfying our Mediterranean tastes. There we found saffron, paprika, white beans, sweet peppers, and a taste of home.

New friends soon filled our house—the tempting aromas from our kitchen made certain of that. There was often a dish of paella in the center of the table, the yellow rice colored and flavored with saffron, loaded with octopus, calamari, and all kinds of *tropiezos,* or "little snags," as the thousand possible garnishes for a paella are known in Spanish. Elsewhere on the table there might be a whole sea bream, glistening with olive oil and garlanded with potatoes and thick slices of onion, or squid, served in all the velvety blackness of their ink. With her talent and blond good looks, Lina Ortiz adapted quickly to New York and imbued herself with its spirit. She had found a place that was made to her measure; her roots showed only in her songs and her cooking. But even that made her a typical New Yorker, since New York is one of the few places in the world where foreign customs are the norm.

After high school, I studied at the New York School of Interior Design. Decoration came naturally to me and when I started working I became quite successful. Wearing a simple gray silk suit and a black beret with a tiny crown pinned to the front, my hair tied back, I arrived at my interview with Dora

Brahms, at the time one of the most famous women in the interior-decorating world. Elegant and sharp-eyed, she looked me up and down and hired me on the strength of a few minutes' conversation. Soon I was her assistant, which meant working at such a pace that days off weren't to be dreamed of—Saturdays and Sundays did not exist. At her side I visited the hotels and elegant restaurants that had commissioned her, and we supervised and created decors in several states near and far from New York City. The experience taught me that when it comes to achieving something in your career, there is no room for distractions. I was coming to know a world of elegance and discretion. I started to live an independent life, in the New York way, and soon had my own apartment only a few blocks from my mother's.

My mother was extremely beautiful. She loved to sunbathe during the hot summers, and when her very white skin grew tanned it brought out her very blond hair and the olive-green of her large eyes. From her I inherited the part of myself that might burst into song at any time. My mother schooled me in the mysteries of makeup, taught me always to keep the skin on my face well moisturized, and showed me exercises to preserve the body's elasticity. She encouraged me to cultivate an attitude of loveliness, and insisted on the importance of simplicity and accessibility. I always think of her with a little hammer in her hand, ready to repair a shelf or a piece of furniture. She said it was a mania she inherited from her father, a cabinetmaker. I often think my aptitude for decoration came to me from all the beautiful things that surrounded me during my childhood, but my mother with her hammer in hand certainly had a lot to do with it, too.

She was always a good friend; she would listen to me for hours and we laughed together over memories of her childhood and mine. Boyfriends came and went. Finally I met the one who seemed right for me, Charles Howard. I liked his intelligence and we shared an adventurous spirit and a taste for good food. Our first son was born. Becoming a mother can make you very emotional; buried feelings come to the surface. That is what happened to me, at least. I yearned to go back to Spain, something that was impossible at the time. I wanted to return to my past. So we went to Havana. We didn't stay long, though. I don't like the tropics; I like big cities.

A thought struck me at the time: as a substitute for the country of my childhood, the best option was Mexico. This isn't the place to describe all I had to do in order to get there. Suffice it to say that one day, with my husband and one-year-old son, I arrived in Mexico City, where I found nothing that reminded me of Spain. Instead, I discovered a world that was very far from anything I could have imagined, even in my wildest dreams. And I fell in love with Mexico.

MEXICO, MEXICO . . .

At the end of the 1950s, Mexico City had a population of about four million, a climate of eternal spring, and a relaxed style all its own. While a house in the south of the city was being renovated for us, we moved into a furnished apartment near the city's great central avenue, the Paseo de la Reforma. My first surprise was that although Spanish was indeed spoken everywhere, it was a different Spanish, spoken with different intonations, accents, and rhythms.

I don't remember if it was days or weeks after our arrival that something happened which is by no means unusual in Mexico City. Dawn had barely broken when my infant son's crib began rolling from one side of the room to another and I found myself unable to get up from bed and go to him. It was an earthquake.

"The Angel fell. Want to see?" the taxi driver who was taking us to our new house asked.

In the heart of Mexico City, a French-style pillar rises in commemoration of Mexico's independence from Spain. A gilded statue of a winged female figure is perched on top, looking as if it's about to fly off into the sky. It's called the Angel of Independence, though in fact it represents Victory, the city's emblem. Beneath this monument the heroes of Mexico's liberation from colonial rule are buried; for that reason, the angel carries some broken chains in her left hand and a crown of olive leaves for the heroes in her right hand. When we saw it that day, the enormous statue was lying on the ground. Even the sight of a real fallen angel, if it were ever possible to see such a thing, couldn't make me feel greater sorrow.

I identified with the people around me; I felt the same way they felt. I soon discovered an interesting coincidence. I was born on Mexico's Independence Day, September 16. What a fate!

Mexico City's air was clean and bracing then; it really was the place "where the air is transparent," as the title of a novel by Carlos Fuentes puts it, and the taste of the foods was as penetrating as the air we were breathing. Everything inspired me, aroused my curiosity, seemed to hold out the promise of a great adventure. At every turn I was confronted with the astonishing, complex history of the various cultures that once lived in Mexico and still do.

The Angel of Independence: Erected in 1910 to commemorate the first hundred years of Mexico's independence, this statue has become a symbol of Mexico City. For the people who see it every day, the figure is an angel, not the winged victory it was intended to be.

The fallen angel: The earthquake of July 28, 1957, shook the angel from her pedestal in the sky.

The mix of ethnic groups that have inhabited the region of Mesoamerica from remote times created a unique world, impossible to understand if measured by ordinary standards. While the Inca culture was developing in South America, groups of curious, creative people were living in towns and cities in the narrow region of Central America, devoting themselves to agriculture, and making their first great contribution to mankind: the domestication and cultivation of corn. They invented implements for grinding, cooking, building, worshipping, and decorating, tools by which they left their mark.

The vegetable dyes their artists used to color statues and murals have lasted through the centuries. Knowledge of the uses of plants, the movements of the stars, and mathematics was common in these cultures. The people observed the natural world around them closely, and their discoveries–handed down from the Olmecs to the Toltecs to the inhabitants of Teotihuacán to the Maya and from there to dozens of other ethnicities, until they reached the Aztecs–resulted in cultures that have fascinated and baffled generations of scholars. New discoveries are continually being made of their elaborate buildings and artifacts, which are perfect in structure and harmony. Throughout Mesoamerica the traces of these ancient peoples can be found, their pyramids and the hieroglyphs that speak to us of their leaders, discoveries, conquests, and history.

In 1960 archaeologists working in the valley of Tehuacán (a semidesert region that covers the southern part of the state of Puebla and the northern edge of Oaxaca) discovered many things that allow us to imagine the winding path of the immigrants of many different races who are believed to have traveled from Siberia across the frozen Bering Strait to create the pre-Columbian cultures of America possibly as early as 35,000 B.C. The groups of nomads who came to America ate herbs and roots, and used the same hunting and fishing techniques they had learned in Siberia. The bodies of their dead have been found, wrapped in nets and placed inside woven baskets. In the valley of Tehuacán, avocado seeds, chile seeds, and the seeds of a kind of domesticated squash called *curbite mixta* were discovered in the strata that archaeologists believe correspond to the period around 5200 to 3400 B.C. By around 3000 B.C., the inhabitants of the valley had found a way of growing a plant that yielded a small form of corncob; this was the beginning of domesticated corn. Once they were better nourished, they discovered ceramics and began creating clay vessels.

"Well, tell me. Is this Aztec, Mayan, Olmec, or Toltec?"

An amusing confusion: To learn Mexico's secrets, you need more time than a tourist usually has.

MEXICAN MARKETPLACES

Despite ongoing struggles over territory and power, the people of these different cultures established places where they could gather together and exchange goods and knowledge: marketplaces. According to Michael Coe, an expert on Mesoamerican culture and history, Christopher Columbus reported seeing canoes filled with merchandise paddling along the coasts of the Yucatán Peninsula in 1502. These were probably the Putún Maya, known as the Itzaes, whose language was Chontal. They were the dominant group of a commercial network that stretched from the Yucatán Peninsula to the very heart of modern-day Mexico. The central hub of all this activity was Xicallanco, a place that in today's terms could accurately be described as an international business center. Representatives of groups from as far away as what is now Honduras and others from the central region of Mexico gathered there.

Today, throughout Mexico, the traditional marketplaces are fighting desperately to survive the encroachment of enormous supermarket chains with their modern forms of commercialization. (In Mexico, even a supermarket sometimes has characteristics of its own that set it apart from super-

An abundance of lemons in different colors and with differently flavored juices.

An unusual combination of dried shrimp and cinnamon, just to attract attention.

Chiles and more chiles to liven the soul.

A bare and succulent papaya on display.

In most Mexican markets, ecologically sound packagings are on sale along with fresh produce. These artistically presented cornhusks will be used to wrap thousands of tamales.

Called *chiquihuites,* these baskets of ancient design are used to keep tortillas hot.

Zucchini and tender young *chayote* squash.

They aren't easy to learn about, to prepare, or to eat, but you have to admire them. Chiles of all different colors, flavors, and levels of heat.

Part of chile culture is knowing how to arrange them on display.

The squash flower in all its splendor.

***Chayotes,* as spiny as hedgehogs, are a Mexican specialty.**

markets in Europe or the United States.) During the 1950s and 1960s, the traditional marketplaces predominated. The first one I visited was in Mixcoac, which served the neighborhood of San José Insurgentes at the southern end of Mexico City, where our house was located. In Mixcoac, I had my first glimpse of the marketplace world of colors, sounds, smells, and people, all absolutely different from anything I had known before. Walking through narrow aisles, I could see stands of fresh produce, conveniently and harmoniously arranged. Vendors sprinkled their products with water from their fingertips, and hawked their wares, inviting prospective buyers to have a look. "Come on over, *güerita*," they called out to me (*güerita* is an affectionate word Mexicans use for light-skinned women).

Everything was within reach of my hands–fruits, vegetables, meats, plucked chickens dangling from hooks, virtually the entire gastronomic wealth of the valley from which the city sprang. One section of the market was reserved for prepared foods. Here were rows of little kitchens, one after the other, with women cooking over clay pots filled with bubbling sauces, some of them green, some bright red, others dark red. A few tables were arranged in front of each stall for the passersby who allowed themselves to be persuaded by the invitation to take a seat.

Soon after that I went to what was then the city's principal marketplace, La Merced. I remember my surprise at the dried chiles piled into pyramids and organized by variety, color, and shape, from the largest ones, almost black, to a variety that were tiny, round, and wine-colored. They gave off a smell like that of chocolate. This extraordinary sight had a humbling effect on me; I thought I would never be able to learn the differences between one type of chile and another, the secrets of their preparation. How was it possible to transform those stiff, dry chiles into a sauce? Along the aisles lined with fruits, there was always a perfectly ripe specimen cut open to reveal its glistening center. Many of the fruits were unknown to me, but the vivid colors of their flesh held a fascination. There were other long aisles of beans and grains in a huge variety of colors and sizes, and corn in every conceivable form, from fresh ears to the dry kernels used in preparing masa for tortillas. I was also struck by the aisle set aside for banana leaves and cornhusks, which are used for wrapping tamales, fresh cheeses, and dishes to be baked. At that time, the Merced marketplace was sur-

The *xololotzcuitles,* or little dogs, weren't just for playing and warming up the beds of the sick. They were also a highly prized culinary treat.

rounded by warehouses that began receiving shipments of all types of foodstuffs and products from across the country at the crack of dawn.

Soon I was able to connect what I had seen in Mexican marketplaces to the descriptions of the humble soldier Bernal Díaz del Castillo, who accompanied Hernán Cortés in the invasion of the New World. A skilled writer, Díaz del Castillo rose to the challenge of putting into words "things never seen before, nor dreamed of." The great city of Tenochtitlán, capital of the Aztec empire, which was situated on the same spot where modern Mexico City subsequently arose, is described in Díaz del Castillo's *True History of the Conquest of New Spain,* one of the seminal sources of information about the history of the New World.

Bernal Díaz del Castillo's account of what he saw in what was then the Aztec empire's principal market was confirmed by many other sources, including one known only as the "anonymous conquistador." That market, Tlaltelolco, was one of the final expressions of the pre-Hispanic culture that had developed in Mesoamerica. The conquistadors saw a marketplace where each product was displayed along its own aisle, in perfect order: cooking pots, serving dishes and griddles, all made of clay; colored feathers from tropical birds; tools and vegetables; the voiceless, hairless dogs with gleaming skin called *xololotzcuitles,* which were used for warming up beds and comforting the sick. All sorts of game were on sale, from peccary to venison to little birds and turkeys, along with medicinal herbs and many things that were unfamiliar to Europeans. Women at open-air food stands offered cooked foods in their sauces, white, blue, and red tortillas, different types of tamales, and various flavors of the thick corn drink called *atole,* all prepared on small portable grills called *anafres.*

GOOD THINGS COME FROM CORN: TORTILLAS, TAMALES, QUESADILLAS

TORTILLAS

The first time I ever ate a tortilla was during the early days of my stay in Mexico City. My husband and I went to a restaurant called El Caballo Bayo, located just beyond the most populous area of the city, near the racetrack. It was a very spacious place, decorated with an equestrian theme in a Spanish colonial style. In the entryway, standing next to the Mexican version of a griddle—an enormous round sheet of blackened metal with a fire underneath it called a *comal*—a group of women were flattening little balls of masa between their hands. Once they had achieved the desired roundness, thinness, and size, they laid them out on the comal. After a few minutes, the tortillas were turned over with a light touch of the fingertips. In seconds, they puffed up, and at that precise instant they were removed from the fire and placed by those same dexterous hands in a basket lined with a very white cotton cloth. Each new arrival at the restaurant was offered some of these small tortillas stuffed with one filling or another and rolled up—a little appetizer that struck us as absolutely delicious. From that moment the smell of tortillas was something I recognized.

Tortilla-making machines, or *tortilladoras,* have saved many women from drudgery.

Whether I was walking in the city's central avenues or its narrowest back alleys, the smell followed me. I must confess that the taste of the tortilla was not easy for me to understand. It took me a while to discover the pleasure of its flavor—at first it didn't seem to have any flavor at all—and I had to concentrate to enjoy the softness as well as the roughness of its texture. I truly believe that in order to reach any kind of understanding of Mexico, you have to begin with the smell and taste of the tortilla.

Something funny happened to me around that time. The large house we were renting on the Avenida Insurgentes, which runs the length of the city from north to south, came equipped with the services of two very sweet, quiet young ladies who saw to it that everything was kept clean. Since I have always enjoyed cooking, I prepared our food, with the best recipes and ingredients I could find, in the European and U.S. styles we were used to. Of course, we shared everything we ate with them. But one day they left the house without saying good-bye. I couldn't understand why. What had we done to offend them? I quickly learned the answer. A neighbor lady knocked at the door and after a series of extremely formal salutations and circumlocutions, she gently revealed, "Señora, please forgive me for troubling you, but I must tell you that the girls said they left your house because you make food that is very strange to them, and they felt very sad because in your house there are never tortillas or beans or even one little chile. Please forgive me for saying this, but it's just that those girls really aren't happy with salmon." From that moment on, tortillas have never been lacking in any house I lived in, even in New York.

A tortilla can contain anything; it is a serving dish and a spoon. Tortillas are the bread of Mexico, and have been part of the culture of the Mesoamerican peoples from the dawn of their civilization. The creation of the mobile "stove," the anafre, gives us an indication of their long journeys, which lasted for generations, while the round flat comal they invented was perhaps what led them to create tortillas. All the implements they used in preparing food were made from fragile clay; many of them have been discovered by archaeologists at gravesites. Those who died were buried with their belongings and thus left traces not only of their bodies but of everything they used and possessed. The use of clay comales is still common, but perhaps the greatest achievement of those ancient peoples was a flexible, smooth masa,

The Aztec empire had rules that governed the distribution of food. In times of famine, tortillas were distributed to all subjects in quantities that varied according to age. A three-year-old had the right to half a tortilla. Four- and five-year-olds received a whole tortilla. After the age of six, children were entitled to a tortilla and a half. In the Mexican diet, then and now, many other foods were eaten with tortillas.

Fresh tortillas on display. In just a few hours they will disappear.

without the tough hull of dried corn. A precise quantity of lime is added to water in which corn is soaked for several hours, then the corn is boiled and rinsed, and left soft and clean for the grindstone. This technique of adding lime and soaking to create the softened corn called *nixtamal* has the benefit of adding nutritionally valuable calcium to the corn.

The tortillas of central Mexico are different from those of the coastal regions, the southern state of Oaxaca, or the Yucatán Peninsula, where the tortillas are thicker and smaller than elsewhere. Along the coast of the Gulf of Mexico, a layer of masa is traditionally spread out on a banana leaf with the heel of the hand. Depending on the specific area, these tortillas can be thick or very thin, and the masa can be made with blue, yellow, or white corn. Red corn is also sometimes used for tortillas, but not very commonly since it has very little pulp. Ana María Vásquez Colmenares, and expert on gastronomy who has written several books, among them one on the cuisine of Oaxaca, told me that more than twenty different types of tortillas are made in that region alone. Given the scarcity of other types of food, the women of Oaxaca have expressed their creativity by continually finding ways to give different

***Tortillerías* are small family businesses that nourish millions of Mexicans.**

forms, thicknesses, and textures to the tortillas they make from the corn they harvest. In addition to making tortillas that are generally larger, they make a special type of toasted tortilla called a *clayuda,* which is enormous and very thin. All the tortillas of Mexico have in common the masa made out of nixtamal from which they are prepared. Scholars of Aztec civilization claim that the emperor was served tortillas decorated with beautiful designs, enriched with turkey eggs and colored with vegetable dyes.

Traditionally, tortillas are made by women. The historian and journalist Armando Ayala has an interesting interpretation of the role of women in the early years of Mesoamerican civilization:

> *Women participated in the gathering of wild plants; they searched for roots or tubers; they gathered pawpaws and nopales; they knew where to find honey to use as a sweetener; they hunted for insects; they knew where the birds built their nests and they pilfered their eggs; they knew how to tell the difference between edible and harmful herbs and how to harvest the aguamiel from the heart of the maguey.... And they*

made tortillas, which had been in use since prehistoric times (the Formative Horizon between 1500 and 1000 B.C.). This can be deduced from archaeological excavations which consistently uncover pieces of broken clay comales.

The Mendoza Codex was created after the fall of the Aztec empire by Spanish scholars who were investigating and interpreting the culture of the indigenous peoples. According to Jacques Soustelle, in *The Daily Life of the Aztecs,*

> *In it are shown a series of figures divided into two columns (children on the left and women on the right); it depicts the education of Mexican children, an education which seems to have been one of the principal concerns of adults and which was carried out very strictly. It also shows the portions of food that were given to a child: at three years, a child was given half a corn tortilla; at four or five years, a whole tortilla; from six to twelve years, a tortilla and a half; and after age thirteen, two whole tortillas. The portions are identical for the two sexes.*

To make a good taco, you have to put in just the right amount of filling and you must know how to roll up the tortilla.

The industrial production of tortillas began with the first tortilla machine, invented by a man named Romero. A different model was designed by Octavio Peralta, but it was rendered obsolete by the machine invented by Fausto Celorio. Señor Celorio said that when he tried to sell the tortillas produced by his machine in his native Veracruz, he had to run across the town's rooftops to keep out of sight of the women who sold handmade tortillas in the streets, because they would have attacked him. Mexicans prefer to eat freshly made tortillas, and long lines form at the doorways of *tortillerías*—the shops that sell machine-made tortillas—in the morning and at lunchtime. But the classic, handmade tortilla still has the best taste, color, and texture.

The tortillas I most enjoyed were

the ones I used to eat at a famous spot called La Poblanita. They were thin, soft, almost transparent, with a taste so delicate they didn't interrupt the flavor of the filling, but with just enough elasticity to contain it and add a new texture to it. For a long time I preferred them to the thicker tortillas that are more common, until I had a chance to visit Yucatán, where I ate some thick tortillas that were delicious.

TORTILLAS IN NEW YORK

Managing to make the kind of tortillas I like in New York City was a real challenge. I used corn flour that had been "nixtamalized," followed the instructions on the package, and learned to calculate the exact amount of water needed. Anyone who works with flour of any kind knows that the amount of liquid varies according to the type of flour and the amount of humidity in the air, and I can't deny that determining the right amount of liquid was pretty complicated. Finally I found it, and now the tortillas at Rosa Mexicano are enjoyed by foreign visitors from countries across the world—including Mexico!—and by many New Yorkers as well.

Experience has taught me that making good tortillas is an art that cannot be learned by just anyone. I've discovered that Mexican women seem to be the only ones who can easily learn to make them. Mexican women who come to New York and tell me they don't know how to make tortillas have no problem understanding my instructions, even though I don't make tortillas well, while other people, even women from other Latin American countries, never quite succeed. It is as if the old gods bequeathed the gift and the mystery of the tortilla to each new generation.

Toasting tortillas over a charcoal fire gives them a different flavor and texture.

WHITE CORN TORTILLAS

MAKES 24 TO 30 TORTILLAS

You will get great satisfaction from making tortillas. Tortillas are simple to make but require a little patience and practice in the beginning. They freeze well in packages of 6 in zip-lock bags. Children love tortillas warmed and rolled up. (I think microwave ovens were invented to warm tortillas!)

2 cups masa harina (see Note)
1⅛ cups water

---

two 4-inch squares of plastic wrap
tortilla press
flat iron griddle or cast-iron skillet (or comal from Mexico)

1. Mix all the ingredients in a bowl and knead to make a soft dough. Knead for 2 to 3 minutes. If the dough feels too dry, wet your hands and continue kneading. Place the dough in a bowl, cover with a damp cloth, and allow to rest for 20 to 30 minutes.
2. Keep a small bowl of water available to dip your hands into. Moisten your hands, take a piece of dough, and roll it into a sphere slightly smaller than a golf ball. Place this ball on a piece of plastic wrap on the bottom of the tortilla press. Place the other piece of plastic wrap on top of the ball and gently press down with the top of the tortilla press. The flattened tortilla will be just smaller than the press.
3. Carefully peel back the top layer of plastic wrap and place the tortilla in the palm of your hand (dry at this point). Carefully peel back the other layer of plastic wrap and lay the tortilla on the heated griddle or cast-iron skillet. Allow to cook for 30 to 45 seconds on each side. Remove the cooked tortilla and place on a dry kitchen towel or napkin; fold the corners to keep the tortilla warm. Tortillas should have little brown spots; if they are brown all over, the griddle is too hot.

Note: Buy a package of masa harina and follow the instructions on the package.

RED TORTILLAS

2 guajillo chiles (ancho or pasilla, according to taste)
½ cup plus 1 tablespoon water
1 cup masa harina

Toast the chiles. Seed and devein the chiles and grind in a spice grinder. Sift through a fine sieve. Mix 2 tablespoons of chile powder with the water and mix with the masa harina. Knead well to evenly distribute the color from the chiles in the dough. Follow the instructions for white corn tortillas.

GREEN TORTILLAS

2 tablespoons hoja santa powder (or ground dry avocado leaves, both have an anise flavor)
½ cup plus 1 tablespoon water
1 cup masa harina

Mix the ingredients together and knead for 2 to 3 minutes. Knead well to evenly distribute the color of the hoja santa powder. Follow the instructions for white corn tortillas.

ESQUITES

I discovered the little snacks Mexicans call *antojitos* (roughly, "little things that tempt the eyes") after we moved into our first house and I began settling into the rhythm of daily life in Mexico. In the afternoons, I only needed to cross an avenue that intersected the Avenida Insurgentes to reach a branch of the first supermarket chain in Mexico City, called Sumesa. Just outside its door, street vendors had set up their stands, and the corner had become a small open-air market. To one side was a woman standing in front

In a culture centered on corn, fresh corn is a wonderful snack. Kernels can be served on their own, or ears of corn will be grilled or boiled. Meaty or crunchy, corn is always on hand, everywhere.

of an enormous, steaming caldron full of corn kernels that she was hawking by calling out "Esquites!"

The bubbling corn, cooked and flavored with *epazote,* caught my eye and awoke my curiosity. (Epazote is a hearty leafy wild green or purple herb used either fresh or dry, but is better used fresh.) The grains were served in paper cups with plastic spoons and were topped with a sprinkle of dry chile powder and lemon juice to taste. Next to the caldron was a narrow board on which stacks of boiled corn on the cob were displayed; lying one on top of the other, the ears of corn showed off their pearly interiors while their husks hung down at one end. The same woman was offering grilled corn on the cob; the ears rested on a metal grill over a charcoal fire in an anafre.

It was a whole symphony of corn. When a customer asked for an ear of corn, the vendor handed him a sharp stick to hold it with and the customer chose among the seasonings. The ears of corn were covered with clotted cream or mayonnaise, then sprinkled with grated cheese. You could also have the grilled corn with lemon juice and chile powder, which was most often the choice. Each customer was handed a beautiful, tender ear of corn on a stick, either red with chile powder or white with cheese, a perfect snack for anyone who needed to eat and walk.

The dish with grains of corn is called *esquite,* a Nahuatl word derived from *tequesquite,* a mineral traditionally added to the corn as it cooks. Tequesquite softens corn and makes it spongy. It has many virtues and uses in Mexican cooking. Tamales come out spongier when made with tequesquite, and fruits become much easier to peel if they are parboiled in a little tequesquite. Some food historians believe that in Aztec times the grains of corn for esquite were boiled in the beverage extracted from the maguey cactus called *pulque,* a drink I'll have much more to say about later. Others say that only a small tequesquite stone was added to the boiling corn.

ESQUITES AT ROSA MEXICANO

When young corn is in season and I can find some not too sweet and yellow but more on the white side, with a balanced degree of sweetness, I offer my customers, as a courtesy of the house, esquites with the taste of those sold on the streets of Mexico City. No one has ever refused them and they are part of my daily effort to teach people more about the flavors that my children and I, and all Mexicans, adore.

ESQUITES / CORN SNACKS

SERVES 6

Esquites, pronounced es-KEE-tes, are sold in cups by street vendors in most cities in Mexico during sweet corn season.

8 ears fresh sweet corn
1/3 pound butter, unsalted
1 serrano chile, seeded and chopped very fine
salt to taste
3/4 cup fresh epazote, chopped fine (reserve 1 tablespoon for garnish)
1/2 cup mayonnaise

1. Cut the kernels from the cobs.
2. Heat the butter in a 2-quart saucepan. Sauté the corn for 2 to 3 minutes in the butter until hot and bubbling.
3. Add the serrano chile, salt, and just enough water to cover the corn. Simmer for 2 minutes. Add the chopped epazote and simmer for another minute. Remove from the heat and add the mayonnaise.
4. Ladle into small glasses or cups and garnish with chopped epazote.

CORN IN ANCIENT MEXICAN MYTHOLOGY

Many anthropologists agree that the inhabitants of the entire Mesoamerican region shared what was essentially a single religion, and that the figures of all their gods, though they adopted slightly different forms, had basically similar meanings. There were many deities dedicated to corn. Just how important corn was to those ancient peoples is shown by a beautiful Mayan legend. The Maya inhabited a region that stretches from the Yucatán Peninsula to the country known today as Honduras. Their sacred book, the Popol Vuh, describes the creation of the world.

The legend goes that once the gods had organized the waters and the lands and the animals that lived on them, they decided to create a superior being who would understand and appreciate the goodness of life. First they tried to create a man of clay, but he was weak and inept. The second attempt was to create men and women made of bark, but they lacked both intelligence and gratitude toward their creators, and for that reason they were destroyed, Finally, they created beings whose flesh was made of corn and had the same colors as corn: red, black, yellow, and white. These beings could think and knew how to thank the gods. Their language was perfect and thus the first human beings emerged on the earth.

Often, as I'm biting into a tamale, I think of the sweet legend of how the bodies of ancient Mexicans were first formed out of corn.

TAMALES

I first tasted tamales on that same street corner outside the ultramodern supermarket whose entryway was transformed every afternoon into what would become for me a kind of ongoing exposition of new foods. In fact, the dishes sold there were very much like the ones enjoyed by the ancient inhabitants of that same valley, the Aztecs.

If a designer working in the fast-food industry were assigned the task of inventing a dish with its own inexpensive and environmentally safe disposable container, a dish that would be nutritional and natural, that would amply satisfy a sudden hunger, and could be kept either under refrigeration or on the shelf for a short while, he or she would be hard-pressed to come up with anything better than the tamales that are sold in the streets and food shops of Mexico. Wrapped in ecologically correct cornhusks, the soft and spongy dough encloses a delicious filling, making the tamale the perfect food which, in its wide variety of textures and flavors, can satisfy a craving for either sweetness or savoriness.

I can vividly remember the woman who stood in front of a steaming barrel calling out, "Tamales, tamaaaales, sweet ones, red ones, green ones, or with chile!" When customers approached, she lifted the lid and fished for the desired tamales among the cloud of steam that emerged, then closed the lid again and quickly rolled the dripping cornhusks in a newspaper she held by the edges. It didn't take long before I had succumbed to the temptation to buy some tamales. I asked for one of every kind and went home to discover a dish that filled me with enthusiasm from the first mouthful.

In his book *The Daily Life of the Aztecs* (chapter VII, *Civilized Life*), the French anthropologist Jacques Soustelle cites Fray Bernardino de Sahagún, author of the *General History of the Things of New Spain*, who described the manners that were instilled in Aztec children:

> *Be careful how you enter (the master's house) for you are being watched there. Come in with respect, bow down and salute him. And when you eat do not make faces and do not yawn, and do not eat carelessly like gluttons and greedy people, do not gulp the food down hurriedly, but eat it little by little.... If you are given mole or any sauce to eat, or if you are given water to drink, do not make a slurping noise, for are you little dogs, after all? Do not eat with all your fingers, but only with three fingers and do it with the right hand. Neither should you cough or spit, so as not to stain anyone's clothing.*

These manners, instilled in Mexican children since ancient times, can still be observed in the way contemporary Mexicans, like those I watched for the first time on that street corner, eat their tamales.

An ecologically correct wrapper with a delicious filling inside, the tamale is the epitome of good design.

TAMAL EN CAZUELA / GRITS WITH PORK AND TOMATOES

SERVES 6

This is based on the traditional recipe for tamale en cazuela, which is made with masa harina. This is a fast version which I feel is a suitable substitute and takes only 15 to 20 minutes to make. Tamal en Cazuela has many uses. Spread it on a platter, wrap, and allow to cool overnight. Cut into squares and sauté in vegetable oil. Serve with shredded chicken and mole sauce.

4 tablespoons vegetable oil
½ pound pork loin, cut into 1-inch cubes
about 1 cup chopped white onion
2 garlic cloves, finely chopped
3 vine-ripened tomatoes, roasted, peeled, seeded, and chopped
1 bay leaf
⅛ teaspoon thyme
3 cups chicken broth
1½ teaspoons salt
1 cup cold water
1 cup quick grits

1. Heat the oil in a 2-quart saucepan. Sauté the pork over medium heat, stirring to brown all sides. Add the onion and continue to sauté for about 5 minutes until the onion is transparent. Add the garlic and tomatoes and sauté for 3 minutes more.
2. Add the bay leaf and thyme. Stir in the chicken broth and salt and simmer for 10 minutes. Remove the pork with a slotted spoon and reserve for another use.
3. In a small bowl stir the water into the grits to make a paste. Crumble half the paste into the simmering broth and stir with a whisk to prevent lumps from forming. Add the remaining paste in the same way. Lower the heat and simmer for 10 to 15 minutes. Stir occasionally with a wooden spoon until at

the desired consistency. Add more broth if necessary. Discard the bay leaf before serving and season to taste.

4. Allow to cool slightly. Blend until smooth.
5. Reheat in a double boiler.

TAMAL EN CAZUELA DULCE / SWEETENED CORNMEAL WITH CUITLACOCHE DESSERT SAUCE

SERVES 6

Though most people in the United States think of tamales as a savory dish, tamales can also be sweet. These sweet tamales are served with a sauce made of cuitlacoche, a unique Mexican ingredient that you can read more about on page 44.

4 cups milk
½ cup superfine sugar
½ teaspoon pure vanilla extract
1 cup quick grits

1. Heat the milk with the sugar and vanilla over low heat for 10 minutes. Remove from the heat and set aside. Mix the grits with a little water to make a thick paste. Add the paste a little at a time to the warmed milk, whisking constantly to avoid lumps. Return to the heat and simmer slowly for 6 to 8 minutes to thicken, whisking occasionally so it does not stick to the bottom of the pan. Allow to cool and blend in a blender until the consistency of crème anglaise.
2. Spread approximately a ¼-inch layer across the surface of a small plate and decorate with a spiral of cuitlacoche dessert sauce.

■ ■ ■ CUITLACOCHE DESSERT SAUCE

MAKES APPROXIMATELY 1 CUP

1 tablespoon butter
4 ounces cuitlacoche, frozen or canned
¼ cup sugar
¼ cup heavy cream
½ ounce sherry

1. In a saucepan (preferably enamel-lined), melt the butter. When the butter is hot, sauté the cuitlacoche for 8 to 10 minutes over medium heat until most of the liquid has evaporated. Stir in the sugar until it melts, and set aside to cool.
2. Pour the cooled cuitlacoche in a blender and add the cream in a stream until blended. Strain into a bowl.
3. Add the sherry if the sauce will be served immediately. If not, store the sauce and add the sherry at the last minute. Just before serving, strain the cuitlacoche through a fine sieve again.

Note: This dessert sauce is also delicious with coconut ice cream and tropical fruits.

TAMALES, TAMALES, AND MORE TAMALES

Mexicans have more than 150 different ways of making tamales. Even the outer container of the tamale varies greatly, and tamales can be wrapped in many things besides the traditional dried cornhusks that have been softened in water, from banana leaves (a custom that originated along the coasts) to the green leaves of the herb known as *hoja santa* or *acuyo* in Veracruz and Yucatán. There is a type of tamale called *brazo de reina* or *tamal de boda* (wedding tamale) that is wrapped in chaya leaves, stuffed with hard-boiled eggs, and covered with a tomato and pumpkin seed sauce. (For more information about hoja santa and *chaya,* a wild vegetable similar to spinach in texture and flavor, see "The Many Herbs of Mexico," page 174.)

The texture of the corn dough also varies. A monumental tamale called a *zacahuil,* eaten in Hidalgo and other regions, is made with cracked corn and is so huge that it is stuffed with a whole pig or sheep and cooked in a specially constructed oven. Individual-sized tamales are the classic dish for the celebratory lunches or afternoon snacks known as *meriendas* that are traditionally given after the church service at which a child celebrates his or her first communion.

Across Mexico City you can still see stands, set up at strategic locations like bus stops or subway entrances, that sell tamales and *atole,* a drink originally made from masa diluted with water and boiled with any kind of fruit puree. Another very popular one is made with chocolate instead of fruit and is called *champurrado.* For economic reasons, atole is now prepared with flavored cornstarch, known in Mexico by the brand name Maizena. The same stands also sell teas made from herbs such as orange leaves or chamomile. Tamale sandwiches, or *tortas,* as sandwiches are called in Mexico, have also become popular: A thick tamale is served inside a special roll called a *telera.*

Today, as in ancient times, tamales bring nourishment and satisfaction to hungry Mexicans. In some areas of Mexico City, and in smaller towns throughout the country, the cry of the *tamalero* can be heard in the morning as he pushes his little cart and calls out, "Tamales, tamaaaaaleeees, tamales for sale!" Pre-Hispanic custom dictated that in times of drought the *tlatoani*—the principal ruler of each community who was appointed by the emperor himself—had to give tamales and atoles to his campesino subjects in order to alleviate their hunger pangs and their anguish.

QUESADILLAS

Next to the supermarket was an enormous *panificadora,* or bakery, called La Veiga; in Spain, fertile plots of ground near rivers are called *veigas,* and many Mexican bakeries are owned by Spaniards. After my first visit there, I often returned to buy sweet rolls and the still-warm *bolillo* and telera rolls that emerged fresh from the oven at merienda time. (A bolillo is a small roll that is crusty on the outside and soft on the inside.)

Every time I visited the bakery, I noticed long lines of people standing

Quesadillas are a sublime taste sensation when they are made on a *comal.* They can also be fried.

in front of a tiled wall that had three perfectly even little windows in it. Each customer left with a steaming paper bag. One day I decided to join the line. When I reached one of the windows, I was finally able to see what went on behind the wall. There was an enormous kitchen back there; its walls were covered with white tiles and everything was scrupulously clean. This almost industrial-size kitchen was bustling with men and women dressed in white who were making *quesadillas.* In the middle, on a large stainless steel table, a group of people were preparing masa to be rolled into tortillas, then stuffed with a variety of different fillings and cheese. A line of enormous oblong caldrons stretched toward the back of the room, all filled with boiling oil into which the quesadillas were plunged. After being fried, the quesadillas were placed on racks to drain, then wrapped up for the customers, and every customer always received exactly the kind of quesadillas he or she had requested. They could be stuffed with cheese, mushrooms, squash flowers, shredded meat stewed in tomato sauce, chicken, or a variety of other things. I was amazed by that kitchen's organization and cleanliness, and by the sheer quantity of its output. People emerged from La Veiga with enormous paper bags full of bread and hot quesadillas that filled the air with their mouthwatering smell.

The most popular type of quesadilla is made with a freshly cooked masa that is returned to the comal for a few more seconds, or with a raw tortilla that is stuffed and folded over, then cooked on both sides. In addition to the stuffings mentioned above, quesadillas are frequently made with the corn mushroom, *cuitlacoche,* which I'll have a lot more to say about. To give even more flavor, a fresh leaf of the Mexican herb called epazote is added.

Quesadillas are a favorite antojito of every Mexican. At noon or at dusk, street vendors set up their anafres, light the charcoal, and get ready to cook their quesadillas either on a comal or in a woklike utensil filled with oil. The various fillings are arranged in small clay bowls or plastic containers. A salsa, usually either a green salsa made with tomatillos or a red salsa made with dried chiles, is added to the quesadillas that need it, generally those made with cheese, potatoes, or beans, since the other fillings are cooked in sauces that include chiles.

For a long time my own fastidiousness kept me from sampling the quesadillas that are cooked and served in the street. Recently I visited the city of Tlaxcala with a friend, and we made a stop on our way back to Mexico City to admire one of the legendary sites of the Olmec culture, the caves of Cacaxtla, which are known primarily for their colorful murals depicting the wars and victories of the region's former inhabitants. Outside the caves, a woman was making quesadillas on an enormous comal. The atmosphere in the caves was so overwhelming that I felt as if I had traveled to pre-Columbian times, and as I emerged into the sunlight the smell of the quesadillas was too tempting to resist. I'm glad I didn't because they were the best quesadillas I have ever tasted. The woman patted a ball of perfectly white masa between her hands to form a large tortilla, then filled it with squash flowers and placed a tender young epazote leaf on top. She cooked the quesadilla on the comal, turning it once. I enjoyed every bite of that delectable combination of textures and flavors. The tortilla, which was a little on the thick side, crumbled in my mouth, in contrast to the chewiness of the squash flower and the epazote leaf, which added its aroma to all the other flavors.

CUITLACOCHE: THE CORN MUSHROOM

During those early months in Mexico City, my husband and I often ate out at what were then the city's best Mexican restaurants: La Fonda del Refugio, a house furnished in exquisite taste with Mexican handicrafts; La Fonda del Recuerdo, where we had seafood and fish prepared in the style of the coast of Veracruz; El Caballo Bayo, which I've already described, and La Fonda del Pato. But we hadn't yet eaten at any of the less elegant neighborhood restaurants. There were also many "fancy" restaurants that served "international" food, but we had learned that in Mexico in those days, everything had a Mexican flavor.

One afternoon my husband burst into the house with an amazed and incredulous look on his face and said, "I've just eaten the most amazing, delicious soup that's made with a mushroom, or something like that; you have to taste it." However hard he tried to describe the soup and its flavor, I couldn't connect it with anything we had ever eaten. The next day we went to La Fonda del Refugio and I waited with great anticipation for them to serve me their unique cuitlacoche soup. I was presented with a dish of black soup, black as squid ink, with a slight aroma of corn, flavored with epazote. Morsels of the strange mushroom dissolved in my mouth; every spoonful brought new surprises to my nostrils and taste buds. I decided I needed to know more, much more, about cuitlacoche.

Cuitlacoche is a fungus that grows on corn; one of the names it is known by in English is "corn smut," and it can become a plague that destroys entire cornfields. The corn's kernels swell up hugely, its outer husk splits open, and large pieces of cuitlacoche with silvery skin and black pulp appear. Some people find cuitlacoche in its natural state grotesque to look at, and perhaps only the curiosity or hunger of the ancient Mesoamerican peoples could have made them dare to eat it. The idea of combining it with epazote is another of their great culinary success stories.

Cuitlacoche is a Nahuatl word meaning black excrement, which may seem like a somewhat violent description for such a delicately flavored mushroom. But the people who subsist on corn do not exactly welcome the mush-

The corn mushroom: When an accident of nature becomes a delicacy.

room's appearance; they always prefer to harvest their corn whole and without any defects. Etymologically, the word literally means sleeping excrement, from *cuitlatl,* feces, and *cochi,* to sleep. The indigenous Mexicans also called a certain type of crow cuitlacoche because it is somewhat similar in shape, size, and color to the black ears of corn afflicted with the mushroom. Or it may be that the black ears of corn got their name from their resemblance to the bird, which, in addition to being black, is reputed to sleep in dung heaps. My favorite explanation of the name is that the crow called cuitlacoche often visited cornfields and, according to the Indians, infected the corn with its droppings, causing it to produce cuitlacoche. Still, the fact is that cuitlacoche is truly delicious. It tastes so good that it is sometimes called "excrement of the gods."

My friends, who know I'm always looking for more information about Mexican ingredients, sometimes bring me books, which is how I learned that the University of Arizona Press had published *Hopi Cookery* by Juanita Tiger Kavena, a Hopi woman. Among the delicacies the ancient Hopi loved eating was cuitlacoche, which the Hopi called *nahana.* According to Ms. Tiger Kavena, though the modern-day Hopi rarely eat it, nahana is part of a game played during the corn harvest. The game originated among children, who ran between the rows of corn at harvesttime with nahana in their hands; when one of them managed to catch another, the winner painted the other's face with the black mushroom. The game is still played, and now, when the trucks have been loaded up with the harvest, young Hopi men catch the young women and paint their faces black.

By chance, I learned of another place where cuitlacoche is eaten as well. One day, a couple of young men came to my house to deliver a new chair. Without knowing I spoke Spanish, they started commenting on the pictures of cuitlacoche that are hanging in my living room. "Hey, look at that," one said to the other. "Do you think other people eat it, too?" I interrupted at once, and learned they were from Ecuador, where the people who live in the mountains eat cuitlacoche, which they call *atopa.*

"Do they eat it in tacos?" I asked. "No," they answered, "we don't eat tortillas in Ecuador. It's used in stews." So cuitlacoche is eaten in other places besides Mexico—who knows how many . . . ?

Once I had made it my mission to introduce and promote Mexican food in New York, I urgently wanted to give people a chance to taste cuitlacoche. After my experience in 1982 running a *taquería* in New York called La Fogata, I tried to find the mushroom in the United States. A young woman who was interested in learning more about the art of Mexican cooking offered to help me track some down. She started phoning all across the country from her office trying to find us a supplier of cuitlacoche. For days and days, her secretary listened to her repeating the strange Indian word. Finally, the secretary asked, "Who is this Rita La Coche woman that they won't let into the country because she's a smut?"

CUITLACOCHE AT ROSA MEXICANO

In the first year or two after I had opened Rosa Mexicano, I wanted to put cuitlacoche on the menu. But it was difficult to have it shipped in fresh from Mexico and though it was available in cans, in those days there was no way of getting it. Fortunately, a man known as Tomato Bob, who supplied me with delicious New Jersey tomatoes, showed up at the restaurant one day with a packet of fresh cuitlacoche. His neighbor, an organic farmer who raised corn without using any pesticides, had found corn smut on some of his plants. Tomato Bob decided that my restaurant would be the best place to sell it. Profiting from the plague, I got ready to include on the menu the dish that I thought would best suit my customers' tastes: cuitlacoche crepes with a gratin of mascarpone cheese, as a substitute for the thick clotted cream the crepes are made with in Mexico. I trained the staff to explain to our guests what it was, what it looked like, and how we prepared it, and I also spent a lot of time going personally from table to table to give all kinds of descriptions and, of course, samples.

I've always enjoyed being able to serve people a new dish and, even more, a new ingredient. Offering people their first taste of cuitlacoche was doubly exciting because it gave me a chance to describe and demonstrate the ingenuity and creativity of the ancient peoples of Mesoamerica and their capacity for making full use of their culture's basic grain, corn. Still, the appearance of cuitlacoche in New Jersey was purely accidental and temporary; I had yet to find a way of obtaining it regularly throughout the year. In New

York anything can happen, and one day I met Christina Arnold. Young and extremely energetic, Christina was a New York City supplier of exotic ingredients whose company was called El Aficionado. She adored cuitlacoche and, given the difficulty of importing it from Mexico, was determined to produce it regularly in the United States. She became my supplier and I made a commitment to support her in her project of producing it in Florida. Today I have cuitlacoche all the time; the ears of corn are injected with the fungus, which then grows on them. I even had the opportunity to create an all-cuitlacoche* dinner for the James Beard Foundation, in which every dish, from the appetizer to the dessert, was prepared with cuitlacoche.

JOSEFINA HOWARD
AN ALL-HUITLACOCHE DINNER
SEPTEMBER 12, 1989

ANTOJITOS

* * *

COLD PÂTÉ DE HUITLACOCHE

SOPA DE HUITLACOCHE

CREPAS DE HUITLACOCHE

BUDÍN DE HUITLACOCHE

SALAD

HUITLACOCHE ICE CREAM

WITH

RASPBERRY AND COCONUT SAUCE

Domaine de Vaufuget Vouvray 1986

Torres Coronas 1985

An entire menu based on the corn mushroom. The ice cream can also be made with truffles.

*Cuitlacoche can also be spelled Huitlacoche.

CREPAS DE CUITLACOCHE / CREPES FILLED WITH CUITLACOCHE, GRATINÉED WITH MASCARPONE AND MANCHEGO CHEESES

SERVES 6

Home cooks in the United States can sometimes find cuitlacoche at stores specializing in Mexican products or at gourmet shops.

CREPES:

2 cups milk

5 large eggs

1 pinch each of sugar and salt

2 ounces flour

2 ounces butter, melted

¼ pound butter, clarified

1. In a medium-sized bowl, whisk the milk, eggs, sugar, and salt. Sift the flour into another bowl, add a little of the liquid, and stir to make a paste. Incorporate the rest of the liquid and the melted butter, and mix just enough to combine. If there are lumps of flour, strain through a fine sieve. Allow the batter to sit for ½ hour before using or, for best results, overnight.
2. In a nonstick pan or 6-inch sauté pan, melt ½ tablespoon of the clarified butter over low to medium heat. Tilt the pan to coat the surface with the butter and pour out any excess. Ladle approximately 2 tablespoons of the crepe mixture into the pan. Quickly rotate the pan so the mixture evenly covers the bottom. Cook for 1 to 1½ minutes and gently flip with a spatula, being careful not to tear the crepe. Cook for 30 to 45 seconds and remove from the pan. Repeat the process until the batter is finished. Stack the crepes on a plate and cover with a kitchen towel.

CUITLACOCHE FILLING:

3 tablespoons vegetable oil
2 tablespoons butter
½ medium white onion, chopped
1 garlic clove, finely chopped
1 serrano chile, seeded and very finely chopped
1½ pound cuitlacoche, frozen or canned
¾ cup small kernels of corn, fresh or frozen
salt to taste
2 tablespoons chopped epazote

GARNISH:

4½ ounces mascarpone cheese
4½ ounces manchego cheese, grated
small leaves of epazote, for garnish

1. Heat the vegetable oil and butter in a 10-inch sauté pan. Sauté the onion for 4 to 5 minutes, add the garlic, and cook over medium heat until the onions are translucent. Add the chile, cuitlacoche, corn, and salt, and cook until most of the liquid has evaporated. Stir in the chopped epazote; set aside to cool.
2. Place 2 to 3 tablespoons of the cuitlacoche filling across the center of the crepes. Roll the crepes and place 3 on each plate, seam side down.
3. Place approximately 1½ tablespoons mascarpone cheese on top of each plate of crepes and sprinkle with 1½ tablespoons manchego cheese.
4. Place under the salamander or broiler to heat and melt the cheese. Garnish with the epazote leaves.

Note: Mascarpone cheese is substituted for the clotted cream or triple cream found in Mexico.

ALAMBRES DE CALLOS DE HACHA CON SALSA DE CUITLACOCHE / SKEWERS OF SEA SCALLOPS WITH POBLANO CHILES AND CUITLACOCHE SAUCE

SERVES 6

SAUCE:

3 tablespoons vegetable oil
2 tablespoons butter
1 cup finely chopped white onion
1 garlic clove, finely chopped
1 pound cuitlacoche, frozen or canned
1 tablespoon finely chopped epazote
1½ cups heavy cream, scalded
½ cup chicken stock
salt

---

6 poblano chiles, roasted, peeled, and seeded
30 jumbo sea scallops (marinated in olive oil, a little lemon, and a pinch of thyme)

---

6 cups cooked white rice
4 tablespoons finely chopped Italian parsley for decoration

FOR THE SAUCE:

1. Heat the oil and butter in an 8-inch sauté pan. Sauté the onion for 4 to 5 minutes, add the garlic, and cook over medium heat until translucent, approximately 2 to 3 more minutes. Add the cuitlacoche and epazote and sauté for 10 minutes, stirring occasionally. Set aside to cool.
2. Scald the heavy cream and set aside to cool.
3. Place the cuitlacoche mixture in a blender and blend with a little chicken stock and puree. Add the heavy cream and pulse the blender. Season with salt. The sauce should be of medium thickness.

SKEWER ASSEMBLY:

1. Cut the roasted chiles into circles the same size as the scallops (approximately 1 to 1½ inches in diameter). Place 2 circles of the poblano chiles (the interior part of the chiles should face each other) on the skewer. Skewer a scallop followed by 2 more circles of poblanos. Continue alternating poblano circles with scallops until there are 5 scallops per skewer (4 if very large).
2. Place the skewers on the grill and brush with the olive oil and lemon marinade. Cook for 10 to 12 minutes; rotate the skewers to cook evenly. The scallops should be golden.
3. To serve: Heat the sauce and cover the bottom of each plate (preferably an oval plate) with it. Place the skewer on the plate and gently pull out the skewer. Place a line of white rice on either side of the scallops. The sauce should form a ring around the plate. Sprinkle the chopped parsley over the rice.

HELADO DE CUITLACOCHE / CUITLACOCHE ICE CREAM

MAKES 1 QUART

1 ounce unsalted butter
6 ounces cuitlacoche, frozen or canned
pinch of salt
1 cup milk
3 cups heavy cream
9 ounces sugar
¾ cup egg yolks (from 9 to 12 eggs)
1 jigger (1 ounce) sweet sherry
2 ounces shredded coconut

1. In a heavy saucepan, melt the butter. Add the cuitlacoche and cook over a medium flame for 10 to 12 minutes. Add the salt and mix thoroughly. Set aside to cool.
2. Puree in a blender. If necessary, add a little milk to make the blades turn. Strain through a fine sieve. Return the cuitlacoche to the same saucepan and add the milk, heavy cream, and sugar; bring to a boil. Remove from the heat.
3. In a small bowl, whisk the egg yolks. While whisking, slowly add 1 cup of the hot cuitlacoche mixture to temper the yolks. Return the tempered yolks to the saucepan with the rest of the cuitlacoche mixture. Cook over low heat, stirring with a wooden spoon, until the mixture thickens and coats the back of the spoon, approximately 6 to 8 minutes. It should not boil.
4. Strain through a sieve again and allow to cool in a container over ice, stirring occasionally.
5. Pour into an ice cream machine and follow the instructions for the machine. As the ice cream begins to thicken, add the sherry.
6. Scoop the ice cream into the serving containers and sprinkle with coconut.

LA CASA DE LAS BRUJAS

We started making friends as soon as we arrived in Mexico, but during the early part of our stay we weren't yet in touch with the real Mexico. So we decided to take advantage of an opportunity to rent a small ranch, where we planned to spend weekends. It was in an area called the Ex-Hacienda de Coapa, which was easily accessible from Mexico City. We took a road called the Calzada del Hueso to get there, turning off onto another supposed "road" known as the Calzada de las Brujas or Witches' Road. The Calzada de las Brujas was actually no more than a track that ran between a couple of alfalfa fields. The house needed repairs, and a man named Señor Balderas came to help us with them. A quiet, formal man whom we liked immensely from the first moment, Señor Balderas was the first real Mexican we got to know. We enjoyed listening to his opinions and the answers he gave to our many questions. Balderas helped my husband with his Spanish, which he was picking up very quickly, and the two men became good friends. I spent my time buying handicrafts and furniture for the ranch.

As Balderas worked on the house, placing one brick on top of another, he expressed his concern: He was worried that we were living in such a remote, isolated spot. We suggested that the only way to protect us from danger was for Balderas to bring his family and live with us. He had a hard time convincing his wife, Ana, to make the move; she resisted making such a big change in her and her children's lives. She was a tall, slender woman. One evening—I will always remember it—I saw her sitting on a rock with her two beautiful daughters. All three of them were enveloped in their rebozos, and with their profiles outlined by the last rays of the setting sun they looked like three madonnas. The mornings, afternoons, and evenings were an uninterrupted pageant.

In the kitchen Balderas cleaned and painted the walls, and he and Charles constructed a *bracero*—a row of large burners built into a tiled countertop—which was inspired by a thirteenth-century painting I had seen. I liked the idea of having burners that would be able to support enormous caldrons. It was the first time I had furnished a home for my family in Mexico with all the local arts and handicrafts that I loved, and the house grew more beautiful every day. Balderas was finally able to pursuade Ana to move, and all of us went to live in Coapa.

By then I already had several decorating jobs in Mexico City. My visits there were a continual series of adventures. The center of the city had, and still has, an atmosphere so extraordinary that I sometimes felt I was in a European city, outside of time. It was a place unlike anywhere else, with mysterious alleyways and ruined palaces inhabited by ragged children, standing next to modern buildings and large, lovely homes—a world that was completely contradictory, neither old nor new.

MY FIRST ENCOUNTER WITH WORMS . . . AND MAGUEY

In search of antiques and special pieces to use in my decorating work, I visited the flea market known as La Lagunilla, where I could easily imagine myself in an Asian bazaar crowded with friendly, playful characters who talked as if they were singing and shouted as if they were crying, against a backdrop of vivid colors, daringly and harmoniously combined. You could find anything there, from worn-out shoes to antique furniture. For me, it was like a visit to Wonderland or Ali Baba's cave; you could never tell if the things on display had been bought or stolen, and objects of exquisite beauty sat side by side with hideously ugly trash.

As I was walking through the food section of the market on one of my first visits to La Lagunilla, I noticed that one of the small "pyramids" the vendors like to make with their wares seemed to move with a life all its own. When I made a closer inspection, I stopped in my tracks: Some small pink worms had fallen from the pile and were crawling into the aisle in front of me. These, I quickly learned, were maguey worms, one of the gourmet products of central Mexico. There are two types of maguey worms: the small pink ones I saw, and another kind that is fat, white, and shaped like a centipede, which Mexican gourmets consider a greater delicacy. The idea of edible worms didn't strike me as altogether strange; my food-loving father used to delight in letting delicious pieces of the blue cheese called Cabrales ripen until they filled with tiny white worms. This was a treat he ate with such pleasure that as a child I had to eat it, too, at first with a certain apprehension, then just in order to keep

The maguey, a treasure Mexicans have made use of for centuries. Today it is in danger of extinction.

him company, and, finally, with pleasure of my own. It was part of the education that lovers and connoisseurs of cheese gave their children's palates.

In central Mexico, the cultivation of maguey worms is just one aspect of the cultivation of the maguey plant, virtually every part of which is put to one use or another. In his *General History of the Things of New Spain*, Fray Bernardino de Sahagún described the many uses Mexicans made of the various products they derive from the maguey. From this cactus, a kind of sap called *aguamiel* was and still is extracted; in its unfermented state it was mixed with other ingredients to make medicines. According to Sahagún, the sap of the maguey mixed with chile and pumpkin seeds was used as a tonic for those who were recovering from illness, to be taken after bathing. The juices that the maguey's stalks gave off when roasted were used in poultices as a salve. Another chronicler of the customs of Mexican Indians, Fray Toribio de Benavente, known as Motolinia, described the many ways in which the maguey was used in building houses: Its fibers were used as a construction material, its juices as a kind of glue, and the sharp tips of its stalks as needles for sewing.

During the rainy season, worms breed in the heart of the maguey.

Nowadays, they are usually fried in oil or butter. As they fry, they puff up and become crackly. They have an exquisite flavor, and a slight vegetable aftertaste which is the taste of the maguey. They are eaten in tacos with an avocado sauce or by themselves as a snack. In Mesoamerica, as in other regions of the world, eating insects is a tradition that goes back a long way. The ancient people known as Mexicas or Aztecs, who arrived like the Israelites at the outskirts of the promised land, pursued by enemy tribes, had to eat all sorts of insects and creepy-crawlies simply in order to survive. They took them from the great lake on which they later built their city, Tenochtitlán, making use of the little eggs of a mosquito that lived on the lake. Plagues of locusts were good sources of food and the Aztecs made a virtue of their presence by roasting them on an open fire; they cooked tadpoles and ants with their little eggs the same way. These ancient tactics for survival have been incorporated into the cuisine of modern Mexico and today exactly 273 varieties of insects that Mexicans enjoy eating in their respective seasons have been cataloged.

I often notice news articles about nutritionists who are evaluating insects as a good option for obtaining animal protein in the future. The many and various ways in which Mexicans prepare and serve insects could become our everyday culinary delights in some distant future. Cooking and eating insects and worms may be more common or more acceptable among people who have highly sophisticated palates, since the conquest of superfluous things brings greater spiritual excitement than the conquest of things that are merely necessary. The discovery of cacti of all kinds, insects, worms, and other uncommon ingredients has been an exciting part of my Mexican adventure, which has lasted so many years and still continues. . . .

EARLY GLIMPSES OF THE LANDSCAPE

Every day I made new discoveries in the marketplaces and across the city, and every evening, on my way back to the Casa de las Brujas, I carried in my mind, in my eyes, and on my lips something to tell and share. The endless pageant of nature in the Mexican landscape was a constant source of wonder. I remember how we used to get up at five in the morning, fill a thermos with café con leche and drive toward the volcanoes, or to some other spot from which we could watch the daily display of color and magic. "Every evening, as I crossed the avenues and entered the alfalfa fields of the Ex-Hacienda de Coapa the car's headlights lit up the little posts along the roadway. An owl was perched on every one of them, and, even more extraordinary, the owls were of several different species. Today, alas, the Ex-Hacienda of Coapa is only a memory buried beneath city streets; nothing is left of the alfalfa fields, the owls, or what was once my house.

Back in those idyllic times, our Casa de las Brujas was surrounded by a wall; next to the gateway hung a ceramic Talavera tile which showed four little witches flying on their broomsticks, one in each corner. To one side of the main house was another, smaller house we had outfitted for the Balderas family. Between the two buildings was a well, with a tile roof to protect it that was sitting atop four posts. I planted four honeysuckle vines, one around each post, and they grew faster than I had ever seen plants grow before. Farther along was an orchard of plum trees that seemed always to be in blossom. Behind the house was a garden with a little pond where two geese lived. When I stretched out on the hammock, one of them would sit quietly in my lap.

I liked the solitude, the smells of the countryside, and the sight of the Mexican sky, which was always intensely blue. Only occasionally did a few white clouds float across it, and the snowy peaks of the two volcanoes could always be seen, presiding over the high plateau of that place where the air was once so clear. The volcanoes, Popocatépetl and Ixtaccíhuatl, are filled with energy; the snow on their heights absorbs the first rays of sunlight and transforms them into rosy sparks. Once during a trip to Puebla, I saw the sparks of light that ricochet off the volcanoes like shooting stars when the full moon appears.

One evening as I was driving home along Avenida Tlalpán, I caught sight of a man who was leading a burro. The burro, in turn, was pulling a little cart with a baby burro in it. I couldn't resist, and stopped the car.

"Is the little one old enough to be separated from its mother?" I asked.

"Sí, señora," the man answered. So I bought the baby burro for a hundred pesos.

When I got home, I couldn't seem to stop stroking his silky fur, shiny gray like silver, soft and curly. He was a very affectionate burro. More like a dog than a donkey; whenever I arrived home, he would come bounding to the door to greet me. I called him "Platero" (silversmith). It wasn't a terribly original name, because there is a very famous book I read as a small girl called *Platero y yo* (Platero and I) in which the poet Juan Ramón Jiménez describes his wanderings through Andalucía with a donkey named Platero. Jiménez, winner of the Nobel Prize for Literature in 1956, also translated one of my favorite books, a series of stories or fables called *Letters to Pepita* by the Indian writer Rabindranath Tagore. In my memory, that book transported me to other worlds, though I never imagined that one day I would be living in the shadow of the volcanoes of Mexico.

THE BOUNTY OF VOLCANIC REGIONS

When they reached what is today Mexico City, its first inhabitants, the Aztecs, the founders of the great city of Tenochtitlán, discovered a huge lake filling the basin that had formed around those two high volcanoes. Their height created a circulation of warm and cold air fronts that met and generated rainfall. The ash that drifted down the sides of the volcanoes made the land very fertile. The Aztecs found not only a large lake but excellent soil and a temperate climate—the best possible conditions for establishing a settlement and, ultimately, a culture.

In prehistoric times, the lake was probably more than fifty miles long and twenty miles wide, covering a surface of almost one thousand eight hundred square miles. To the north, it extended to the slopes of a mountain range called Pachuca, to the south, it reached Xochimilco and Chalco; on the west it went as far as the outskirts of Teotihuacán and Texcoco and on the east as far as Atzcapotzalco. The edges of the lake were filled with water lilies, bulrushes, giant reeds, and a great variety of aquatic herbs. On its banks, which sloped toward the mountains, grew cacti, rushes, and forests of oak, pine, and *ahuehuete* trees. A large number of streams emptied into the lake, which, in turn, nourished them with its own waters. The lake was guarded by the snowy peaks of Popocatépetl and Ixtaccíhuatl; from time to time, the former would emit clouds of smoke and make fearsome subterranean noises.

If you look at a map of Mexico, the population density is always

Nieves are eaten year-round, and today they are sold in many flavors.

greatest around the volcanoes, because that's where the soil is most fertile. Almost twenty-five million Mexicans live and work in the foothills surrounding volcanoes. In 1943, a volcano called Paricutín erupted in the state of Michoacán, and for a time the whole area was in a state of upheaval. El Bajío, a volcanic region where the finest vegetables are grown, covers parts of the states of Michoacán, Guanajuato, and San Luis Potosí. Another volcanic region is Uruapan, where avocados, peaches, and other fruits are grown; they are so beautiful that they have made the place famous.

On my visits to the wholesale market at Hunt's Point, where most of the produce for New York City is sold, I've been surprised to notice how many products are marked "grown in Mexico." Raspberries, strawberries, asparagus, artichokes, and many other fruits and vegetables come in boxes that are stamped with names in French and other languages but that originate in Mexico. Unfortunately, the U.S. public is often unaware of where these fruits and vegetables are from because once they are removed from the boxes for retail sale it's not always possible to tell.

With the exception of sturgeon caviar, everything can be produced in Mexico; I found out that there's even a secret place where truffles are grown! But the ancient inhabitants of the lake basically nourished themselves with the bounty of its waters: turtles, ducks and other aquatic fowl, frogs, axolotls, and a type of freshwater shrimp called *acocil,* as well as a very nutritious kind of algae called *spirulina.*

In Mexican mythology, the legend of the two volcanoes I liked to watch, Popocatépetl and Ixtaccíhuatl, is a little like the story of Romeo and Juliet, a story of two lovers who have died together. The girl, "the sleeping women" (Ixtaccíhuatl), was lying on her back (you can imagine the shape of the volcano), and the man (Popocatépetl) lay down beside her head, carrying a lighted torch. They have been that way for centuries, and the snow has covered them. But the torch may one day be lit again and the lovers reborn and joined as they were centuries ago.

Legends aside, the ancient inhabitants of the region certainly knew how to take advantage of the snow on the peaks of the volcanoes. We know that they walked up to snow level to gather it, then carried it down and ate it to help stave off the summertime heat. They also mixed it with fruit and honey or sap to give it flavor and color. Long before Europeans arrived in Mexico, the Aztecs had invented the sorbets Mexicans call *nieves* (snows).

Mexicans use seasonal fruits for making nieves, which are traditionally prepared almost entirely by hand. A metal cylinder containing fruit, sugar, and water is placed inside a wooden box full of crushed ice. As the cylinder is rotated, the ingredients freeze. Unlike ice cream, nieves contain neither milk nor cream; they are light and refreshing. In Mexico, specialists in nieves make them in all sorts of different flavors; I prepare the nieves I serve my guests at Rosa Mexicano with the herbs that are used in certain Mexican dishes, with delicious results. I present them in a hollowed-out mango, the kind Mexicans call a *petacón.* We cut the mango the same way Mexican fruit vendors do when they sell fresh mango on a stick; the flowerlike cut enables the customers to enjoy the mango without getting its juice all over them.

In the late 1980s Mexican scientists from the Universidad Nacional Autónoma de México (UNAM) began monitoring the two volcanoes, putting instruments in strategic locations to measure their seismic movements. Since 1994 Popocatépetl seems to have a crest, a column of ash rising out of its crater that volcanologists are watching very closely. The people who live on its slopes call Popocatépetl "Don Gregorio," in memory of a popular *curandero* or shaman who practiced certain rituals to keep the volcano calm. In the past several years, since the curandero's death, the volcano's activity has worried many Mexicans, though the inhabitants of its slopes have heard from their fathers and grandfathers that "nothing will happen."

ASTURIAS IN MEXICO

On my way back to Coapa one evening, I made a surprising discovery. Someone had told me that I had to see the Colonia Asturias. Along the Avenida Tlalpán, and very close to the Clasa film studios where for years many great Mexican films were produced, a community of immigrants from the Spanish region of Asturias had sprung up. On the days of their traditional celebrations, they held typical Asturian festivals called *romerías*. The sight was like a dream or hallucination, transporting me to a wistful childhood with my mother's perfume wafting through the air. There I was surrounded by people from Asturias, where I had once spent so much time; they were speaking their language, wearing their regional costumes, playing their traditional instrument, the *gaita* (bagpipe), and performing their folk dance, the *jota* (jig), traces of their Celtic background. They paraded their Virgin through the neighborhood—and all this was happening not far from where we lived, near Xochimilco! I also found the little rolls stuffed with hazelnut paste known as *queisadiellas*, one of the classic foods of Asturias. They were sold at stands during the romerías. Similar rolls can probably still be found at a *panadería* called La Luna, a traditional Mexico City bakery located halfway between the Colonia Asturias and Coapa. Then as now, the romerías in the Colonia Asturias were advertised over the radio at the end of August, and everyone was invited to come and enjoy.

We made new friends, and very gradually the Casa de las Brujas became a gathering place. Every Sunday we held an open house. My big bracero enabled me to cook in enormous caldrons, which I also used for serving the food. Sometimes we fed as many as two hundred people. I made spaghetti, salads, and some recipes that I had learned from my mother such as chicken rubbed with garlic, lemon, and thyme and roasted on a wood fire, and *chuletas adobadas,* pork chops cooked with paprika, garlic, and olive oil. Spanish paprika was easy to find in Mexico, but I had the daring idea of using a powder made from dried ancho chiles instead. At Rosa Mexicano I still serve chuletas adobadas; it's become a favorite dish of many of my guests who won't let me take it off the menu.

CHULETAS DE PUERCO ADOBADAS / MEXICAN PORK CHOPS MARINATED IN A PASTE OF GROUND CHILES AND SPICES

SERVES 6

This dish gives me great pleasure because my mother taught me how to make it when I was a little girl in Spain. Her recipe called for paprika. Later I discovered that paprika is a chile. When I included it on the menu at Rosa Mexicano, I simply substituted ancho chile for paprika and the recipe became Mexican. It turned out to be our most popular dish.

3 pounds loin pork chops (approximately 1 inch thick, 8 ounces each)
salt to taste
8 large ancho chiles
4 garlic cloves, peeled
¼ teaspoon freshly ground black pepper
¼ teaspoon ground cinnamon
½ teaspoon dried oregano
¼ teaspoon dried thyme
4 whole cloves
⅓ cup white vinegar
1½ teaspoons salt
3 tablespoons vegetable oil

1. Lightly pound the chops with a meat mallet. Make a ½-inch insertion into the edge near the fat. Season with salt to taste.
2. Toast the chiles and remove all the seeds and veins. Place in a bowl and generously cover with boiling water. Soak for at least 1 hour. Soaking the chiles reduces the heat of the chile; the longer they are soaked, the milder they become.

3. Remove the anchos from the boiling water and place half of them in a blender. Add the garlic, pepper, cinnamon, oregano, thyme, cloves, white vinegar, and salt and blend for 30 seconds. Add the remaining anchos and 1/4 cup of the chile soaking liquid and blend for 30 seconds. Add 1/4 to 1/2 cup more of the soaking liquid, enough to make a smooth, velvety paste. Add 1/4 cup more of the soaking liquid and blend for 30 seconds.
4. Dip each pork chop into the paste to totally coat and place in a medium-sized bowl. Pour any remaining ancho paste over the pork chops, making sure the pork chops are totally covered. Refrigerate overnight.
5. Heat the vegetable oil in a 12-inch sauté pan or cast-iron skillet. Scrape off any excess ancho paste (or it will burn) from the pork chops and place them in the pan. Over the highest flame, brown the chops and rotate in the pan to cook evenly. Baste with any excess chile paste. Flip the pork chops after 3 minutes. Reduce the heat to medium and cook for approximately 10 minutes, turning after 5 minutes. Reduce the heat if the chops are getting too brown.
6. Serve with rice.

■ ■ ■ BOILED RICE SERVES 6

3 tablespoons vegetable oil
1 medium white onion, peeled and coarsely chopped
1 garlic clove, peeled and finely chopped
1 1/2 cups long-grain white rice
3 cups chicken stock
salt to taste

1. Heat the oil in a 2-quart saucepan and sauté the onion and garlic for 2 to 3 minutes. Add the rice and stir to coat the rice with oil. Cook for 2 to 3 minutes; continue stirring to slightly toast the rice. Pour out any excess oil. Add the chicken stock, season with salt, cover, and bring to a boil. Once it reaches a boil, reduce the heat to simmer and cook for 20 minutes, or until rice is tender and the stock has been absorbed.

XOCHIMILCO, THE MARKETPLACE AND THE CANALS

It was my good fortune to begin my acquaintance with Mexico near Xochimilco, a place that still seems to retain the memory of the once great city that the Spanish invaders conquered, though today it is fully incorporated into Mexico City and is very easy to reach. Its canals wend their way between cultivated fields and people's homes. As they were in the ancient city called Tenochtitlán, canoes that slip slowly across the still, silent waters are the primary means of transportation. A leisurely journey on one of those canoes, among trees and trilling birds, can transport you to distant days when time seemed to move at a more leisurely pace. The trees that line the canals of Xochimilco are called *ahuecatls,* and it is their roots that support the floating islands, or *chinampas.*

To supply the house with food during the week, Señora Balderas edu-

Fresh produce is still grown in Xochimilco, and Mexicans glide along its canals in boats, singing, drinking, and eating.

cated me in the art of buying at the Xochimilco marketplace, where farmers came to sell the produce and flowers they grew right there in Xochimilco on the chinampas. The open-air market has one area reserved for plants and flowers, and another for vendors of fresh produce. All of these stands are clustered around a covered market where baskets and lovely clay pots of all sizes are on sale, and where there are food stands selling prepared meats and a variety of dishes with such a range of tempting aromas that I always tried some tacos whenever I was in the vicinity.

In the Xochimilco market, I got to know the vendors and their language quite well. Some of them spoke only a few phrases of Spanish; among themselves they conversed in indigenous languages. I discovered stands that sold tiny, unripe olives by the measure—the measure was a tin can that had once held sardines. In bottles made of recycled glass, an intensely green virgin olive oil was on sale. I soon learned that in Xochimilco and other areas the first Spaniards had planted olive trees and vineyards. Later, during the colonial era, the production of wine and olive oil was prohibited in Mexico because the local products competed with those imported from Spain.

The Xochimilco market was where I first learned about the Mexican taste for *nopales* and the way they are prepared. The nopal is a cactus that was taken to Europe by the Spaniards and now also grows along the coasts of the Mediterranean and in southern Spain near Africa; it produces sweet, refreshing fruit called *tunas* or, in English, prickly pears or pawpaws,

Roots of the *ahuecatl*, the tree that supports the *chinampas*.

eaten wherever nopales grow. But I have no doubt that Mesoamerica is the only place where the cactus's spiny leaves are also eaten. In his book *Cocina Mexicana*, a well-known Mexican poet, writer, and gourmet named Salvador Novo, a winner of the National Prize for Literature, describes the courage of the first inhabitants of what later became the great city of Tenochtitlán, when they braved the cactus's thorns not only to eat the prickly pears but to taste its leaves. Every time I came home from Xochimilco, the trunk of my car was full of food and fresh flowers to decorate our house and I had exhilarating memories of new adventures.

NOPALES AT ROSA MEXICANO

Nopales could not be absent from my menu. Mexicans usually enjoy the cactus in salads, but there are many other classic recipes that call for it, some of them traditionally served during Holy Week, when a religious custom encourages people to avoid eating red or white meat. Out of consideration for the financial and nutritional needs of its believers, the Catholic Church officially did away with the tradition, since, on those days, fish consumption and fish prices became inordinately high. Nevertheless, Mexicans still like to prepare the traditional dishes that are associated with the different times of the year.

One such dish is called *nopales navegantes;* the nopales, which have been cut into little cubes or lengths and precooked, "navigate" in a sauce made from dried chiles. The dish also includes little flat cakes made of dried shrimp that has been salted, ground up, and mixed with eggs. After the egg is added, the shrimp powder becomes spongy and is fried in small portions. The slightly sweet and intensely red sauce penetrates the salty, spongy little cakes and the nopales add an acidic flavor which, along with the accompanying tortillas, make it a dish replete with flavors and textures. I also remember eating nopales that were stuffed with cheese, dipped in beaten egg, fried, and served with tomato sauce. But for my guests at Rosa Mexicano, I serve nopales in a salad.

ENSALADA ZACATECANA / CACTUS SALAD FROM ZACATECAS

SERVES 6

It is essential to be extremely careful when you clean cactus. Place your finger at the end of the thickest part of the cactus pad, being careful not to touch the thorns. Use a sharp knife or vegetable peeler to scrape the thorns from the surface of the cactus pad. Be careful not to remove too much of the skin of the cactus.

4 cactus leaves (5 to 7 inches long)
4 tablespoons olive oil
1 medium white onion, cut in half and sliced very thin on the diagonal
1 small head Boston lettuce, leaves torn into small pieces
salt to taste
2 tablespoons dried oregano

1. Bring 1½ quarts of salted water to a boil in a 3-quart saucepan. Cook the cactus leaves until tender, test with a fork or the tip of a sharp knife, which should insert easily into the cactus pad.
2. Strain and cool. The cactus and the remaining water will be slightly viscous. Cut in thin strips on the diagonal, almost julienned.
3. Heat the olive oil in an 8-inch sauté pan and sauté the onion for 5 to 8 minutes until translucent. Add the cactus strips and cook for 2 to 3 minutes more. Add lettuce leaves and cook until wilted. Season with salt. Remove from the heat.
4. Toast the oregano in a dry sauté pan; be careful not to burn it. Allow to cool. Place the oregano in the palm of your hand and, using your thumb, rub the oregano until it is almost a powder and sprinkle over the cactus. Toss and place on serving plates. Serve warm.

NOPALES CON QUESO / ROASTED CACTUS PADS FILLED WITH CHEESE

SERVES 6

It is essential that you be extremely careful when you clean cactus leaves. Using a sharp knife or vegetable peeler, scrape the thorns on the surface of the cactus pad, being careful to keep your fingers away from the sharp spines.

The *nopal* cactus grows in various parts of the world, but the ancient Mexicans were the only ones who dared eat its thorny leaves.

12 cactus leaves (5 to 7 inches long)
2 ounces Oaxaca cheese, very thinly sliced (or use a cheese that melts well, such as farmer, Monterey Jack, or mozzarella)
1 cup flour
2 eggs, beaten
1 cup bread crumbs, very fine
4 tablespoons vegetable oil
salt

1. Place the cactus leaves on a hot grill or over a gas burner. Turn them over several times using tongs and cook until roasted and tender. The cooking time depends on the size and thickness of the cactus. Remove from the grill when tender and fully cooked. Place the cheese on 6 pieces of cactus leaves and place the remaining cactus leaves on top of the cheese.
2. Dredge both sides of the cactus sandwiches in flour. Carefully shake off any excess. Dip in the beaten eggs. Roll in the bread crumbs to coat the sides.
3. Heat the vegetable oil in an 8-inch sauté pan and sauté the cactus, approximately 2 minutes on each side. Season each side with salt and serve with tomato broth.

XOCHIMILCO: A BRIEF HISTORY

The nopal cactus appears on the national seal of Mexico, which shows a nopal with an eagle perched atop it, devouring a snake. Legend has it that the Aztec people, following the prophecies of their spiritual guide Huitzilopochtli, set out from a place that has yet to be identified with any certainty, and had to cross great distances in order to find what they had been told to seek: an islet in a lake where an eagle was resting on a nopal, eating a snake. And that, according to legend, was what they found in the place they named Tenochtitlán.

Some historians put the founding of the Aztec city in the year 1318, while others date it to 1325 or 1370. The city was called Tenochtitlán in honor of Tenoch, the priest who led the Aztecs. Its inhabitants were known as *tenochcas*. One of their first priorities was to build a temple to Huitzilopochtli, and since they had neither stones nor wood, they built it out of the same things the lake gave them as food: fish, frogs, tadpoles, little shrimp, mosquitoes, water snakes, little worms, and all the birds that lived on the lake.

According to Armando Ayala, the history of their wars, strategies, and betrayals is as complicated as that of any other people in history, but the surprising thing is that less than a century had passed before they had toppled the Maxtla empire that preceded them and made themselves the absolute rulers of the region. In that short time, the Aztecs put their many slaves to work and created a city so splendid that it dazzled the European invaders with its great size and perfect order. But first, the Aztecs tried to erase every surviving trace of the cultures that went before them in order to create their own mythology.

In Nahuatl, the language spoken by the Aztecs, Xochimilco means "the place planted with flowers." Some scholars have said that when Xochimilco was invaded by the Aztecs, its inhabitants burned their library, which contained the history of the region. Others maintain that after it was subjugated by the Aztecs, Xochimilco became the repository of the codices that recorded all the histories, discoveries, and knowledge of the Aztec empire. These codices were burned by the Spanish invaders, who considered them dangerous and pagan: The history of many Mesoamerican peoples went up in smoke. When the King of Spain asked to be shown the codices, they were reconstructed by the few indigenous scribes left, and translated into Spanish by people who did not fully understand the original texts.

We know that the ancient inhabitants of Xochimilco specialized in carving stone, and that their market was always thronged with people. Precious metals and stones were on sale there, as well as mirrors, obsidian for making knives and spearheads, seashells and tortoise shells, bones, sponges, herbs, roots, leaves, seeds, medicinal plants, ointments, and syrups. But the economy of Xochimilco was primarily based, for many years, on the products of its lake and *chinampas* (man-made islands where flowers and vegetables are grown). Its vegetables were transported by canoe along the canals to the city of Tenochtitlán. After the invasion, the Spaniards pursued and implemented a policy of friendship with the inhabitants of Xochimilco. For many years, there was very little colonization, and only a few haciendas were founded: The Spaniards wanted the chinampas to go on producing. And during Mexico's colonial period, the chinampas did produce root vegetables, onions, tomatoes, leafy vegetables, and vast quantities of corn. And not just the chinampas. In the first half of the sixteenth century, more than a million fish were taken from the lakes of Texcoco and Xochimilco each year.

For years, Xochimilco remained veiled in mystery, but today it is a tourist attraction where visitors glide through the canals in canoes that are wreathed in flowers on Sundays. In other canoes, groups of mariachis or trios of musicians offer their songs to passersby, and vendors patrol the waters in smaller boats filled with pots of mole with chicken, rice, and beans, as well as other dishes and soft drinks. Mexican families often celebrate special occasions or simply enjoy a day in the country with music and song on the waters of the Xochimilco canals.

At one point, Xochimilco was almost destroyed by neglect and unbridled development. Nevertheless, the unique charm of its canals and the customs of its original inhabitants have helped it to survive. It was designated a Monument of Humanity by UNESCO several years ago, and endless efforts are being made to rescue its waters from the choking lily pads and to preserve the few green areas that remain.

In Xochimilco there are still a few patches of *huauhtle,* or amaranth, a seed with a nutritional value similar to that of sesame, which the Spaniards prohibited the Indians from growing because of its links to a pagan custom. The pre-Columbian peoples traditionally made gods out of amaranth and honey on the days when they remembered their dead. When the period for those sacred and deep-rooted festivities had ended, they ate the amaranth in slices. For many years, amaranth seemed to have been lost; only the people of Xochimilco still had it. But the Day of the Dead was "Christianized" and today it is celebrated throughout the country in a striking combination of indigenous customs and Catholic rituals.

Amaranth, a seed the ancient Greeks called *amarantus,* is a food that has survived for millennia. The word *Amarantus* is engraved in the ancient Greek temple at Delphi; it means literally "plant always alive." This does not mean that amaranth lives for many years, but refers instead to the longevity it is believed to confer. Amaranth has also been eaten in India since ancient times. According to Dr. Benito Manrique de Lara, an expert who researches, creates, and promotes food products made with amaranth, the ethnobotanic origin of amaranth was in Mesoamerica. Its presence in other regions may perhaps be attributed to the plant's tiny, light seed, shaped like a minuscule flying saucer, which may have been carried by currents of air or migrating birds halfway around the world. Many researchers have fallen under the spell of these still unsolved mysteries involving plants that go from one part of the globe to another. The experts assign such plants their origin on the basis of what they call "biological diversity"; in other words, a given plant's origin will be attributed to the place or region where the plant has been domesticated, planted, and harvested, and where it displays the greatest degree of genetic variety. Thus we know that rice, though produced and consumed in tremendous quantities in the Far East, actually originated in India because that is where it has the greatest genetic variety, after having been cultivated for so many centuries. The same thing can be said of wheat, which is believed to have originated in Egypt. Certain plants don't seem to have a single place of origin, but are commonly found under a given set of climatic conditions; an example of this is the coconut tree, which grows near the sea in warm climates.

In Mesoamerica, amaranth was and is part of the culture of several ethnic groups. The Coras, who live in the north of Mexico, believe that amaranth gives strength and long life to their bodies, and also to their houses; they add ground-up amaranth to the mixture of clay and adobe they use in building their homes. All the different ethnic groups that know and use amaranth consider it a source of good nutrition. They also use the seed in their sacred rites. The Huicholes, who are known for their ability to run for whole days on end, make a powder out of amaranth seeds (which they call *pinole*); it fuels them on days when they run twenty-five to thirty miles in search of another sacred plant, peyote. Amaranth is related to another grain called quinoa, which was one of the basic foods of the Incas.

I've always been interested in searching for the historical roots of the present and I'm intrigued by the how and why of the myriad destinies of different kinds of food. Despite having passed through a period of restriction, amaranth is going into the twenty-first century as a seed considered by the U.S. National Academy of Sciences and the World Food Organization to be "the best food of vegetable origin for human consumption." Considered to have special magical powers over the human body in antiquity, amaranth has now been scientifically proven to have extraordinary nutritional value. Which just goes to show that in science as in history, it's sometimes important to go back and learn more about the past in order to move ahead into the future.

Mexicans consider amaranth their own, and it was one of the five basic grains of their pre-Hispanic diet. (The others were corn, beans, cacao, and *chia*. The chia is a tall plant with blue flowers. Its seed, which is spongy, oily, and a grayish-coffee color, is used to create a popular, refreshing drink.) When a Mexican scientist was given the opportunity to travel in space, he took some amaranth with him in order to study how the grain would react under zero-gravity conditions. But in Mexico City, no one asks any questions about amaranth; people just enjoy eating the delicious sweets made with amaranth and honey that street vendors sell along with brightly colored rice paper wafers. Amaranth seeds that are heated on a comal, or in a frying pan, puff up like popcorn.

GRABBING A FEW QUICK BITES

My work as a decorator frequently took me into the city, where I became acquainted with *comederos,* makeshift, unlicensed restaurants, usually run by widows in modest private houses. One type of comedero that could be found in every neighborhood then was simply called broths, *caldos.* The most famous was Caldos Zenón, in the central area known as the Zona Rosa, on calle de Niza, a street named after the French city of Nice. For many years Caldos Zenón was famous for being the place where people went to have soup in the wee hours of the morning after a night's revelry, in much the same way Parisians used to go to Les Halles. It was once no more than a street stand, but when its street was being repaired, Caldos Zenón finally set up a real shop with white tile walls, metal chairs, and tables draped in red-and-white-checked plastic. A sign above the counter listed the chicken parts that were available: wings, legs, necks, or breasts. Behind the counter was an enormous caldron of simmering chicken broth, which was served in a large cup along with the chicken part the customer had requested. At each table, there were small pots of onion, cilantro, and finely chopped chiles as well as avocados cut in half, and you could flavor the broth as you liked. And, of course, there was always a napkin full of hot tortillas. Caldos Zenón's broths were so good, the saying had it, that they could raise the dead.

Another favorite comedero was on a back street called Atocpan, near the southern stretch of the Avenida Insurgentes where an enormous movie theater, the Manacar, was located; amid all the banks and office buildings was a simple little house where a widow opened her doors at lunchtime. Seven or eight tables in the living room and part of the garage were made available to anyone who wanted to enjoy her delicious home cooking at truly economical prices. She served a soup, rice that was sometimes red with tomato and sometimes white but always included peas and cubed carrots, a main dish that varied from day to day, beans, a dessert, and a beverage, usually one of the drinks made with fruit juice that Mexicans call *aguas frescas.* A basket full of tempting bolillo rolls stood on each table to accompany this delicious food, which was the classic cuisine of an inn or *fonda.*

That was where I first ate *sopa seca,* the Mexican pasta soup that has always made me sit up and take notice. First you sauté some extremely fine vermicelli noodles, which are sold in bunches, until they begin to darken, then you drain them on absorbent paper. Next, puree some ripe tomatoes with a clove of garlic and a slice of onion, place the resulting smooth sauce in a pan with a little oil and cook it until it changes color. Add the noodles along with some good chicken stock and simmer the soup until the noodles have cooked and absorbed the stock (that's why it's called "dry soup"). This is the most popular soup in Mexican homes.

Some people like to alternate mouthfuls of soup with bites of green chile and rolled-up tortilla. But at that time, the proprietresses of comederos like the one where I enjoyed having lunch always offered their guests bolillos, oblong rolls that have a round golden tip at each end and a raised, golden line across the top. Always fresh and crunchy, they are truly delicious. They were originally inspired by French baguettes and Spanish *bollos,* but those European origins have been completely Mexicanized. I still wonder what happened to the bolillos like the ones we used to eat. Maybe in some small town in the depths of Mexico they still make them like that. But it wasn't until much later that I began to understand Mexican bread.

Another quick lunch I discovered, or my nose discovered for me, was the *comida corrida,* strictly a take-out affair. Near the present-day Hotel Camino Real is the Avenida Melchor Ocampo (which bears the name of the lawyer who wrote the wedding vows used by Mexican couples who are married by a judge). A mouthwatering smell led me to a place where a row of huge pots contained a tempting variety of dishes. My desire to taste everything there as soon as possible was frustrated by the man who was serving a line of women. "There's no table service here; you have to bring a *portaviandas.*"

It was the first time I had ever heard of such a thing. A portaviandas consists of a series of metal pots that fit neatly one on top of the other and are held in place by two long handles. Cold foods and the dessert go in the lower pots, then, in ascending order, beans, rice or sopa seca, a meat stew, and finally, in the top pot, hot soup. Such was my longing to try this food that the next day I showed up with a plate; the man at the head of the line lent me a fork and I sat on a park bench and enjoyed myself. Whenever I saw a sign

A *comida corrida*, or quick lunch, can be had in every corner of the city, from the humblest to the grandest old building. For people who need to eat and run back to work.

that said "Comida Corrida," I gave it a try. It was a neutral, universal cuisine, with a Mexican stamp on it, but no chile, though hot sauces were available for those who wanted them.

Around that time I enrolled in the cooking school run by Señora Josefina Velázquez de León. It was in the central part of Mexico City, on the second floor of an old building on the calle de Uruguay, if I recall correctly. At that time, it wasn't very common to take cooking classes; they were generally attended by young, newly married women who wanted to learn to make dishes and plan menus for their everyday meals. I asked for a very specific kind of training: I wanted to learn the techniques for preparing sauces and the proper uses of the chiles that had made such an impression on me. I learned about some of the more common varieties of fresh and dried chiles, and how they are roasted, deveined, soaked, and ground up. The lessons were very basic, but they did their part to open my eyes to the essential principles of Mexican cooking. At Josefina Velázquez de León's Culinary Academy, I took the first steps that would one day lead me to a much deeper understanding of Mexico's great cuisine.

THE HOUSE ON CALLE AMBERES

Our leisurely life in the country lasted only a short while. The city called us back. With a friend, I started a company that produced and sold fabrics for interior design, while my husband was asked to do some important work as a sound engineer, which was just one of his many specialties. But the most important reason we had for leaving La Casa de las Brujas was that I was pregnant again and needed to be near medical care. This time we decided to go to the very heart of the city: the Zona Rosa.

In Mexico City every neighborhood has a theme. There are neighborhoods whose streets are named after composers, philosophers, or the great authors of world literature, and other neighborhoods where the names of Mexican heroes predominate, or characters from ancient Greek mythology and literature, or the names of Aztec emperors, or of cities in Spain or across the world. Throughout the country there are avenues named after the most important Mexican president, Benito Juárez, as well as presidents such as

Francisco I. Madero or Lázaro Cárdenas, and almost every other head of the Mexican government.

In what was then only beginning to be called the Zona Rosa—in reality, part of the Colonia Juárez—the streets were named after European cities. We moved into a house on the calle Amberes, a street named after the Belgian city of Antwerp. The house was built in the Mexican style known as *porfiriana,* in an area of the city created during the long dictatorship of Porfirio Díaz (he was president 1877 to 1880 and 1884 to 1911). Mexico underwent many changes during those years, and a European and particularly French style of architecture predominated. The house on calle Amberes had a facade with two balconies and an iron door, very much in the French manner, which somehow disguised the spaciousness of the interior. Its two floors were constructed around a central courtyard. We moved from one room to the other along the arched galleries surrounding the courtyard, and its flowerpots filled with plants and flowers could be seen from every room. My toddler son loved to lean out the balcony and watch the street, and he was so small that once or twice he got stuck between the columns.

My work as a designer allowed me to become better acquainted each day with Mexicans and their customs. I was often invited to family lunches. In Mexico lunch is eaten between 2:00 and 4:00 P.M. This didn't seem strange to me, because lunch is eaten at the same hour in Spain; what did surprise me was that the meal could go on until nightfall. Every lunch offered its own surprises. I was served delicious, delicate dishes with flavors I had never tasted before. Every time I was invited to such a meal, I went home and reproduced what I had tasted. And, of course, I kept on inviting our old and new friends, who grew in number from day to day, to our house. Mexican food continually amazed me, but I still didn't dare serve it to friends. I was sure I would never be able to achieve the right flavor. So I went on cooking my own dishes, similar to the ones I had served in Coapa.

COOKING LESSONS

At that point in my life, I used to serve a Russian cake that some Russian friends in New York had taught me to make: *pashka.* You don't need an oven to make this cake, only a special, pyramid-shaped wooden mold. The base is square, with an opening in the center, the sides fit tightly together and are held in place by two elastic bands, and a lid covers the top. In order to make pashka, you need a good quantity of egg yolks into which you beat a similar quantity of sweet butter, fresh cream, cream cheese, and sugar. After that, you line the mold with cheesecloth, then pour in this rich mixture and let it rest in the refrigerator with a saucer underneath the opening and a heavy board pressing down on the lid. During the night, the whey drains off drop by drop. When the mold is opened, an extraordinary cake appears, which is decorated with pieces of dried fruit arranged to form Russian letters, a tradition of the Russian Orthodox Church. It was a very attractive and almost ceremonial cake, and my friends and clients were delighted with it. Pashka is one of those delicacies that aren't often eaten nowadays because they seem like a bombardment of cholesterol, not to mention the risk of salmonella one is exposed to. But in the 1960s people didn't think much about those things.

My friends were excited about pashka and wanted to learn how to make it. I decided to make a deal with them: Each of them would teach me one recipe, and in exchange I would teach them to make the Russian cheesecake. Those who didn't have a wooden mold like mine could use a new flowerpot with a hole in the bottom, lined with cheesecloth and covered with a heavy lid that would exert pressure. It took two consecutive sessions to make the cake. I formed groups of five, and each of the five would offer me one of the classic recipes she knew. Many of the dishes I savored and learned to make in the splendid houses of that time are now served at Rosa Mexicano.

My friend Lucía Acevez, a native of the town of Alvarado in Veracruz, one of the best-known ports on the Gulf of Mexico, showed me some of the most elegant ways of preparing *lenguado,* a type of flounder. Lenguado is almost as flat as a sheet of paper and has two eyes, one very close to the other, on the top. Lucía, whose nickname was *la Picheca,* showed me how to make delicate lenguado fillets rolled around small boiled shrimp, then poached in fish broth. My friend served them with béchamel sauce; I add a light poblano chile sauce and each mouthful is a treat. As I was taking my first bites of this delicious dish, Lucía described every step of its preparation to me, and I still have the piece of paper I noted the recipe down on. It is one of my guests' favorites.

Among other Mexican seafood delicacies, I also learned to make *chilpachole,* a Nahuatl name for a soup made of crab and shrimp cooked with ancho chiles. *Chilpachole* means "little pieces" in Nahuatl. In a thick red broth flavored with aromatic herbs like cilantro and epazote, crabmeat, well picked over, is cooked with shrimp and sometimes oysters.

The original recipe for this soup taught me one of the culinary secrets of Mexico: the use of masa as a thickening agent. When the broth has reached a full boil, you add little balls of masa that you poke with a finger on one side to form them into the shape of little pots: they're called *chochoyotes.* When they are boiled in a broth or sauce, the chochoyotes release some starch and the preparation is thickened. The use of cornstarch, which is so popular in Chinese and French cooking, is in fact one of Mexico's contributions to the world's repertory of culinary techniques. The essential difference is that Mexican cooking uses masa, which adds a more definite flavor than simple cornstarch. A classic dish that comes down to us from pre-Columbian times is *testahuil,* a broth made with dried or fresh shrimp that uses their shells for added flavor. The use of masa as a thickening agent results in a soup that is a little like a French bisque.

Generally my clients would offer to let me visit their kitchens, where their cooks would teach me to make the foods that interested me. My work as a decorator gave me the chance to visit the city's most magnificent houses, owned by Mexico's wealthiest families, who extended their friendship to me. Their cooks usually prepared an international cuisine, but since they knew of my interest in Mexican food, they would serve me their Mexican specialties.

TESTAHUIL DE CAMARONES / MEXICAN SHRIMP BISQUE

SERVES 6

This soup is a pre-Columbian dish from the Pacific Coast. Many people who taste it compare it to a bisque.

6 cups water
1 tablespoon salt
1 pound very small shrimp with shells
½ cup masa harina
2 guajillo chiles
additional salt to taste

1. Bring the water and salt to a boil in a medium saucepan. Cook the shrimp for 1 to 2 minutes in the boiling water (until the shrimp turn pink). Strain and return the liquid to the saucepan.
2. When cool enough to handle, peel and devein the shrimp and set aside. Put the shells back in the boiling water and let simmer for at least 30 minutes. Strain the broth and discard the shells.
3. In a small bowl, mix the masa harina with ½ cup of the warm shrimp broth. Stir to make a soft dough. Add more broth to dissolve the dough to a creamy consistency. Add the mixture to the remaining broth and stir with a whisk. Allow to simmer over a low flame until the soup has thickened slightly and has a consistency similar to cream.
4. Toast the chiles in a dry pan until pliable. Let cool slightly. Seed, devein, and grind the chiles in a spice grinder. Sift through a fine sieve to make a chile powder.
5. Add the chile powder to the broth. Stir and simmer for about 10 minutes. Add the shrimp. Bring to a quick boil and remove from the heat. Season to taste with salt.

Note: This recipe can also be made with crab or lobster.

ROLLOS DE LENGUADO / FLOUNDER ROLLS FILLED WITH SHRIMP AND SCALLOPS IN POBLANO SAUCE

SERVES 6

One of my clients, Lucía "La Picheca" Acevez, from Veracruz, served this to me for lunch one day. She invited me back to learn to make it with her cook. I learned to make this dish twenty years ago, and people still ask me, "Is this nouvelle cuisine?"

2 tablespoons butter
2 tablespoons vegetable oil
1 small white onion, chopped
1 small garlic clove, finely chopped
1 vine-ripened tomato, roasted, peeled, seeded, and chopped
6 ounces small shrimp, cleaned, deveined, and chopped into small pieces (save the shells)
6 ounces scallops, chopped into small pieces
salt and pepper to taste
6 fillets flounder, approximately 2½ pounds
juice of 1 lemon
4 cups fish stock
shells from shrimp
bouquet garni: 2 to 3 sprigs thyme, 1 garlic clove, 1 bay leaf, 2 to 3 sprigs Italian parsley
Poblano Chile Sauce (see page 85)
1 red pepper, roasted, seeded, deveined, and julienned

1. Heat the butter and oil in a 10-inch sauté pan. Sauté the onion for approximately 5 minutes until translucent. Add the chopped garlic. Add the chopped tomato and cook for approximately 1 minute, stirring continuously. Add the shrimp and scallops, sauté until the shrimp are pink and the scallops are cooked, approximately 4 to 5 minutes. Season with salt and pepper to taste and remove from the heat. Allow to cool completely.

2. Cut the flounder fillets lengthwise following the line on the fish. Place the fillets between two pieces of plastic wrap and carefully pound to an even thickness. Season with salt and pepper and squeeze a few drops of lemon juice on each piece. With the skin side up, place a spoon of the cooled filling on the first 1/4 of the fillet. Roll up the fillets and hold the rolls together with toothpicks.
3. In a saucepan, heat the fish stock with the shrimp shells and the bouquet garni. Bring to a boil, reduce to simmer, and cook for 10 minutes. Strain the stock and return to the saucepan. Arrange the flounder rolls in the fish stock and poach for 5 minutes or until fully cooked.

To serve: Ladle a layer of Poblano Chile Sauce on a plate and place two pieces of rolled flounder on the sauce. Carefully remove the toothpicks. Decorate with two crossed thin strips of roasted red pepper.

BUDÍN AZTECA AT ROSA MEXICANO

Another of the Mexican dishes I learned to make in one of those memorable "cooking classes" and that has stayed on the menu of Rosa Mexicano at my customers' insistence is the *budín* or *torta azteca.* I was presented with a pile of tortillas, one atop the other, with chicken layered between them, all bathed in a barely cooked tomato sauce, with a lovely white crest of cream, grated cheese, and chopped onion. This Aztec torta was served in a colorful ceramic dish and it looked wonderful!

The texture of the tortilla was softened by the sauce, and the preparation of the chicken heightened its flavor. The thick cream made it look like a cake, and from time to time my mouth made a new discovery: strips of poblano chile that were slightly piquant when chewed, or bits of white onion, the most pungent ingredient. I adapted the budín azteca for Rosa Mexicano. To introduce my guests to the taste of poblano chile, I replaced the tomato sauce with a poblano sauce. And for both practical and aesthetic reasons, I make it in a springform pan. This pie or torta can also be made with other fillings and sauces.

BUDÍN AZTECA / MULTILAYERED TORTILLA AND CHICKEN PIE

SERVES 6

I was eating this dish at the home of one of my clients. I asked, "What is this? It's delicious." Manuela, the cook, taught me how to make it. There are at least four versions of this recipe. One resembles lasagna: layers of tortillas with picadillo, cheese, and tomato sauce. I make my version in a springform pan so it comes out perfectly round and makes nice slices.

1 cup vegetable oil
18 white corn tortillas
approximately 2 cups boiled and finely shredded chicken: the yield from two 3-pound whole chickens
3 pounds queso fresco, grated
3 cups Poblano Chile Sauce (recipe follows)

1. Preheat the oven to 350 degrees.
2. Heat the oil in an 8-inch sauté pan. Dip the tortillas in the hot oil, turn with tongs, and coat each side. Each tortilla will take only 30 seconds; they should be soft, not crispy. Layer the tortillas on paper towels to absorb the oil and they will remain soft.
3. Place a layer of tortillas on the bottom of a 10-inch springform pan. The tortillas should overlap slightly to cover the bottom of the pan. Place a layer of chicken on the tortillas followed by a layer of cheese. Ladle some sauce over the cheese. Place another layer of tortillas and continue until all the ingredients are finished. The top layer should be cheese.
4. Place the springform pan in another larger pan with about 1½ cups of water. Place in the oven for 25 to 30 minutes.
5. Allow to cool completely. Remove the ring of the springform pan and cut the pie into 10 wedges.
6. Place the wedges on a greased baking pan slightly separated. Loosely cover the pan with aluminum foil and reheat for 15 to 20 minutes. Serve with warm Poblano Chile Sauce. The dish can be reheated in a microwave.

■ ■ ■ POBLANO CHILE SAUCE MAKES APPROXIMATELY 4 CUPS

3 poblano chiles
4 tablespoons butter
4 tablespoons flour
3 cups milk, scalded
salt and pepper to taste

1. Roast the poblano chiles over an open flame until the skin is blistered. Turn to blister all sides. Place in a plastic bag for 10 to 15 minutes. Cut off tops of the chiles. Peel, seed, and devein. Blend in a blender with enough milk to make the blades turn.
2. Melt the butter in a 6-inch saucepan. Add the flour and stir with a wooden spoon to make a roux.
3. Remove the saucepan from the heat and add 1 cup of milk. Whisk until smooth. Return to a low flame and whisk in the rest of the milk and the chile puree. Season to taste with salt and pepper.

WOMEN IN MEXICAN COOKERY

In the homes of my friends and clients, the cook was revered. She knew the secrets of seasoning food, she learned the habits of the house, and she knew how to please each member of the family. The fact that women were employed as cooks was one of the things that surprised me about Mexico; in my grandmother's and my parents' homes I had seen mostly men in charge of the kitchens.

My grandmother hired a man who was given enough money to buy food for the house for an entire year; he prepared the menus for lunches and dinners. In my parents' house there was also a male chef; in fact, it was my father's male chef who taught my mother to cook. But in Mexico, women presided over the kitchens, not only in the great houses I visited but also in restaurants. In La Fonda del Refugio, which I visited and whose fine-tuned organization I admired, I found only women in the kitchen. Even today, almost all the restaurants that serve regional foods or Mexican specialties are largely staffed by women.

We shouldn't forget that the majority of male chefs throughout the world, even if they had additional professional training, were essentially taught the art of good cooking by their mothers or grandmothers, and in many of the kitchens of Mexico the women are still there. The women who run kitchens are called *mayoras,* or majors, and it is their skill and passion for their work that have allowed them to achieve that position. One of my greatest treasures is a book by Diana Kennedy which she signed for me with a dedication that called me *mayora.* No one knows precisely how the designation originated; perhaps it is used because it still leaves room for a higher rank in the kitchen, the rank of chef. Even when there is a male chef in a kitchen, he will generally consult with the mayora whenever there is a decision to make. Many women accompanied the soldiers during the Mexican revolution, and another theory has it that the rank of major was given to the women who took on the responsibility for preparing food for the troops during the Mexican revolution.

In an industrial area of Mexico City, a restaurant called Nico's has successfully operated for many years. Its decor is very austere and its clientele consists mainly of the executives and businessmen who work in the area. The kitchen serves traditional dishes, various types of moles and adobos, and some specialties such as Sopa Seca de Nata, made from a recipe that was among the closely guarded secrets of a convent in Guadalajara. Sopa Seca de Nata is a true delight: Crepes are alternated with layers of chicken cooked in tomato sauce, strips of poblano chile, and the heavy cream Mexicans call *nata.* This exquisite dish beautifully expresses the way French cuisine was adapted in Mexican kitchens. Nico's serves great food, and the kitchen is staffed exclusively by women. The funny thing is that most of the guests are men, who feel comfortable enough to ask for something "the way my mother used to make it." The mayora always knows just how to satisfy their cravings.

JAIME SALDIVAR, THE CREATOR

The kitchens of hotel chains all have their chefs, but in Mexico at that time, the best known and most respected chef was Jaime Saldivar, who presided over the very exclusive Club de Industriales. The club was located on the second floor of a building near a strange monument to motherhood. I visited it several times. Jaime Saldivar created a space that was the pride of many businessmen. A lover of art and, as he called himself, "a Sunday painter"—though today his paintings sell for high prices in places like Sotheby's—he started a vast collection of paintings and sculptures for the club. But at that point I was more interested in his vision of Mexican cooking. He served dishes such as crepes with cuitlacoche or a delicious, delicate cream-of-young-corn soup to which he added caviar. The kitchen at the Club de Industriales knew how to handle chiles in just the right quantities, so that their flavor was a pleasure. The dishes served there were, in reality, the recipes of the great houses and haciendas of early-twentieth-century Mexico, but presented in a more modern fashion.

I never met Jaime Saldivar in person, but I learned a lot from him; it was he who modernized Mexican cooking through his elegant presentations and the harmonious combinations of ingredients and colors he achieved. In the 1960s Señor Saldivar was already serving what is now known as Mexican nouvelle cuisine. The idea of nouvelle cuisine didn't yet exist, but in my opinion Jaime Saldivar's cooking was an example of it.

SOPA DE MAÍZ CON CHIPOTLE / ESSENCE OF CORN AND CHIPOTLE SOUP

SERVES 6

The recipe for this soup is an adaptation from a recipe by Jaime Saldivar.

4 ears fresh young corn
1 quart milk, scalded
2 tablespoons unsalted butter
1 tablespoon granulated sugar
salt to taste
2 cups chicken broth
chipotle paste to taste (approximately ½ teaspoon chopped chipotle or use the juice from a can of chipotle)
¼ cup heavy cream, scalded (optional)

1. Shuck the corn and remove the kernels from the cob. Puree the kernels in a blender, adding sufficient milk for the blades to turn.
2. Melt the butter in a 2-quart saucepan and sauté the pureed corn for approximately 2 minutes. Add the remaining milk along with the sugar and salt. Simmer for 5 to 6 minutes. Strain and allow to cool. Reserve the liquid.
3. Wet a cheesecloth, wring out the water, and fold it into four layers. Next, wring the cooled corn in the cheesecloth, squeezing the cloth to get all the liquid out of the corn. Discard the squeezed corn.
4. Return the liquid from the corn to the saucepan and heat in the reserved liquid. Just before boiling, add the chicken broth and bring to a simmer.
5. Add the chipotle paste and stir thoroughly. If desired, the soup can be thickened with the heavy cream.

Note: For a luxurious and delicious alternative, make the soup without the chipotle and serve with a tablespoon of caviar.

THE GREAT RESTAURANTS OF MEXICO IN THE 1960S AND 1970S

Like many New Yorkers at that time, I enjoyed wearing high heels, but in Mexico I started wearing flats, and not only for comfort. I discovered that I needed to be a little lower down in order to appreciate Mexicans, who are generally a bit smaller in stature than I am. I liked to walk through the streets and meet people's eyes directly. In only a few thousandths of a second, you can connect with another person, feeling a direct greeting in the steady gaze of someone's eyes. I was truly enchanted by the Mexican people. The city was sometimes a little dirty and at other times glowed with magnificent colors, but it was also very cosmopolitan, particularly in places like the Bosque de Chapultepec, a park that dates back to the splendors of the Aztec empire. *Chapultepec* is a Nahuatl word meaning "hill of crickets." The area first served as the pleasure garden of emperors and kings, and later became a battlefield. Today it is the biggest park and meeting place in the city. In one area of Chapultepec is a lake on whose banks you can still find what was then one of the great restaurants of the world: Del Lago.

The first time I walked into Del Lago it was so beautiful I almost fainted. The entrance is at the top of a hill, and the building is shaped like a cone. When I went in, I found myself on a semicircular terrace filled with enormous colored flowers made by hand out of thin, slightly stretchy paper. As you descended, these flower-filled terraces alternated with terraces lined with beautifully set tables all the way down to the lake. On the lowest level were musicians and a dance floor. Seen through the enormous window that stretched from the dance floor to the roof of the cone, the surrounding woods and the lake became part of a continual spectacle. At night, the moon and stars shone in the sky; by day, the mirrored surface of the lake's waters was disturbed only by passing swans. When it rained, the show went on, with the wind shaking the enormous trees and the pitter-patter of drops against the window. On windless nights, a fountain spouted high jets of water that seemed to dance to the rhythm of the music. The restaurant served the "international cuisine" of that era, and the food was well prepared. Del Lago still exists, and though the decor and food have changed completely, its fountain is still comparable only to the one on Lake Geneva in Switzerland.

Les Ambassadeurs was another of the city's great restaurants, located on the Avenida Reforma, across from an equestrian statue of the Spanish king Carlos IV that Mexicans have nicknamed *el caballito,* or "the pony." Few people are interested in the historical figure, but they still appreciate the quality of the sculpture. Les Ambassadeurs was markedly French and extremely formal. I went there several times, and noticed that the majority of the other guests were businessmen, always very well dressed. In those days, men had to wear jacket and tie in every formal restaurant; they weren't allowed in without them. I realized that what mattered most to all the guests there was the food; everyone seemed to be concentrating on it. I remember a certain elegant gentleman who asked the waiter to bring the ingredients for his salad, then prepared it himself, mixing the oil, vinegar, and other condiments with special pleasure, before serving it to his companions. Since then, *el caballito* has been moved to another square in the city and replaced by a modern sculptor's interpretation of it. The restaurant called Les Ambassadeurs is still there, but it, too, has changed.

Another good French restaurant was the Normandie, located near the center of the city on calle López. To enter, you walked down a staircase. It was the place where the city's gourmets went to eat classic French cooking. Another restaurant of the same type was the Périgord, whose menu included the best-known French dishes of that time. It was on the Avenida Yucatán, which had a strip planted with palm trees running down the middle; the avenue passed through a residential area of the Colonia Hipódromo Condesa, which was the site of a racetrack at the turn of the century and later became known for its Art Deco architecture.

My personal favorite at the time was a restaurant called Acapulco. It is still there on calle López in the same block as the Normandie. It specialized in fish and seafood, which always looked very fresh, spread out on crushed ice in a small stand next to the door, or stored in the refrigerated display case that stood in the entryway. At Acapulco I had something I've always wanted to eat again: avocado stuffed with baby eels. The fresh eels were cooked *a la bilbaina* in olive oil with fried garlic and *guindilla,* a chile that is grown in Spain. Still hot, salted and tender, the eels were placed over half a ripe, cold avocado, and the whole thing was served on a bed of finely chopped fresh lettuce. This is another of the interesting and astute dishes that combine an ingredient not produced in Mexico, in this case, eels, with an indigenous fruit that today is eaten across the world.

TACOS: AN ENDLESS ADVENTURE

Another restaurant that made a big impression on me was the place I first tasted the foods of southeastern Mexico and Yucatán. It was an unpretentious spot whose owners waited on the tables themselves, and I made a point of going there on each different day of the week in order to try every one of the daily specials. My interest in authentic Mexican food was growing, and tacos, in particular, had begun to exert a real fascination on me.

The Avenida Revolución is part of a neighborhood called Tacubaya, where enormous houses with thick walls dating from the turn of the century line narrow streets. Intersecting this avenue is the calle Covarrubias, a little street where a restaurant called La Poblanita is located. The walls of the spacious entryway were covered with tiles, and a long row of pots sat stewing on hot plates, offering a tempting variety of fillings that guests could choose among for their tacos. There were mushrooms, mole, the strips of roasted pepper with cheese known as rajas, sweetbreads, cuitlacoche, chicken livers—

The old Poblanita restaurant was where I first tasted true Mexican tacos.

These enormous copper caldrons are ideal for making *carnitas.*

more than twenty different items to choose from. At the back, a group of women were making soft tortillas cooked on an enormous black comal. The tortillas were small and thin, and provided a delicate complement to the fillings without interfering with their flavors: the perfect wrap.

There was always a line of people at the door of La Poblanita, ready to wait as long as necessary to sample its delights. Elegantly attired couples stood next to people from the poorest neighborhoods. Every social class was represented in the line at La Poblanita, an extraordinary place that has slowly declined. Among what were then the great restaurants of Mexico City, some are still operating, but without their former splendor, and others have completely disappeared.

In my quest to learn more about tacos, it became clear that tacos with the pieces of barbecued pork called *carnitas,* and all the other varieties of tacos with pork, were the place to start. Mexicans sometimes call pork *cochino,* a word that can also mean dirty. The story is told that when the Spaniards first brought domestic pigs over on their ships, the Indians saw some piglets that were asleep and described them as *cuchi cuchi,* the Nahuatl word meaning to sleep. And to this day pigs are called cochinos.

The taste of pork did not come as a complete novelty to the indian inhabitants of Mesoamerica, since they ate the wild pig known as a peccary that is indigenous to the Americas. (I've learned, by the way, that there is currently a project under way in Mexico to raise peccaries on an industrial scale for their meat, which is said to have an extraordinary flavor.) But the peccary must have been difficult to hunt and was therefore sampled by most of the population only as a rare delicacy. Still, the immediate acceptance of pork by the indigenous Mexicans, after it was introduced by the Spaniards, shows that it was not absolutely unknown to them. By a simple process of elimination, it can be inferred that the Indians used one of their preferred methods of cooking when they made carnitas: boiling.

Tacos with carnitas are so popular that they can be found everywhere: on street corners, in markets, in taquerías. In any group of street vendors, there's always one who sets up a portable stove, puts a big pot on top of it, and fills the pot with every part of the pig, from the various cuts of meat to the snout, eyes, intestines, and feet. The taco is made with whatever part of the pig the client requests, finely chopped and placed between one or two hot tortillas. Chopped onion and cilantro are the classic garnishes. The variety and flavor of the sauces set out for customers is what ultimately determines the success or failure of the food stand.

Despite the proliferation of carnitas, it's hard to find any that are really good. After tasting them several times, I think I finally started to like them when I ate them at Aquí es Jalisco, where I washed them down with tequila. Tequila comes from Jalisco and carnitas from Michoacán; the two states share a border in central Mexico, and carnitas and tequila go very well together. Mexican cooking makes use of virtually every part of the pig, wasting nothing, and in that it resembles the traditional cuisines of many European countries, with their stews and cold cuts.

CARNITAS / PORK FILLING FOR TACOS

SERVES 6

2 pounds pork shoulder with fat, cut into 2-inch squares
½ medium white onion, chopped
1 bay leaf
½ orange, cut in slices, with the peel
salt to taste
12 white corn tortillas

1. Place the pork in a 3-quart saucepan and cover with water. Bring to a boil with the onion, bay leaf, orange slices, and salt. Reduce to simmer and cook for 1 to 1½ hours. Add more water if necessary.
2. Remove a piece of pork from the pan and check for tenderness. Cook for another 15 minutes if the pork is not tender. When it is tender, pour out any excess water and allow the pork to fry in its own fat. Stir to brown on all sides.
3. Remove from the pan and serve with fresh hot tortillas for making tacos.

TAQUITOS DE TINGA POBLANA / SHREDDED PORK FILLING FOR TACOS

SERVES 6

3 tablespoons vegetable oil
½ medium white onion, chopped
1 garlic clove, chopped
2 vine-ripened tomatoes, roasted, peeled, seeded, and chopped
shredded pork
½ teaspoon paste from a can of chipotle chiles
salt to taste
12 fresh white corn tortillas

1. Follow the recipe for Carnitas (page 94), omitting the orange segments. Remove the meat when it has finished cooking, and shred.
2. Heat the vegetable oil in a sauté pan and cook the onions for 5 to 6 minutes; add the garlic and cook for 2 to 3 minutes until the onions are translucent. Add the tomatoes and cook for 2 minutes.
3. Add the pork and cook for 3 to 4 minutes, stirring occasionally with a wooden spoon.
4. Add the chile paste (to taste) and stir well to evenly distribute the chiles. Season to taste with salt.
5. Serve with fresh hot tortillas for making tacos.

MORONGAS AND MORCILLAS

The menu at Rosa Mexicano had to include a selection of tacos like those I loved to eat in Mexico. I decided to serve a plate of three small tacos stuffed with three different foods: *tinga poblana, cochinita pibil,* and *moronga.* Unfortunately, not many of my guests order this particular item, but I keep it on the menu because I want to demonstrate the variety of flavors that Mexicans use in seasoning pork.

Foods made with sheep or pig blood are very popular in Mexico. Moronga, which is made with pig blood, is the dish my guests have the hardest time with. It's rather audacious of me to serve moronga, I know, since the United States is one of the few places where blood sausage is not accepted. Almost everywhere else I've lived, the blood of certain animals is commonly eaten. The vendor at the Fuente del Berro in the Iturbide neighborhood who sold a large sausage made with sheep blood known as *budín* (a word derived from the English *pudding*) is a very vivid figure in my childhood memories of Madrid. For a centavo, he would slice off and serve us a delicious slab. In Spanish cuisine, sausages made from pig blood are called *morcillas;* they are made with rice or onions, then sliced up and grilled, to be used in stews or as appetizers. The Irish also have their black pudding, made with pig blood, as do the French—the famous *boudin noir*—and many other cultures.

During the first years of my stay in Mexico I couldn't believe that something as delicious as the Spanish morcilla could have an acceptable

Mexican interpretation. But one day I learned. During a lunch given by my friend and client Lucía, I met a gentleman who at that time was the owner of one of the city's best-known restaurants, La Cava. Naturally the conversation turned toward food, and we started talking about morcilla, which I defended with full patriotic fervor, and moronga, which he claimed was one of the great sausages of the Mexican nation. Since I hadn't yet tasted moronga, I accepted his challenge to try it. When the lunch was over, he took me to the nearby market of San Ángel. We walked past the line of stands specializing in moronga and with great expertise he steered me toward the one where we bought the first moronga I ever tasted. And there was nothing to do but admit that he was absolutely right. The texture of Mexican moronga is different from morcilla or from Irish black pudding or the blood sausages made by the Germans, Russians, Hungarians, or French. Grainy, slightly gelatinous, and extremely aromatic, it turned out to be a real novelty and delight for my palate.

My memories of the Fuente del Berro and the morcilla I used to eat have brought back to mind the plague of sparrows that once descended upon Madrid. The beautiful acacias that adorned the street we lived on were infested with sparrows, the streets were blanketed with sparrow droppings, and suddenly a vendor appeared offering a new taste sensation: grilled sparrows. He carried a large pot piled high with small birds, perfectly cleaned and roasted. It was a real treat to bite into the morsel of flesh and the little bones, everything delightfully crunchy. But soon the plague of sparrows was over. The last time I visited Madrid I asked about grilled sparrows, but nowadays there are so few sparrows around that no one touches them.

MORONGA AT ROSA MEXICANO

We make chorizo sausage ourselves at Rosa Mexicano but moronga is a much more complicated endeavor, and I've been told that making it is prohibited by New York State law. After some investigation, I managed to locate a Mexican family, longtime residents of Chicago, who make moronga and send it to me. It's interesting to see how often guests at Rosa Mexicano who are of Irish descent order moronga; I often guess their origins by their choice.

MY MEXICAN SON

My pregnancy was advancing and one day I went to the English Hospital, where my second son was born. At that time, the hospital was located on the spot where one of the largest and most architecturally interesting hotels in the city, the Camino Real, now stands. The hospital was officially named the American British Cowdrey or ABC. In the 1970s it had vast corridors with huge white floor tiles, lit during the day by the brilliant sunlight that streamed in through the windows and at night by large white lamps that hung from the high ceilings. The rooms were large and their wooden doors and windows looked out onto the spacious gardens. It was like something out of a film about the First World War.

MY FIRST POZOLE

My clients generously continued to allow me to consult and practice with their cooks, but always warned me that I could ask them all the questions I wanted as long as I didn't hire them away. Among those cooks I particularly remember a woman named Manuela, who took the time to explain every step in the preparation of various dishes to me. That Manuela was off-limits to me, but one day I was lucky enough to find another Manuela of my own.

The Manuela I found was a hardworking woman who had been employed for several years in the kitchen of a café called the Konditorei, which specialized in a variety of European pastries and also served lunch. The Konditorei was only a few streets away from my house, and I often ate there. Manuela grew attached to my children. We agreed that she would live in our house and take care of the children when she wasn't working at the Konditorei so that I could continue with my work as a decorator.

I often brought home the ingredients for preparing whatever Mexican food I had just learned about or tasted. One day I came home ready to make a *pozole*. I had bought a good piece of pork loin and special corn for pozole, and was getting ready to prepare the recipe. Manuela watched me for a while, then asked, "What are you making, Señora?" "Pozole," I told her. Her answer was an immediate standing invitation. "If you want to know what pozole really is, you have to come to my village and my house. We'll show you what a true pozole is."

A few months later, my family, Manuela, and I headed for the state of Jalisco. To the west of Mexico City lies the city of Guadalajara, the capital of Jalisco. We traveled along the banks of Lake Chapala and passed through a little lakeside town called Ajijic, inhabited mainly by retirees from the United States who enjoy the landscape and the special charm of the place. We continued on a road heading north until we entered a region that was desperately dry. The cornfields were withering under the sun's rays, and there seemed to be no trace of life in those solitary hills except for the hut that was Manuela's family home.

After many hours of traveling in a little Fiat van, and very much in need of a rest, we found ourselves in a house that consisted of a single room. On one side was a bed, and on the other a space for the fire, where a large pot rested on iron bars. Manuela's family had already prepared the meat and other parts of a pig they had butchered the day before to use in the pozole. After welcoming us with a series of very formal introductions and greetings, they discreetly withdrew and left us their bed and their hut. I've always wondered where they went in all that emptiness. That night, the fatigue of the long journey won out over the excitement of the day's surprises and we fell exhausted into bed. Very early the next morning, Manuela and her family began making pozole.

First they lit a wood fire; next, in an enormous clay pot full of fresh water, they placed the whole pig head, which had been cleaned quite thoroughly, but which still had its snout, teeth, ears, and eyes. The head cooked for several hours until it had completely softened, then the pot was removed from the fire and left to cool for a while. Next they gently removed the head from the broth and proceeded to separate the meat from the bone, returning to the broth, in long strips, the ears, without a trace of hair left on them, the cheeks, the tongue, the snout, the brains, and everything that was edible, without wasting a single morsel.

Then they put the pot back on the fire and when the broth started to boil again, they put in the cuts of meat from the rest of the pig. The contents of that enormous pot boiled merrily on the fire in the corner of the hut while we slept another night across the room. Finally the meat became tender, and they added other soft parts of the pig along with a large amount of a specially treated dried corn that had been cleaned and soaked. These grains of corn, called *cacahuazintle*, are larger and meatier than most and have been used for dishes similar to pozole since pre-Hispanic times. Several more hours went by until the corn and everything else had become completely soft. During that time, fresh water was added periodically to keep the broth from cooking away.

While the corn slowly softened, Manuela's family quartered up a fat hen, cut it in pieces, and added it to the pot. By noon, the grains of corn had burst open and looked like little flowers. Only then was salt added to the mixture, because it is believed that the corn absorbs the liquid better if the broth has no salt. Soon after that, the members of the Howard family were regaled with plates of succulent pozole. We were also served the classic garnishes: powdered oregano, radishes and chopped onion, dry chile powder and chopped fresh lettuce. And *tostadas* made with small tortillas.

There are several variations on the white pozole I learned to make with Manuela's family, including a red pozole made by adding dried chiles and a green variety seasoned with green chile and *acelga* leaves. Acelga is a vegetable similar to spinach which was brought to Mexico from Spain. But in my opinion, the white pozole of Jalisco is undoubtedly the best example of a food in which a product brought from Spain (in this case, pork) was added to corn, and European and indigenous cooking techniques were combined.

There are those who claim that the indigenous peoples already had a pozole before the Spaniards arrived, and it's possible that they did, since their repertoire of cooking techniques consists basically of roasting, steaming, and, above all, boiling in broths or sauces. Though they didn't have pork, they did have peccary and other game that could have been prepared the same way pozole is made today.

POZOLE AT ROSA MEXICANO

The pozole we make at Rosa Mexicano is the same as the dish I learned to cook in that lonely hut in Jalisco, but the pig's head is finely chopped so my guests won't be shocked at finding a pig's ear or snout on their plate. In fact, it shouldn't be that shocking: People forget that every part of the pig is used

A celestial choir.

in sausages and all other kinds of charcuterie. But—except in the case of head cheese, where the pieces of meat are visible in the aspic—it's difficult for the consumer to know what sausages really contain, since everything has been thoroughly ground up. Günter Grass, the famous German writer, has written a poem called "The Jellied Pig's Head," which is practically a recipe for pozole. It is included in his book *The Egg and Other Poems*, and I recommend it to anyone who's interested in cooking as a theme for literary poetry.

For my pozole, I use canned cacahuazintle kernels, with excellent results. When pozole is poured into a mold and refrigerated, it solidifies into a kind of gelatin that can be delicious sliced up and served cold. Pozole is one of the signature dishes of Rosa Mexicano. I still have a card signed by a French gentleman who once ate at Rosa Mexicano with an entire table of people who ordered pozole. They congratulated me effusively after their meal, and said they had been told to try the pozole at Rosa Mexicano because it was one of the great dishes of international gastronomy, comparable to cassoulet, bouillabaisse, and—they hesitated for a moment—paella. As they were leaving, the man I mentioned took out a blank card on which he scribbled in French "To the high priestess of Mexican food" along with a completely illegible signature. Someone told me he was well known, though I still don't know who he was, but I keep the card with special appreciation.

POZOLE

SERVES 12 TO 15

Pozole is a stew made with various cuts of pork, chicken, and hominy, and served with an assortment of condiments. If you make it, either have a party or freeze it in containers. It becomes gelatinous when cold, and is similar to head cheese.

1 pig's head, washed well and cut with a butcher knife into 4 pieces
6 pig's feet
5 to 6 garlic cloves
2 large white onions, peeled and cut into quarters
salt to taste

4 pounds pork shoulder, cut into cubes
2 chickens, whole
2 6-pound cans of hominy, strained and washed

Garnishes:

3 lemons
2 ripe avocados, diced
1 cup red radishes, diced small
½ cup jalapeño chiles, seeded, deveined, and finely chopped
1 large white onion, finely chopped
2 tablespoons dried oregano

1. Place the cut-up pig's head, the pig's feet, garlic, onions, and salt in a large stockpot with 8 quarts of water, or enough water to cover the ingredients.

2. Bring to a boil. Reduce the heat and simmer for 2 hours.
3. Strain the stock and allow to cool. Remove all the meat from the pig's head, discarding the skin and carcass.
4. Return the stock to the pot and bring to a boil. Add the pork shoulder and the two chickens. Simmer for 1 more hour. Strain. Allow to cool.
5. Remove the meat from the chickens and cut into small pieces. Return the stock to the pot, add the chicken pieces and the pork shoulder and the drained hominy. Bring to a boil. Season to taste with salt.
6. Serve in large soup bowls with an adequate amount of chicken, pork, and hominy in each bowl.

   Serve with individual plates of garnishes. Place half a lemon in the center of each plate. Place a small amount (approximately 1 tablespoon) of each garnish around the lemon. Garnishes should be sprinkled into the pozole according to individual taste.

Note: Pozole is also delicious blended. Blend the broth with the chicken, pork, and hominy for a thicker soup, adding a little cream or milk to make it lighter.

LA VENTILLA

In Mexico most people have always made a tremendous effort to own a home; the primary goal of families at every social level was and is to acquire a place of their own. Perhaps because of my particular history and nature, I've never owned a building. At that time, I was more interested in having the freedom to set up house wherever I wanted.

We moved from the city to La Ventilla in Teotihuacán, where the great pyramids are located, motivated by a book written by Fanny Erskine Inglis Calderón de la Barca, the Scottish wife of Marquis Ángel Calderón de la Barca, who was Spain's first ambassador to Mexico after it gained its independence. The fifty-four letters she wrote to her family from Mexico were collected in a book entitled *Life in Mexico.* Written between 1840 and 1860, the letters give a frank description of the horrors she endured during her long trip in a carriage from the port of Veracruz to Mexico City, and of her stay in the city she came to love.

La Ventilla was the last stop she made before the city, and her description of the place and the marvels of Teotihuacán fascinated me so much that when I once happened to pass by the strange inn, constructed in a vaguely Spanish style, I was completely charmed by it. When the possibility of living there arose, I jumped at it.

La Ventilla was a Mexican interpretation of a castle: Enormous stones had been laid one atop the other like bricks, and adobe mixed with chips of *tezontle* had been used as mortar. Tezontle is a porous red rock found in many parts of Mexico; its permeability makes it an excellent base for gardens, and also for roads or highways, which are covered with it, then paved with asphalt. The family that owned La Ventilla offered to rent us part of the building. At that point, half the place was in ruins, and part of it was occupied by the owners, who rented out a section that was separated from theirs. In our part of the house, the kitchen ceiling was almost two stories high; it was supported by enormous wooden beams, from which dangled cords with hooks on them for hanging pots. Against a wall at the back of the kitchen was a large bracero made of polished cement that was tinted red, with several large gas burners. On the wall across from the bracero, a small window gave onto a view with a well in the background; behind it and throughout the property stretched my favorite kind of garden. It was wild and abandoned; grass grew everywhere and roses, irises, and many other flowers were scattered through the grass, adding their beautiful colors to its surface. Those flowers were born and died without ever being cut. The kitchen reminded me of my grandmother's in its spaciousness and size, though obviously its surroundings and layout were very different.

In addition to the garden, La Ventilla was at that time surrounded by beautiful countryside, creeks full of fish, and enormous ahuehuete trees. I was surprised not only by the size and grandeur of those trees but also by the way their roots grew out of the ground. You could easily climb on one, walk along it, and from there grab hold of one of the tree's spreading branches. An old bridge, probably built in the nineteenth century, and named after Maximilian, the Austrian prince who was emperor of Mexico, spanned a river that was dry but always threatened us with a flash flood. In the distance we could see the tip of the great Pyramid of the Sun, one of the remains of the Teotihuacán culture, which, along with many others, preceded the Aztecs in this region. We bought a telescope, which we installed in the top part of the house. The first time I looked through its lens I saw a beautiful red cardinal. The magnetism of the pyramids seemed to envelop us.

The sites chosen by the ancient inhabitants of Mesoamerica have an aura, an energy that I can sense and that affects me profoundly. I feel I have been identified, that I'm caught up in something, and I'm sure that the peoples who constructed their religious centers there had special reasons for doing so. I've experienced the same thing in Oaxaca, when I've visited the ruins of the Mixteca and Zapoteca cultures, or in Veracruz, standing before the remains of the grandiose and extremely ancient culture of the Totonacas. In Teotihuacán, as in all the places where the vestiges of Mesoamerican cultures are found, I've felt the energy that emanates from them. The works of Michael Coe, an eminent scholar of the pre-Columbian world whose books I often turn to, have confirmed my feelings. The pyramids of Teotihuacán have many secrets they have not yet revealed, and every new discovery or theory of modern archaeology awakens new possibilities. In Nahuatl, *Teotihuacán* means "Land of the Gods," and that is the feeling the place gives you.

The Aztecs didn't know much about Teotihuacán either, and they are said to have called it the "Land of Giants" because they believed that only a

Only a race of giants could have built the pyramids of Teotihuacán.

race of gigantic men could have constructed those enormous pyramids. Fifteen hundred years ago, it was a living city whose buildings were decorated with brilliant colors—red, blue, yellow, and turquoise—and with thousands of inhabitants. Their homes surrounded the great ceremonial center. A Center for Teotihuacán Studies has been created, where people from Mexico and across the world come to excavate and learn more about the influences of Teotihuacán culture on other Mesoamerican cultures, and new discoveries are continually being brought to light. When we lived there, campesinos plowed the lands around Teotihuacán with their tractors, and you could see small children running between the furrows behind the tractors and filling baskets with what for a time I thought were stones. To my amazement, they turned out to be clay figures; the children had impressive quantities of pre-Columbian figurines to sell, though few of them were intact; there was usually only the head.

The owner of La Ventilla was an extremely kind woman. When she learned of my interest in Mexican cooking, she tried to serve me something new every day. In the mornings, she made us *huevos rancheros,* a lightly fried tortilla topped with two fried eggs, yolks still very soft, and covered with a cooked tomato sauce seasoned with onion, garlic, and green chiles. *Huevos a la mexicana* are eggs scrambled with *salsa mexicana*—so called because it contains the colors of the Mexican flag—made with chopped fresh onion, green chile, cilantro, and tomato. Once she showed up in my kitchen with a tray of antojitos, which are made of masa formed into different shapes. They can be round or thin, and are stuffed with a variety of beans; their flavors vary according to their shape and their filling. The names also change according to the region. Among the innumerable varieties of antojitos, my landlady introduced me to what she called *tlacoyos,* whose Nahuatl name derived from the word *tlaxcalli,* meaning tortilla. They were boat-shaped and rather thick pieces of masa, lightly cooked. Their raised edges held in a layer of *frijoles martajados* or pounded beans topped with a layer of crumbled cheese. They looked absolutely delicious and in their contrasting interplay of textures, they tasted even better. The tips of the tlacoyos were shaped into fine points and the masa was cooked there to the point of being slightly golden and crunchy in contrast to the smoothness of the frijoles martajados. They were sometimes topped with salsa, which gave them a necessary touch of freshness.

BEANS

The wonderful smell of delicious beans boiled for several hours in a clay pot still comes back to me. Beans are a prehistoric legume originating in the American hemisphere. Experts have discovered vestiges of cultivated beans that date from 7000 B.C. Christopher Columbus is said to have first encountered them in a place called Huevitas on the island of Cuba; he took them from there to Europe. The French word for beans, *haricots,* comes from the Nahuatl word *ayacotl,* which was what the peoples of the Mesoamerican region called beans. The dictionary of food compiled by Waverly Root gives a history of American beans. They were found by Cortés in Mesoamerica, by Cabeza de Vaca in Florida, and, a little later, by Jacques Cartier at the mouth of the St. Lawrence River. Clearly, beans can thrive in almost every climate.

Before Columbus, one of the best-known legumes in Europe was the fava bean, which is difficult to digest. American beans were first accepted by the Florentines at the behest of Alessandro de' Medici, who planted beans on Pope Clement VII's recommendation. From then on, Florentines have had to endure the nickname "bean eaters" because it took many years before the rest of Europe came to appreciate this extraordinary food. Catherine de' Medici took them with her from Florence to France in 1533 when she married Henry II, and almost a hundred years later they began to be cultivated near Saissons, which gave its name to the type of beans grown there. But for many years the French disdained beans. Brillat Savarin, the famous French gastronome who wrote *The Physiology of Taste,* was contemptuous of American beans.

In Mexico, beans are extremely popular. They are grown in all sizes and colors. Among them is a variety still called *ayacotes,* which are large and robust, with a sturdy hull; they can be up to an inch long. No matter what the season, there is a space reserved for beans in every Mexican marketplace, offering a wealth of colors, shapes, and sizes—sometimes ten varieties or more at the right time of year. There are round ones, small ones, long ones, fat ones, and flat ones. Some beans are a single deep color, so shiny they seem to give off blue sparks, while others are speckled with tones going from white to pink and from blue to purple. As far as colors go, the infinity of tones ranges from black to yellow, red, brown, pink, and purple, and even white. There are gray beans and beans in variegated brown tones, while others are black and white. There are even beans that naturally have lovely designs outlined on their surface.

Regional preferences are very marked. In the state of Nayarit to the northwest of Mexico City, a white bean called *azufrado* is preferred; on the east coast, black beans are the favorite. Even the names that Mexicans have given their beans are lovely: *garbancillos, canarios* (so called because of their canary yellow color), *perlitas,* or little pearls (which are spherical and brown), *ojos de cabra,* or goat's eyes (light brown with dark-brown stripes), *panzas de puerco,* or pig bellies (light gray and round). Beans taste best when they've just been cooked: You can tell they are fresh by their smooth, shiny surface.

I learned to cook beans in the following way: The beans are soaked, then rinsed before being cooked with a piece of onion in fresh water. Once they have softened, they can be salted. After they are cooked, the beans can be served in their broth or made into refried beans, which gives them a new flavor, texture, and appearance.

The versatility of this legume is not as great as that of the soy "bean" (which isn't really a bean at all), from which so many products are derived. But from a purely gastronomic point of view, the American bean is particularly flexible. In addition to being refried, beans can be served *martajados,* that is, pounded so that they lose their shape but still keep some of their texture. Ways of preparing beans vary by region and personal preference. I've always been fond of *huevos tirados,* a specialty of the state of Veracruz in which refried beans are added to eggs, producing a very original dish. Across the country, beans are eaten in many different ways, primarily as

These beans still bear the original name by which beans were known in Mesoamerica: *ayacotes.* They can grow to almost an inch long.

I saw them on the road to Zacatecas, and they can be seen across Mexico: Beans being shipped by truck and ready to come out of their shells.

an accompaniment to meat, fish, and poultry. As a side dish, beans help tame the hotness of chile and cleanse the palate in preparation for the next dish or dessert.

Beans are also the principal ingredient in certain cassoulet, or stew-type, dishes. When they are served on their own, cooked with chile, cilantro, tomato, chopped onion, and pieces of *cerdo gordo* or *chicharrón* (pork cracklings), they are called *frijoles charros,* or cowboy beans, and are very popular in the north of Mexico. One of the classic dishes of southwestern Mexican cuisine is *frijoles con puerco,* beans with pork, which restaurants in Yucatán offer as the day's special once a week.

SUN-DRIED BEANS

One day I greeted Ruperto, our chef, with a bag of bean powder, enthusiastic about the possibilities for new creations. Ruperto took me aside and told me a story from his early childhood.

My father was an arriero. *[In Mexico, arrieros are men with burros who transport and distribute new food products from one place to another on their burros, across winding mountain paths or to remote communities.] He would leave our village with his five little burros and walk to a village near the volcanoes, San Nicolás de los Ranchos, where they made* metates *(grinding stones). Each burro could carry three of the enormous metates, and after loading them on, he headed for the coast of Guerrero, passing through a town in Oaxaca called Pinoteca on the way, and selling the metates one by one. For this long trip, which took almost a month, my mother would make him* frijoles del arriero. *A good quantity of recently harvested beans were sun-dried and grilled on the black comal, along with some* guajillo *chiles and some avocado leaves to give color and taste. I watched my mother grinding all she had grilled to a uniform, aromatic powder, throwing in a pinch of salt from time to time. My father carried this bean powder in a jute bag. Of course he couldn't go without tortillas, and so* totopos *were made in a special way. Tortillas that were slightly bigger than usual*

In addition to recently harvested beans, you can buy jams, fruit juice, wines, honey, and other regional specialties on the road.

were laid out on the comal, but were cooked only on one side, until they were crunchy. The evening before the day my father would set out on his journey, the tortillas were placed upright with their still uncooked surface facing the fire so that they would dry out thoroughly. The totopos were added to the jute bag, and my father also carried a clay pot that hung from the pack on one of his burros. When he got hungry, he would tie his burros to a tree, build a fire out of branches, fill his clay pot with water, and add a portion of the bean powder, which quickly turned into a thick soup that he ate with his totopos . . .

Ruperto had returned to his childhood and was filled with memories. He told me with great emotion that in the countryside in those days, a family's cupboard usually held only onions, chiles, and corn, but there was always something good to eat. Ruperto remembered the sauces that would take on different flavors and aromas according to the ripeness of the chile they were made with, the homemade tortillas, the ingenious stews, and everything he had loved to eat. After milking the cow, they heated the milk, then added sugar and cinnamon and, when it was just beginning to boil, broken-up pieces of tortilla. Out of a gourd called a *jícara* that is decorated and used as a bowl or mug, he and his six brothers and sisters enjoyed a breakfast similar to the one eaten by peasants in Spain, except that in Asturias the peasants add slices of bread to the milk and call it "bread soup."

FRIJOLES A LA CHARRA

SERVES 6 TO 8

This dish is served in the winter at Rosa Mexicano. When I served this at my former restaurant, La Fogata, it was described as a hefty bean-and-pork dish which seemed to have crossed the border and become chile con carne.

1 pound pinto beans, soaked overnight in 2 quarts water
1 pound pork shoulder with some of the fat left on, cut into 1½-inch cubes
3 ounces smoked slab bacon, cut into 1-inch cubes

2 smoked ham hocks
½ medium white onion, quartered
salt to taste

4 tablespoons vegetable oil
1 medium onion, coarsely chopped (approximately 1 cup)
1 garlic clove, finely chopped
3 large ripe tomatoes, roasted, peeled, seeded, and coarsely chopped (approximately 1½ pounds)
1 serrano chile, finely chopped
⅛ teaspoon dried thyme
6 cups water

1. In a large saucepan, heat the beans in the water that they have been soaking in overnight. Add the pork shoulder, bacon, ham hocks, and quartered onion. Cover and cook over low heat for about 1 hour or until the beans are tender. Add the salt and allow to cool. Set aside. Remove the ham hocks.
2. Heat the vegetable oil in a 12-inch sauté pan. Sauté the chopped onions for 5 minutes over medium heat until translucent. Add the chopped garlic and cook for another 1 to 2 minutes. Add the bacon and pork and cook to brown the meat, stirring with a wooden spoon. Add the tomatoes, chile, thyme, and water. Gradually add the cooked beans. Cook over low heat for 25 to 30 minutes or until the beans thicken slightly.

SALSAS AND CHILES

In Mexico, the daily staple of the campesino is a taco with beans; this might seem a bland diet, but with the addition of salsas made with a variety of chiles, the taco can acquire new dimensions of flavor. Mexican salsas with chiles do more than add a touch of freshness and variety to a diet that could otherwise be monotonous. Modern nutritionists have found that the combination of corn and beans is an excellent source of protein, something that is generally true of any mixture of grains and legumes. In the classic taco, made with a corn tortilla and beans, the addition of a salsa completes the body's nutritional requirements with the vitamins from the vegetables. Nutritionists have called the taco eaten by the poorest Mexicans "a nutritional find."

SALSA

During my stay in La Ventilla, I learned that a salsa, as it is understood in Mexican cuisine, is a condiment added to a simple preparation immediately before it is eaten. The very specific role of salsa is to enhance the flavor of the most basic foods. In tacos, salsa is most important if the filling is fried with roasted meat, poultry, or fish. But a taco that is filled with a stewed dish doesn't need any salsa because it already has its own juices and the broth it was cooked in. The mixtures of chile, garlic, onion, spices, and herbs that go into this type of condiment salsa function like the broths in which meats or vegetables are cooked. The *molcajete,* or mortar, is ideal for preparing salsa.

MOLCAJETE: THE VOLCANIC UTENSIL

The molcajete that is now in use is exactly the same as those used daily by the indigenous women of the Mesoamerican region and very similar to various types of mortar used across the world. The molcajete is a piece of volcanic rock (though today other types of rock are sometimes used) carved into a bowl shape. The ingredients of the salsa are ground up against the rough, porous rock under the pressure of a pestle, or *tejolote,* a Nahuatl word that means "stone" or "pressing hand." Eventually, with daily use, the molcajete begins to wear down and small particles of lava come off, containing tiny quantities of iron, copper, and other minerals, which, mixed with whatever is being prepared, enrich the diet of many Mexicans, ancient and contemporary, who do not have access to a nutritionally balanced variety of foods or to industrially manufactured vitamins.

Garlic and onions are crushed first until they have completely lost their shape, then the softer chiles are ground in; salt is added, which helps with the grinding, and finally the tomato or tomatillo is pounded into the rest. For this type of salsa, it is best to roast the ingredients first, except the fresh herbs that are added last; the chiles, tomatoes, or tomatillos can also be boiled. *Salsa de molcajete* is served in the molcajete itself immediately after being prepared. Although many people are addicted to chile and consume it in exaggerated quantities, a well-prepared salsa uses it in moderation, only as a condiment. If the chile is excessive, it overpowers the flavor of all the other ingredients and numbs the palate.

***Molcajetes* are much more than kitchen utensils. They are works of folk art that speak to us of the innate grace and subtle artistry of the Mexican people.**

THE PSYCHOLOGY OF CHILES

Arturo Lomeli, a friend of mine who has kindly allowed me to reprint his dictionary of chiles at the end of this book, tells me that chiles have been a remedy and a consolation for innumerable generations of Mexicans. He theorizes that across the centuries chiles have functioned as a highly effective social pacifier because the boring diet of Mexico's poor, which otherwise might make them revolt in fury, becomes interesting and appealing thanks to the baroque variety of chiles.

Furthermore, chiles are an effective medicine. They are rich in vitamin C and can ward off colds and flu or help sufferers get through it more quickly. One chile contains 94 mg of vitamin C and 310 mg of vitamin A, while an orange has only 37 mg of vitamin C and 146 mg of vitamin A, and a grapefruit has only 13.5 mg of vitamin C. Chile is a terrific expectorant as well as a digestive stimulant. I've read that in Thailand it has even been used as a psychiatric medication because it startles catatonic patients out of their lethargy.

As if that weren't enough, it has been scientifically established that chile is a very effective analgesic because capsicum, the chemical that produces chile's hotness, acts on the nerve endings to block pain. Given its medicinal value, it is easy to understand why eating chile becomes a kind of addiction for many people. But obviously such an addiction, like any other, is not compatible with eating well.

There is no doubt in my mind that in the majority of Mexican homes where good food is appreciated, chile is used sensibly with a moderation that is almost an art. The women of country towns are especially expert at combining the flavors of chiles, tomatillos, or tomatoes with herbs such as cilantro or *pipetza,* a wild grass with a very definite aroma. I usually avoid the word *exotic,* but I will say that pipetza is exotic; its flavor is very hard to describe and can't be compared to any other.

CHILE IN CHINA

I once had a long and useless argument with a woman of Chinese origins, a well-known gourmet, who couldn't accept my statement that chile originated in Mesoamerica and had been transported from there to China, where it gave rise to Hunan and Szechwan cuisine. Fortunately her companion brought the discussion to an end by giving her a gentle kick. I can't seem to locate the exact book where the following story is told but I will include it here since it shows chile in such a good light. It appears that the communities of Szechwan and Hunan had for many years suffered defeat and humiliation at the hands of their neighbors because the people were weakened by the lack of certain vitamins. When they began adding chile to their food they believed that it made their warriors stronger and more daring, and after that they emerged victorious from battle. . . .

	VITAMIN C	VITAMIN A
CHILE	94 MG	310 MG
ORANGE	37 MG	146 MG
GRAPEFRUIT	13.5 MG	166 MG
LEMON	39 MG	10MG
AVOCADO	10 MG	2.15 MG

This chart shows the high vitamin content of chiles compared to other fruits.

GREEN CHILES

Mexicans have had millennia to refine the place of chiles in their cuisine; in Tehuacán, in the state of Puebla, traces of chile seeds seven thousand years old have been found inside the remains of the bodies of the ancient residents of that area. Green chiles are roasted, fried, or ground up raw, depending on the type of chile in question or the dish that is being prepared. The most popular types of green chiles are, in order, serranos, jalapeños, poblanos, and chiles de árbol. Serrano chiles are a central ingredient in *salsa cruda* (raw salsa), or salsa mexicana. They are also used in green salsas and cooked salsas. The very fresh smell of serrano chiles reminds me of grass. When I started serving guacamole at Rosa Mexicano, it was still difficult to find serranos in New York, so I substituted jalapeños, which were readily available. The two varieties are interchangeable, but not exactly the same. Jalapeño chiles are classically used for *rajas en escabeche* (canned pickled chile strips), and for making stuffed chiles. Because of their long and robust form and their abundant flesh, poblano chiles are ideal for preparing sauces to cook other foods in and for the traditional *chiles rellenos, rajas,* and *salsa de poblano.* Today they are available almost everywhere. Green chiles de árbol, which are much hotter, are used in condiment salsas, *chilacas,* which are also fiery, and are used for making rajas.

But undoubtedly the fieriest and most aromatic of the fresh chiles are those called habaneros. They can be green, yellow, or orange. Despite their name, they did not originate in Havana or in Cuba, but along the Caribbean coastline and in the Yucatán peninsula. They are treated with a great deal of respect because if you handle them with bare hands you may continue to feel their heat for several days. They are grilled on the comal, minced, then mixed with minced onion; a little lemon or bitter orange juice is added and they are served as a condiment, especially with the regional foods of southeastern Mexico.

A similar chile, but larger, fleshier, and with black seeds, is the variety called *manzano,* which is slightly less hot. But poblano chiles are undoubtedly the most popular fresh chiles throughout Mexico.

CHILES RELLENOS / POBLANO CHILES FILLED WITH CHEESE AND SERVED WITH TOMATO BROTH

SERVES 6

12 medium (or 6 large) poblano chiles, roasted, peeled, and deveined
2 to 3 cups queso fresco, grated
6 egg whites
5 egg yolks
1 cup all-purpose flour, for dredging
3 cups vegetable oil, for frying
salt to taste
Tomato Broth (recipe follows)

1. Roast the chiles to char the skin and peel. Make an incision in the chiles and carefully remove the seeds and veins. Be sure to keep the chiles intact. Set aside. Stuff the poblanos with cheese.
2. Whisk the egg whites until they have soft peaks. Whisk the egg yolks and fold the whites into the yolks.
3. Dredge the stuffed chiles in flour; carefully shake off the excess flour.
4. Heat the oil in a 2-quart saucepan. Dip the stuffed chiles into the egg batter and allow the excess batter to drip off; then gently lower the chiles into the hot oil, turning them carefully so that they brown on all sides. When the chiles are browned, remove from the oil with a slotted spoon and drain on paper towels. Season with salt.

■ ■ ■ TOMATO BROTH MAKES 6 CUPS

½ medium onion, chopped
1 garlic clove, finely minced
2 pounds vine-ripened tomatoes, roasted, peeled, seeded, and chopped
3 cups chicken stock
3 tablespoons vegetable oil
salt and freshly ground black pepper to taste

1. Put the onion, garlic, tomatoes, and chicken stock in the blender. Blend until smooth.
2. Heat the oil in a 2-quart saucepan. Add the tomato puree. Bring to a boil and reduce to simmer. Season with salt and pepper and simmer for 10 minutes. Adjust seasoning if necessary.
3. Strain through a fine sieve.

To serve, place a layer of the sauce with one chile relleno on each plate.

RAJAS DE CHILE POBLANO / SAUTÉED STRIPS OF POBLANO CHILES AND ONIONS

SERVES 6

I call the poblano chile the "noble chile." Rajas is a component of many other recipes, such as Budín Azteca, tamales, and sauces.

4 large poblano chiles
3 tablespoons vegetable oil
2 medium white onions, sliced thinly
2 garlic cloves, finely chopped

1. Roast the chiles to char the skin. Place in a plastic bag for 10 minutes. Remove the skin and wash under running water; seed and devein. Slice into ¼-inch strips.
2. Heat the oil in a 10-inch sauté pan and sauté the sliced onions for 3 to 4 minutes. Add the garlic and poblano strips and sauté for 6 to 8 minutes, or until the onions are translucent. Cool. Refrigerate for up to two weeks.

Note: One of Craig Claiborne's favorite dishes at Rosa is a plate of rajas with cheese melted on top.

POBLANO MOUSSE

SERVES 6

This recipe was inspired by a pepper mousse from Paula Wolfert's book The Cooking of South-West France. *Since peppers are chiles, I thought why not try the recipe with poblanos. It was a success! It is served with the seafood platter at the restaurant and over the whole poached red snapper.*

1 recipe Rajas de Chile Poblano (see page 118)
1 cup heavy cream

1. Blend the rajas in a blender to make a smooth paste.
2. Whip the cream to soft peaks. Fold the chile paste into the whipped cream.

RAVIOLIS DE POLLO CON SALSA DE CHILE POBLANO / CHICKEN RAVIOLI WITH POBLANO CHILE SAUCE

SERVES 6

This recipe is adapted from one in an 1840s poblano cookbook.

1 3-to-3½-pound chicken
1 stalk celery, coarsely chopped
1 medium white onion, quartered
2 carrots, coarsely chopped
8 whole peppercorns
3 to 4 sprigs Italian parsley
4 tablespoons vegetable oil
1 medium white onion, finely chopped
2 garlic cloves, minced
3 vine-ripened tomatoes, roasted, peeled, seeded, and finely chopped
120 wonton skins
3 eggs, beaten
2 tablespoons water
cornstarch
Chili Poblano Sauce (recipe follows)
6 ounces manchego cheese, grated

1. Place the chicken in a large stockpot with the celery, quartered onion, carrots, peppercorns, and Italian parsley. Cover with water and bring to a boil. Reduce to a simmer and cook for 30 to 40 minutes. Allow to cool in the stock.
2. Strain the chicken and reserve the stock for cooking the ravioli. There should be about 5 cups of stock. Remove all of the meat from the chicken carcass and shred it into small pieces.
3. Heat the vegetable oil in a 10-inch sauté pan. Sauté the chopped onion for 4 to 5 minutes, add the garlic and cook until translucent. Add the tomato

and cook for 2 to 3 minutes, stirring occasionally. Add the chicken and cook until most of the liquid has evaporated.

4. To assemble the ravioli: Place a spoonful of the chicken filling into each wonton wrapper. Brush with edges of the wrapper with a mixture of the beaten egg and water and place the second wonton over the filling and seal the edges. Carefully remove any air from within the ravioli. Pinch the edges together to seal. Place the ravioli on a cookie sheet sprinkled with a little cornstarch. Cover with a slightly damp cloth to prevent ravioli from drying out.

Note: To make Tinga Poblana de Pollo, chicken filling for tacos, stir in 1 to 2 teaspoons of chipotle paste made from pureeing a can of chipotle chiles.

■ ■ ■ CHILE POBLANO SAUCE

6 poblano chiles
4 tablespoons butter
½ medium onion, chopped
1 cup chicken broth
1 cup heavy cream, scalded
¾ cup champagne
salt to taste

1. Roast chiles and place in a plastic bag; allow to steam for 10 minutes. Peel, seed, and devein the chiles and cut into strips.
2. Heat 2 tablespoons of the butter in an 8-inch sauté pan. Sauté the onions for 4 to 5 minutes until translucent. Add the chile strips and sauté for 2 to 3 minutes more. Allow to cool slightly.
3. Place the chiles and onions in a blender. Blend, adding enough chicken stock to make the blades turn.
4. Heat the remaining 2 tablespoons butter in a 1½-quart saucepan. Sauté the chile paste for approximately 5 minutes, stirring occasionally. Add the remaining chicken stock and let simmer for 3 to 4 minutes. Add the scalded

cream and the champagne and simmer for 2 to 3 more minutes. Season to taste with salt.

5. To serve: In a deep saucepan, bring 5 cups chicken broth (the liquid reserved from cooking the chicken) to a boil, reduce to simmer, and cook the ravioli approximately 3 to 5 minutes or until cooked through. Remove with a skimmer and place 5 ravioli on each plate. Ladle poblano sauce over the ravioli. Sprinkle manchego cheese over the sauce and place under a broiler for 30 seconds or long enough to melt the cheese.

FROM THE TREE OF LA NOCHE TRISTE TO CHILES EN NOGADA

Among the many stories and legends of Mexican cooking is the tale of *chiles en nogada,* a dish traditionally eaten on September 16, Mexico's Independence Day. One of the heroes of Mexico's independence was General Agustín de Iturbide. The story goes that he once paid a visit to Puebla, a very colonial and baroque city where convents and monasteries abound. Chiles en nogada were created and served to General Iturbide at a banquet in one of those convents; the dish includes all the colors of the newly independent nation's flag to celebrate and honor the man who won the war of independence.

During the first years of my life in Mexico I met many hardworking, intelligent, receptive, and sensible people. As a free-lance decorator, I was always on the lookout for furniture makers who could carry out my ideas and work in the eighteenth-century English style I specialized in. I had realized that this type of furniture needed to be larger, since it was generally being made in smaller dimensions because the Mexicans had adapted it to their own size.

This was how I met Señor Rueda, Señor Mora, and the craftsmen who worked with them. I must note that in all the decorating work I did for more than twenty years, I never brought anything in from outside Mexico; I always found Mexican craftsmen who understood my projects. My clients were willing to finance any trip abroad that might have been necessary, but I never had to leave. One September, Señor Mora phoned me out of the blue and said, "I'm coming to pick you up and bring you to my house. My wife makes excellent chiles en nogada; it's the time of year for them right now and you have to taste them."

On the way to his house in Atzcapotzalco, site of another former part of the Aztec empire, Señor Mora stopped to show me a place that has been a symbol of triumph for Mexicans for several centuries, the tree of *la noche triste* (the sad night). The story goes that this was the spot—at that point it was on the outskirts of Tenochtitlán—where Hernán Cortés sat down to weep over the defeat of his first attempt to conquer the city. An enormous old tree trunk, with very few branches, was surrounded by a metal fence that held a plaque describing the event and giving its date. The very name of the "sad night" surprised me, since it was, after all, the invaders who called it that.

When we reached the Mora family home I was served a dish that initially seemed more like an odd children's game than food. I started by tasting the sauce, which was at room temperature; it was so sweet I thought I was about to eat some kind of cake. I was told to add some pomegranate seeds, which seemed to be on the plate only as a decoration to the sauce, and I began to like the combination. Then I cut into the chile, and the hot ground beef surprised me with its accompanying texture of nuts, pine nuts, and candied fruit. The combination of savoriness, sweetness, hardness, and crunch produced a lively sensation in my mouth. Then I felt the heat of the poblano chile. When I went home, I couldn't really say if I had liked what I ate or if I had only been surprised by it. But the trip to Atzcapotzalco, an ancient kingdom, and the visit to the tree of the sad night added up to quite an adventure.

CHILES EN NOGADA AT ROSA MEXICANO

We tried to add chiles en nogada to the menu, but there was an obstacle: At that time pomegranates were available in New York only in November and December. So we serve chiles en nogada only then. Each year the arrival of the pomegranates is greatly anticipated; because the dish is so colorful, many of my customers assume it is made for Christmas, and they call up to ask if we have the "Christmas chiles" yet. For Mexicans, chiles en nogada is part of the celebration of their independence day in September; for many New Yorkers it has become a "typical Mexican Christmas dish." In gastronomical matters such as these, the only really important thing is for the dish to taste good, look good, and use quality ingredients.

Chiles en nogada is just a more elaborate version of a very characteristic technique of Mexican cooking: stuffing. In any Mexican home, a lot of stuffed zucchini, nopales, squash flowers, morel mushrooms, and poblano and jalapeño chiles are served, and certain dried chiles are stuffed as well. Chiles rellenos, or stuffed chiles, are a classic of Mexican cooking, a dish we couldn't possibly have left off the menu at Rosa Mexicano. We stuff them either with cheese or with ground meat cooked in tomato broth and seasoned with raisins. They are always dipped in batter, fried, and, just before being served, cooked for a few minutes in tomato broth. The version stuffed with cheese is one of the options for my guests who choose to avoid dishes made with meat.

CHILES EN NOGADA

SERVES 6

This dish was invented for Mexican Independence Day, which happens to also be my birthday. It takes advantage of the fresh walnuts and pomegranates that are in season at that time to create one of Mexico's most exquisite and favorite dishes, with the colors of the Mexican flag. It is a dish full of contrasts and a blend of textures: sweet/sour, warm/cold, salty/sweet.

FOR THE CHILES:

12 poblano chiles

Roast the chiles to char the skin (see page 284). Carefully clean the skin, leaving the chile intact and make an incision to remove the seeds and veins. (Soaking the chiles in hot, salted water produces milder chiles.)

FOR THE SAUCE:

2 cups shelled and peeled walnut halves (if fresh, skin can be peeled immediately)

½ cup farmer cheese

1½ cups heavy cream (approximately)
2 slices white bread, trim the crusts, soak in cold water, and squeeze dry
1 teaspoon sugar

Pour boiling water over the walnuts and soak overnight. Drain and peel (rubbing the walnuts in a rough towel helps). This is somewhat difficult when the walnuts are not very fresh. Chop very fine in a blender or food processor. Add the cheese, cream, bread, and sugar and process until homogenous. The texture will be smooth and slightly thick. Thin with a little more cream if necessary, but be careful not to blend too much or the cream will whip. The sauce should be pourable but thick enough to coat the chiles. Chill thoroughly.

FOR THE STUFFING:

2 pounds pork shoulder, boneless, trimmed and cut into 1½-inch cubes with water to cover
1 medium white onion, peeled and quartered
1 bay leaf
8 black peppercorns
3 whole cloves
1 tablespoon salt
¼ cup vegetable oil
½ medium white onion, chopped
4 garlic cloves, peeled and finely chopped
4 vine-ripened medium tomatoes, roasted, peeled, seeded, and chopped
2 peaches, peeled, pitted, and finely diced (optional)
2 pears, peeled, cored, and finely diced
2 red apples, peeled, cored, and finely diced
½ cup raisins, soaked in hot water and drained
3 tablespoons diced mixed candied fruit
⅛ teaspoon each ground cinnamon and cloves

salt and pepper to taste

---

seeds from 2 small pomegranates
¼ cup parsley, coarsely chopped

1. Place the pork into a 2-quart saucepan with the onion and spices, except the salt, and add water to cover. Bring to a boil, lower the heat, and simmer until tender, 45 to 60 minutes, adding the salt after the first half hour. Allow the pork to cool in its liquid. Chop the pork; reserve ½ cup of the liquid.
2. Heat ¼ cup vegetable oil in a 3-quart saucepan and sauté the chopped onion over medium heat until translucent. Add the garlic and cook for another minute. Add the chopped tomatoes and stir and cook for about 5 minutes. Push to the side, leaving a space in the center.
3. Stir in the chopped pork. Add a few tablespoons of the reserved broth. Cook the mixture for about 15 minutes. Stir in the diced fruits, raisins, candied fruit, and spices; mix in the tomatoes. Season with salt and pepper to taste. Bring the mixture to a simmer and remove from the heat.
4. Stuff each chile with some of the warm mixture; do not pack too tight. To serve: Arrange the stuffed chiles on a platter, seam side down. Chiles should be served warm with cold sauce (preferably not directly from the refrigerator and ice cold). Pour the sauce over the chiles, leaving the stems showing. Sprinkle with the pomegranate seeds and chopped parsley and serve.

GUACAMOLE AT ROSA MEXICANO

Mexican cuisine offers a wide variety of sauces in which foods are cooked. The dishes we serve at Rosa Mexicano are generally cooked as tradition dictates, that is, marinated before being grilled, then served with the sauces they were cooked or marinated in. We almost never serve sauces on the side (though occasionally I serve *chiles encurtidos,* chiles and vegetables marinated in a combination of oil, vinegar, and aromatic herbs).

Guacamole, usually served as a condiment in Mexico (basically it's a salsa cruda with avocado added), has become at Rosa Mexicano an appetizer and one of the signature dishes of the house. By having our waiters prepare it for guests at their tables, I'm trying not only to demonstrate guacamole's freshness and simplicity but to show people how to use the marvelous Mexican molcajete.

GUACAMOLE EN MOLCAJETE

SERVES 2

The key to this basically simple dish is the ripeness and freshness of the ingredients and the fact that they retain their flavors in the chunky consistency. The flavor is best if the ingredients are crushed in a molcajete, a volcanic stone, or in a mortar and pestle.

3 tablespoons chopped white onion
½ teaspoon chopped serrano chiles
1½ teaspoons finely chopped cilantro
½ teaspoon salt
1 ripe Hass avocado
1 small vine-ripened tomato sliced in half, horizontally. Cut out the stem, scoop out the seeds and center with a spoon, and chop

1. In a small bowl, thoroughly mash 1 tablespoon chopped onion, the serrano chiles, ½ teaspoon cilantro, and salt with the back of a wooden spoon until it is a juicy paste.
2. Holding the avocado in the palm of your hand, cut the avocado in half lengthwise around the pit with a paring knife. Twist the top half of the avocado to separate the halves. Carefully hit the pit with the edge of a sharp knife and twist to remove the seed. Slice it lengthwise into approximately ¼-inch strips and then across to form a grid. Scoop the avocado out with a spoon next to the skin. Place in a bowl with the paste.
3. Stir thoroughly to coat with the paste. Add the remaining onion, remaining cilantro, and the tomato, and gently fold to incorporate all the ingredients. Add more chopped serrano chiles and salt to taste.
4. Serve with freshly made tortilla chips or corn tortillas.

Note: Adjust the amount of serrano chiles in the recipe for mild, medium, or hot guacamole.

TOMATOES

Guacamole has two main ingredients, both of them original products of the Mesoamerican region: avocado and tomato, whose name, even in English, evinces its origin. Tomato derives from the Nahuatl word *ictli tomatl,* which means fleshy, globular, and with a belly button. Look at a tomato, and you won't have any trouble understanding why it was given that name.

When I arrived in Mexico I was startled by the way tomatoes were used. The common practice in Europe at that time was to use canned tomatoes; fresh tomatoes were used only after having been boiled for hours and hours to make sauces. I discovered that Mexicans eat tomatoes practically raw much of the time. The Mexican method is to roast the tomato all over on the comal, take off the skin (though sometimes a trace of burned skin is left on purpose), then open it up and take out the seeds. In addition to giving the tomato's pulp a slightly smoky flavor, the initial roasting provides all the cooking necessary for making a sauce to cook with or a salsa pureed in a molcajete or blender.

In Mexico, there are over twenty different types of tomato. There are cherry tomatoes, large tomatoes known as *guajillos,* yellow tomatoes, and the variety that in the United States are called beefsteak tomatoes. I love to bite into a beefsteak tomato as if it were an apple. Delicious!

Tomatoes were taken to Europe aboard Spanish ships, though many years went by before they were fully accepted, especially in France and Italy (think of it—an Italy without tomato sauce!). Because the tomato was so new and different, many qualities were attributed to it: People believed it was an aphrodisiac or was extremely poisonous.

The tomato also met with some resistance in the United States. It was first eaten in Louisiana, which has a long-standing connection to the Mexican port of Veracruz because of the maritime route across the Gulf of Mexico that links the two cities. In 1918, following the First World War, a campaign was waged across the United States to promote a more healthful diet, based on fruits and vegetables. That was when tomatoes finally gained wide acceptance; they were particularly recommended because of the vitamins and minerals they contain. Tomatoes began to be cultivated in Florida and California, but for many years most tomatoes were used for making catsup or canned tomato puree.

TOMATOES AT ROSA MEXICANO

In the years since I started the restaurant, the cultivation of tomatoes has made great strides in the United States. There was a time when the fresh tomatoes from New Jersey supplied by Tomato Bob were available only in the summer, and importing tomatoes from Mexico to New York was a problem. One day, to my great good luck, Lucky Lee, from a company called Lucky Tomato, appeared in my office. Her family, which for generations had worked on Wall Street, had decided to move to Florida to grow high-quality organic tomatoes. Until then, the tomatoes I could get were the same as those sold in supermarkets, picked before they were ripe and transported in refrigerated trucks. Lucky Lee offered me, and other New York restaurateurs, tomatoes that are not picked until they have ripened on the vine; they are placed in a truck in Florida at night and reach our kitchens the next day, without having been exposed to any gas to make them ripen more quickly. For our guacamole and salsas, we seed them and use only the flesh next to the skin; that way, the texture and quality of the tomato is sweeter and fresher. It's how I learned to use tomatoes in the kitchens of my Mexican friends, and it's what we do in the kitchen at Rosa Mexicano.

AVOCADOS AND THE TOWN WITHOUT CRIME

Pear-shaped and with dark, shiny skin, avocados hang in pairs from the tall, leafy tree they grow on. The name *avocado,* which is used in languages across the world, is also of Nahuatl origins: It means tree testicles (since they grow in pairs). When we say tomato or avocado, we're using names and concepts that reflect the images that the indigenous peoples of Mesoamerica had of the foods of their land.

The type of avocado known in Mexico as the *criollo* has skin that is black, shiny, and very thin and a large pit surrounded by a moderate amount of pulp. I first ate one in a town called Chiconcuac in the state of Morelos (not to be confused with the other town of the same name in the state of Mexico), only a few miles from Cuernavaca. The principal product of Chiconcuac is sugarcane. It is a lovely place, with avocado trees and a beautiful aque-

Avocados: Mexico's answer to butter.

duct. In recent years it's become a favorite spot for families from Mexico City to build their country houses.

Erich Fromm, the famous psychoanalyst, once used this town as an example in a study of human behavior. And on my visit, I was struck not only by the almost tropical beauty of the town with its geraniums and profusion of other flowers but also by the unique way the community handled its problems. In the center of the town was the jail, with no bars, locks, or even doors. Anyone who had broken the law in any way—and the infractions were always minor—went of their own accord and sat on the bench in the "jail." They did it calmly and sat out the days of their "sentence" along with others who kept them company on the other side of the wall. Chiconcuac was and is an exceptional place. I don't know if it is still a town without crime or criminals, but I do know that it is still as beautiful as ever.

In Chiconcuac, I saw black, shiny avocados hanging in pairs from the branches of the trees. I was told to eat them skin and all, following the local custom, and I did; their skin tastes a bit like grass, slightly bitter and also sweet and nutty. I've seen people squeeze the pit out and then eat the avocado, including the skin, which adheres very tightly to the pulp, in a tortilla with a little salt. Eaten this way, an avocado taco yields a delightful variety of textures and flavors. In order to produce avocados for export, an initial hybrid called *fuerte* (strong) was developed, with tougher skin and abundant pulp. Several years ago, an agronomist named Hass came up with the avocado that today bears his name; it has a tough, hardy skin and a lot of pulp. In the city of Atlixco, a few kilometers from Puebla, I found a touching monument to the avocado: an avocado tree planted by the California Association of Avocado Producers and marked by a testimonial plaque. I'm waiting for the day when I'll have time to go there, clean the plaque and decorate the monument, because I, too, must pay tribute to this marvelous fruit.

AVOCADOS AT ROSA MEXICANO

When an avocado is split open as we prepare guacamole for our guests, it must be fully and perfectly ripe. The system we have developed consists of putting the avocados away when we first receive them, then moving them to different places depending on the number of days left until they're ripe. We wait almost a week before using the hardest ones, and during that time many of them ripen to perfection. Because of their natural delicacy, others simply rot, and we are continually having to throw avocados away. But our top priority is to make sure that anyone who orders guacamole at Rosa Mexicano will enjoy it in all its splendor, with an avocado that has flesh as soft as butter. I also use white onions, like those used in Mexico, for guacamole. I've always preferred them to yellow onions, which are sweeter.

A CHANGE IN MY LIFE

My stay at La Ventilla was brief, but since I had already been living in Mexico for five years, I could better appreciate and understand the many things I saw there. My marriage went through a serious crisis. We returned to Mexico City for a short time and tried to rebuild our relationship, but in the end we separated. I went back to Teotihuacán alone with my sons. During the time we lived at La Ventilla, I only went into the city on Saturdays. In those years, something was taking shape that would eventually become quite an institution: the Bazaar Sábado, a weekly market where the wares of a highly selective group of well-known artisans were sold. In its early years, the bazaar was located in a little street in the neighborhood of San Ángel. For years now it has filled San Ángel's Plaza de San Jacinto, and it is frequented by Mexicans and foreign visitors alike.

RETURN TO THE MAGIC . . . OF TEOTIHUACÁN

Around that time, I had started selling jewelry designed by Frank Lowenstein, whom I had met in Teotihuacán, and who was one of the pioneers of the Bazaar Sábado. He had worked in the mining industry and was raised in the southern United States, the son of a rabbi. He had been married twice and always had a girl on his arm. He was a wise, knowledgeable man, and a current of sympathy and respect grew up between us, from which a solid friendship was born. Frank enjoyed Mexico and especially San Juan Teotihuacán. Only two or three miles from La Ventilla, he had rebuilt an old hacienda that dated back to the sixteenth century and called it La Posada. He received only a select number of guests, some of them famous Mexicans, but the majority from the United States. Each bedroom at La Posada had been decorated with great care in the Mexican colonial style; the decor at La Posada was in excellent taste, and the inn provided its guests with every service. Frank had set up a small store there to sell his jewelry and a few beautiful handicrafts.

The presence of that small, exclusive hotel and its shop inspired me to rent a house in San Martín de las Pirámides, a house I found only a few steps away from the inn. It was a simple building situated at the far end of a rectangular lot and filling up its entire width. The house was two stories high, and the stairway that connected the two floors had been built in front on the outside; the front door was at the top of the stairs on the right. On the left side of the house's facade, a beautiful ahuehuete tree protected it with its shade. You had to walk quite far across the empty lot to reach the house, and it occurred to me to take advantage of all the stones that were left over from the renovation work on the inside of the house to make more than half the lot into a garden. Among the stones piled against one of the house's walls, I planted a vast and varied selection of cacti. It was an extraordinary garden; some of the cacti quickly began to produce beautiful flowers. I put a speaker from my stereo system among the branches of the ahuehuete, and spent many tranquil evenings sitting out in my garden waiting for the stars to appear while being carried away by the music. Gregorian chants were particular favorites of mine and they elevated my spirit; the torrent of notes harmonized perfectly with the spirituality of that place, which was once the "Sacred City."

My older son was already in his early years of elementary school and the younger one was just beginning to go to school. I enrolled the boys in the town school. I had witnessed the magic of the place during my last stay in the neighborhood of the pyramids, but this time I lived inside it. Around

Nopaleras like these are a frequent feature of the landscape throughout Mexico. Both the fruit—which can be red, green, or yellow—and the leaves can be eaten.

that time, "Sound and Light" displays began taking place at the pyramids, and on weekend nights their peaks shone like brilliant jewels. The fantastic panorama of the sky in the evening, at dawn, and during the day never ceased to amaze me, and my friendships with the people of the town grew closer every day. My sons played with the town's children and with Frank's sons. A dear local woman named Paula came to help me with the housework and the boys, while I worked on smoothing out some details at La Posada and running the shop.

I remember the serene afternoons when the boys came to tell me they were "going to get prickly pears." They came back glowing, with baskets brimming with green, red, and yellow prickly pears. They had learned the art of picking them without getting cactus spines in their hands. They brought back such enormous quantities of prickly pears that we had to make jam. Under Paula's guidance, the boys learned to make prickly pear and nopal marmalade.

In San Juan Teotihuacán and San Martín de las Pirámides, the moon and stars captivated the eye. For a long time, we could do nothing but look up at the facets of the moon, the sparkle of the stars, the cupola of the universe; it was hard to look away. It isn't at all surprising that the place's first inhabitants constructed a pyramid of the moon, which was the first thing they worshipped. Later they built a larger pyramid to the sun, but they also laid down a road, "the road of the dead." And of course they built their homes. The town of San Martín de las Pirámides and its surroundings were full of "mysteries." Everywhere you looked there were rocks marked "Do Not Touch"; they had been set there to mark and guard some archaeological remains of the place's ancient inhabitants that hadn't yet been disinterred. I used to drive along green and beautiful country roads to do my banking in the town of Tulacingo, in the state of Hidalgo, which was the same distance from Teotihuacán as Mexico City, about twenty-four miles. Near the bank in the town's small commercial district was a Sears, Roebuck store that made me laugh. I always wondered, What is that store doing here, in this otherworldly spot? Between the Sears, the bank, and the street was a little hummock of earth with a sign on top: "Do Not Touch."

THE VISITS OF THE SOULS (DAYS OF THE DEAD) IN HIDALGO

The state of Hidalgo, which lies to the northeast of Mexico City, is one of the country's richest silver-producing regions. Across the state traces remain of the British families who for many years were involved in exploiting the region's silver, whether it was to be found in forests and rivers or in extremely arid areas.

A significant portion of the inhabitants of Hidalgo are heirs to the customs and language of the Otomí people. One of my fondest memories of that time is of going to what is called the Fiesta del Xantolo. Every year on October 31 the local families prepare their altars. They first make an arch with green leafy branches, which they decorate with citrus and other kinds of seasonal fruits; beneath the arch they put a table covered with a white, hand-embroidered cloth, on which many different kinds of foods are set out, along with candles, flowers, and colorful paper streamers. They believe that this is the day their dead children—who died innocent, without having known the sins of this life—come to the house and are welcomed with sesame tamales and atole. On that day no meat is eaten, and the living children of each family are the guests of honor. The following day the altar is filled with the favorite foods of the family members who died as adults, to prepare for their arrival.

While the women are cooking and baking breads, the men have to build and decorate the altar. Then the beer and other drinks are brought out. The entire day of November 1 and the entire night, until dawn, is spent singing to the dead, inviting them to come and visit their families. On November 2, after having eaten and drunk again, the whole community carries the food on foot to the cemetery on a hill, where the graves painted in vivid colors stand out in strong contrast to the surrounding green; it was a place that moved me deeply when I saw it and moves me still when I remember it. Who would fear death with so lovely a final home waiting? The life of the inhabitants of these mountains may seem poor, but when they die they certainly rest in heaven. . . .

At the cemetery, the townspeople sing to their dead once more and surround the headstones with flowers and lighted candles. My heart almost burst when I heard them singing "Las Mañanitas"—the Mexican birthday song—to the dead children because it was "their day." *El día que tu naciste, nacieron todas las flores,* the song goes. "The day you were born, all the flowers were born."

The souls of the dead continue their visit for a month, until the last day of November. Then the men of the town cover their faces with masks or handkerchiefs, and some of them dress up as women, and they parade through the town dancing, accompanied by stringed instruments and trumpets. A few little boys dressed up as devils are particularly enthusiastic participants. These dancers are called *"Los disfrazados,"* or "The Disguised"; it's their job to announce that the day has arrived when the souls of the dead must end their visit to the town. The disguises and the masks are to keep Death, which is circling near, from recognizing them. Women do not participate. Again there is a procession to the cemetery, where they pray, remembering each of their dead by name. A special altar is built for those who died in far-off times and no longer have anyone to remember them. After so much eating, drinking, and celebrating for the dead, the people of the town and anyone else who happens to be there can feel that the souls have returned to where they came from and life goes on. . . .

People in Hidalgo like to sing a little tune that goes *Sigamos comiendo y bebiendo aunque salgamos debiendo* (which means something like "Let's go on eating and drinking even if we end up in debt"). In fact, the people there are very proud of always having something to eat, for they have thoroughly mastered the art of making full use of the maguey. Hidalgo is the region where maguey worms are produced in greatest abundance, as well as ant eggs (*escamoles*), and maguey flowers, which are eaten with corn tortillas. One of the regional specialties is the *zacahuil* tamale, which is made with a thick, very coarsely ground masa and then wrapped around a whole turkey or sheep. Needless to say, the zacahuil is enormous and has to be cooked in a specially constructed clay oven.

Pachuca is the capital of the state of Hidalgo, and the town's culinary specialty, in addition to maguey worms when they're in season and a few other antojitos, is its *pastis.* These pastis are the local version of the classic English turnover known as the Cornish pasty, which was brought to Pachuca by British miners, many of whom were from Cornwall. Like the originals, they are usually filled with ground meat and potatoes, though the Mexican pastis are flavored with green chiles. What struck me most about them was the finger-width rim of dough that surrounds the turnover. There is a very interesting and practical explanation for this. The area's numerous miners were fond of eating pastis, and some ingenious woman must have seen them doing so with dirty hands and had the idea of adding a little more crust around the edges so that the miners could hold the pasti by the rim of crust, eat it without getting the dirt from their hands onto it, and then throw away the rim. Fresh and hot from the oven, pastis melt in your mouth in a rich variety of flavors and aromas as the delicately prepared meat contrasts with the soft texture of the pastry. Here is the original recipe for the English Cornish Pasty, which you can Mexicanize by adding a bit of minced chile to the meat. If you're planning on eating them with dirty fingers, be sure to add a rim with which to hold them.

PASTIS

SERVES 6

Strangely enough, these are the same as the pasties made in Cornwall, England.

FOR THE DOUGH:

2 pounds all-purpose flour
1 tablespoon salt
1 pound unsalted butter, chilled
2 to 4 tablespoons ice water

1. Pour the flour onto the counter and make a well in the center. Sprinkle the salt around the well. Cut the butter into cubes and place in the well in the center of the flour.
2. With the tips of your fingers, pinch the cubes of butter and toss with the flour and salt to coat. It is important to work quickly so that the butter does not become too soft.
3. Add 2 tablespoons of water and toss to bring the dough together with your hands. Add only enough water to make a dough that holds together but is

slightly crumbly. It should not be wet. Wrap in plastic wrap and refrigerate for 1 hour.

FOR THE EGG WASH:

3 egg yolks
3 tablespoons milk

Mix well with a fork.

FOR THE FILLING:

1 pound potatoes
4 tablespoons vegetable oil
½ medium white onion, finely chopped
¼ pound ground beef
salt and pepper to taste
2 tablespoons Italian parsley, finely chopped

1. Wash the potatoes and cut into small (⅛-inch) cubes.
2. Heat the vegetable oil in a 12-inch sauté pan. Sauté the onions over medium heat, cook for 4 to 5 minutes or until translucent. Add the ground beef and potatoes. Stir with a wooden spoon, breaking up any clumps of beef as you go. Once the meat is browned, lower the heat and season with salt and freshly ground pepper to taste. Reduce the heat to low and cook for 20 minutes or until the potatoes are done.
3. Add the parsley at the end of the 20 minutes and correct the seasoning. Allow to cool.

ASSEMBLY:

Preheat oven to 325°F. Roll out the chilled dough to a ¼-inch thickness and cut into 4-inch circles. Place a spoonful of the filling on each circle. Brush the edges with the egg wash, fold the dough over, and press to seal. Twist the edges over your finger to make a nice seam. Brush the top with the egg wash. Place the pasties on a cookie sheet lined with parchment paper or brushed with oil. Bake at 325° F. for 15 to 20 minutes, or until golden brown.

LIFE IN TEOTIHUACÁN

Cooking contests were one of our favorite pastimes. Frank Lowenstein was a good cook, and we made dishes from all over the world, in every style of cooking and in large quantities. Mexican food continued to be a marvelous mystery that we enjoyed but didn't dare make ourselves. Spirits were so high during these competitions that my son Esteban decided he felt like participating, too, and I remember very clearly the day he appeared with a plate of oatmeal cookies. Once he even made a classic Jewish kugel.

My visits to the city began to be fewer and further between. On Saturdays, though, I still went with Frank to the Bazaar Sábado, where I displayed and sold the magnificent jewelry he had created. La Posada was almost always full of people, but I found that Sundays were the perfect day, to escape and enjoy life and the food in the marketplace.

The years passed and my life was very different from the one I lived when I arrived in Mexico. The boys were growing and going to school in a place that was very far from where I had grown up, and my senses had grown accustomed to the new world that surrounded me. It seemed perfectly natural to me to walk through that market, choosing—with some expertise of my own by now—among the ingredients that the vendors had for sale every week. A dish called *barbacoa* was often what I ended up opting for; the name might sound familiar, but it's nothing at all like the United States barbecue.

BARBACOA IN TEXCOCO

Barbacoa is made with tender mutton, cooked in a pit dug in the ground. To prepare barbacoa, you need the fleshy leaves, or *pencas,* of the maguey; the dish is a traditional favorite in places where magueys abound. In my day, the barbacoa in San Juan Teotihuacán was known as some of the best around, but the barbacoa in Texcoco was considered even better.

The town of Texcoco lies to the east of Mexico City on the banks of Lake Texcoco, a body of water with which Mexicans are in perpetual ecological conflict. At that time, the lake had been drained so that the lake bed could be used for agricultural purposes. But it turned out to be unsuitable for cultivation, and when March arrived with its strong winds, every throat within a wide radius suffered from the choking dust that was thrown up. Air pollution wasn't a problem yet, but the *polvaredas,* or dust storms, from the Texcoco lake bed periodically fouled the air around Mexico City. Today, the lake is being filled again and appears to be recovering; I hope the efforts to resuscitate it succeed.

Texcoco means "stopping place," so named because members of several different cultures would gather there in pre-Columbian times. Some historians claim that a renaissance of the Texcoco region was brought about by one of its emperors, Netzahualcoyotl, who formed an alliance with the Aztecs that helped his kingdom to flourish. The landscape of Texcoco is very similar to that of San Juan Teotihuacán and San Martín de las Pirámides; it's a characteristic rural Mexican landscape that had been preserved in a dignified, beautiful way. The city of Texcoco was at that time governed by a retired bullfighter named Silverio Pérez, a native of the town, and under his regime everything was in shining order. There was a nice restaurant at the bullring, serving regional dishes.

The kind of barbacoa I enjoyed eating at the Texcoco market is placed in a hole and covered with various layers of maguey leaves and hot coals; the hole is then filled in with dirt. In the early hours of the morning, the moment arrives for the ceremonial "uncovering" of the barbacoa. The dirt is pushed away with a stick, smoke starts coming out of the hole, and little by little the maguey leaves, the charcoal, and more maguey leaves appear, until finally the meat can be seen, clean and aromatic, tender, juicy, savory, and ready to enjoy. It dissolves in the mouth; its fat is like butter, and only a few grains of salt are needed to heighten its flavor. When the sheep's belly appears and is cut into slices, everyone's mouth starts watering in anticipation of another delight, which satisfies all expectations. Fresh tortillas and salsas that stand at the ready in their molcajetes complete the fiesta. The meat is generally served in tacos accompanied by a little jug of its own broth. Barbacoa is a traditional Sunday feast for the inhabitants of the central part of Mexico, where magueys are very common.

The Indians called the cooking technique used for barbacoa *tepachtle* because of the steam that cooks the meat. The technique is said to have originated along the coast, where it is called *taina*. It must have been a very common primitive method of cooking, probably used in many places across the globe before things like stoves and ovens were developed. Barbacoa can be made with any type of meat; barbacoa made with beef and poultry is sold in the marketplace of the lakeside town of Valle de Bravo in the state of Mexico. In Yucatán, banana leaves are used instead of maguey leaves. Sometimes the meat is stuffed with a mixture of different chiles and wrapped in avocado leaves before the layer of maguey leaves is put down.

The barbacoa I tasted for the first time was made with mutton. To cook it in as traditional a way as possible, I follow the instructions given by my much-admired cooking instructor Josefina Velázquez de León in her *Mexican Cookbook for American Homes*, which was published in both English and Spanish. I guard the thirteenth edition like an irreplaceable treasure. On page 260, an immensely lengthy and complex recipe for preparing barbacoa appears, instructing apprentice cooks on how to dig the pit, prepare the coals, and so on. Then, after this whole terrifying recipe for making both the oven and the barbacoa, the following notice appears: "This is the primitive method for making barbacoa. It can also be made in the same way on the bottom of an adobe oven." I would add that if my readers would like to make barbacoa in their homes, they need only cover their ovens with terra-cotta tiles. That's how pizza is made at home, and the special tiles are easy to find. In the United States, anything is possible!

In the marketplaces of Mexico, barbacoa is sometimes served in *flautas*– that is, rolled up inside long tortillas which are then deep-fried and topped with cream, shredded cheese, and *salsa borracha,* or drunken sauce. Salsa borracha is made with pasilla chiles and pulque (an alcoholic drink made from the juices of the maguey). Other marketplace stalls sell *panza rellena,* stuffed sheep's belly, a dish very similar to the Scottish haggis; both dishes use the belly of a sheep or lamb stuffed with all the animal's entrails and both are cooked in very much the same way. The difference between the two lies primarily in the Mexican addition of chile and epazote.

GRASPING THE BASIC PRINCIPLES

A frequent visitor at La Posada was a young man whose last name was Shuster (I don't remember his first name). Despite the foreign-sounding name, he appeared completely Mexican. He was a bohemian at heart who sang in a sweet voice while accompanying himself on the guitar. He was also a good cook; he would show up at the house on Sundays and we would cook lunch together. Shuster stayed in my mind because with him I finally began to understand the basic principles of the art of Mexican cooking.

Shuster made a sauce out of pasilla chiles. He roasted the chiles, softened them in boiling water, ground them up in the blender with a clove of garlic and a little onion, and poured the sauce into a beautiful clay dish that held a little hot oil. The sauce bubbled appetizingly when he poured in a generous amount of chicken stock to make a lovely chile broth. Shuster then broke several eggs, one by one, into the hot broth. When I tasted the eggs, whose yolks were still soft and whose texture contrasted with the flavors of the sauce, I had a flash of illumination. I understood the principle of what Mexicans call a *molito,* which is based on the use of dried chiles.

A molito is a dish you can make every day with whatever happens to be on hand, a dish born from imagination and availability. Almost any meat or vegetable can be cooked in a molito. If there are some guajillo chiles in the house, they are roasted, soaked, and pureed with a clove of garlic; the resulting paste is sautéed with hot oil, a little broth or water is added, a pinch of one spice or another–anise, oregano, even just pepper–and you can cook anything at all in the resulting mixture: chicken wings, zucchini, you name it.

Molitos can be made with an enormous variety of dried chiles (see the dictionary of chiles at the end of the book); a different flavor and a different experience for the mouth are produced by each one. My favorite chile grows in Oaxaca and is dried and smoked in Puebla; it's called Chipotle Navideño, or Christmas Chipotle, and it is a true delicacy. You can use it to prepare an elegant molito with a smoky flavor, or to make chiles rellenos in the style of Naolinco, Veracruz.

FLAVORS AND COLORS OF MOLE

A molito, which can be the basis for a *mole,* is the type of indigenous dish that was described by the chroniclers of the Spanish invasion of Mexico: a broth of pureed chiles in which vegetables and/or meats are cooked. Nevertheless, the first mole to be called mole was created during the Spanish colonial era.

Mole was the dish that I was having the hardest time appreciating at that point in my expanding acquaintance with Mexican food. The combination of chile, spices, nuts, seeds, and sometimes chocolate or fruits is not only complicated to make but also requires a palate that is well educated in the flavors of Mexican food. The sauce that results from this daring combination of ingredients requires a technique all its own and everyone who makes it has his or her personal approach.

A good mole can take several days to make. Just roasting, rinsing, cleaning, pureeing, and sautéing the enormous number of ingredients can take hours and hours, and that's before they are combined and cooked on a slow fire while being stirred constantly. It reminds me of something said in a wonderful Chinese book of essays on food: "A great chef can make no more than four great dishes in one day." Making a good mole can take two or more days, and each cook must find an individual equation for mole. However, one advantage of mole is that it can always be kept in the refrigerator for several weeks. If you make a mole on Sunday, you can be certain you'll eat it on several subsequent days, and moles taste even better when reheated. If the mole has thickened, you need only add a little chicken broth to revive it. There are more than forty different kinds of mole in the state of Puebla alone, and in Oaxaca moles are differentiated on the basis of the colors of the chiles used and the degrees to which they are roasted. But the mole of Puebla, called *mole poblano,* has its own legend, which history has passed down to us.

A LITTLE HISTORY

The word *mole* probably derives from Latin and means a large thing. In Spanish, a *mole* is a mass or bulk, referring to largeness of size and corpu-

Everyone makes his or her own *mole,* and a mole fiesta advertises a menu of alternatives for tasting them.

lence. It also means a large number, a multitude, a weight, or a load. The word was probably applied to the sauce because it includes a large number of more or less secret ingredients. Curiously, *mole* is also an Aztec word, derived from the Nahuatl *mol* or *molli,* which means soup, stew, mixture, or sauce. In Mexico stews or boiled sauces that include chile are called *mole* or *molito. Clemole* is another Aztec word meaning fire stew, and *Chi-mole* refers to a stew that includes chile and is badly made. The word *mol-cajete* also involves the same concept since it refers to the stone or clay mortar in which chiles are ground up—and *guaca-mole* is of course a salsa with avocado.

The original mole poblano is said to have been created in the kitchen of the Santa Rosa Convent in Puebla. This kitchen is famous not only as the site where mole originated but also for its great beauty. Its spacious layout and walls covered with enchanting blue Talavera tiles provide a living image of the traditional kitchens of Puebla. Anyone who happens to be in Puebla can visit it, since it is now a museum open to the public. A typical colonial-era Puebla kitchen can also be seen in the Franz Mayer Museum in Mexico City.

During Mexico's colonial era, which spanned the sixteenth, seventeenth, and eighteenth centuries, one of the viceroys who ruled the country visited Puebla. The city's various convents vied with one another in creating the most delicious dishes in his honor. In the Convent of the Dominican Sisters, Sister Andrea de la Asunción decided to prepare a unique dish that would surprise and delight the esteemed visitor and his entourage. Legend has it that mole poblano should be made with wild turkey, the species of turkey that originated in America. The nun picked out a few wild turkeys and fed them for several days on large quantities of chestnuts. According to

An antique Mexican kitchen on display in a museum in the city of Puebla.

another version of the story, less plausible but more romantic, angels helped Sister Andrea make her mole by placing the ingredients in her hands one by one as she stood at the stove.

MOLE POBLANO AT ROSA MEXICANO

In the early days of the restaurant, I used to serve a buffet brunch on Sundays. A number of Mexican dishes, including a variety of moles, were presented in a line of clay pots warmed by individual burners so that guests could serve themselves. They could also help themselves to fresh tortillas and a variety of aguas frescas.

Sometimes the variety of moles was more extensive (once, I invited a group of cooks from Oaxaca to prepare their moles for us). I wanted my guests to choose among the largest variety of dishes so they could grow accustomed to the different flavors of Mexican cuisine.

OTHER TYPES OF MOLE

We soon began serving other kinds of mole, including the black, red, and yellow moles of Oaxaca. Today, I serve *mole de Xico,* which originated in the small town of Xico in the state of Veracruz. I also serve *mole de ciruela,* made with prunes. The moles we serve at Rosa Mexicano are prepared from scratch in our kitchen.

There are infinite varieties of mole, particularly since every cook has his or her own personal formula, and mole is constantly evolving. Lately I've noticed that moles in Mexico are becoming sweeter and sweeter; where once fruit was added only to diminish the heat of the chiles, now moles are made with sugar or sweetened chocolate. The chocolate Sister Andrea added to her mole poblano must have been pure, unsweetened chocolate that lent acidity and consistency rather than sweetness to the mixture, but today the chocolate added to moles is generally sweetened.

While we're on the subject of moles, we must mention *mole verde,* or green mole. Certain historians consider mole verde a pre-Hispanic dish, because its basic ingredients are all used regularly in indigenous cooking. But like every other aspect of Mexican cuisine, mole verde has evolved from a simple pre-Hispanic paste made from tomatillos and pumpkin seeds.

MOLE POBLANO

MAKES ABOUT 3 QUARTS

There are many ways of making moles. Each person makes it his or her own way. The recipes for moles are lengthy and cooking them is a great weekend activity. Moles freeze well. Mole poblano can be served with various types of meat, but this one is particularly good with chicken or turkey.

12 mulato chiles
10 ancho chiles
4 pasilla chiles
2 small chipotle chiles
1 to 1½ cups vegetable oil
2 tablespoons sesame seeds
2 ounces almonds, skin removed and toasted
2 slices white bread, crusts removed
1 ripe plantain
2 ounces raisins
6 pitted prunes
1 large white onion, sliced
2 large garlic cloves, toasted
4 whole cloves
pinch of ground anise seeds
pinch of ground cinnamon
pinch of dried thyme
4 medium vine-ripened tomatoes, roasted, peeled, and cored
2 corn tortillas, dried out overnight and fried in 2 tablespoons vegetable oil
4 cups chicken stock

pinch of sugar
2 ounces Mexican chocolate (preferably Ibarra brand)
salt, to taste

1. Toast the chiles, remove the stems and seeds, and soak in abundant boiling water for 30 minutes, the longer the better.
2. Strain the chiles and blend in the blender to make a chile paste, adding some of the soaking liquid to make the blades turn. Place the chiles in a bowl and set aside.
3. Heat 2 tablespoons oil in an 8-inch sauté pan. Sauté the sesame seeds, almonds, and bread until golden. Strain any excess oil and drain on paper towels. Place in the blender.
4. Peel the plantain and cut into 1-inch pieces. Heat 2 tablespoons of the vegetable oil in the same pan as in step 3 and sauté the plantain for 5 to 6 minutes or until golden. Remove from pan. Add the raisins and prunes and cook for 3 to 4 minutes more. Strain any excess oil and place the plantain mixture in the blender with the sesame seeds, almonds, and bread.
5. Heat 2 tablespoons of the oil in an 8-inch sauté pan. Sauté the onions for 4 to 5 minutes, add the garlic, and cook for 2 to 3 minutes, or until the onions are translucent. Add the cloves, anise, cinnamon, and thyme and roasted tomatoes and cook for another 2 to 3 minutes, stirring with a wooden spoon. Strain any excess oil and place the spices in the blender with the rest of the ingredients. Break up tortillas and blend, adding enough chicken stock to make the blades turn.
6. Heat the remaining oil in a large, thick-bottomed pot. Sauté the chile puree for 4 to 5 minutes over medium heat, stirring with a wooden spoon. Add the blended ingredients and cook for another 4 to 5 minutes, stirring occasionally. Add the remaining chicken stock and a pinch of sugar, stirring well to incorporate it. Simmer for 35 to 45 minutes.
7. Add the chocolate, stir to melt it, and mix well into the sauce. Season to taste with salt; the mole should not be too sweet.

■ ■ ■ ENCHILADAS DE MOLE POBLANO

1 3-to-3½-pound chicken, poached
1 recipe Mole Poblano (page 148)
½ cup vegetable oil
12 white-corn tortillas
4 ounces queso fresco, grated
1 small white onion, sliced paper thin
boiled rice (see recipe on page 64)

1. Remove and shred meat from poached chicken.
2. In a 12-inch sauté pan, warm the shredded chicken with 2 cups of the mole poblano.
3. In the meantime, heat the vegetable oil in a 10-inch sauté pan. Fry the tortillas briefly in the oil, approximately 2 to 3 minutes on each side. Drain the tortillas on paper towels. They should be soft.
4. Place a spoonful of the chicken and mole on each tortilla and fold in half. Place two filled tortillas on each plate (plates should be ovenproof) and cover with a generous ladle of heated mole sauce.
5. Sprinkle with queso fresco and place under a heated broiler until the cheese melts.
6. Garnish with the thinly sliced onion and serve with boiled rice.

MOLE NEGRO DE XICO CON POLLO / BLACK MOLE FROM XICO WITH CHICKEN

This mole is also delicious made with turkey or pork and is usually eaten with plain tamales. It is an adaptation of a recipe by Carolina Suarez Suarez, from her store, El Xiqueño.

1 large (3-to-3½-pound) chicken, cut into 8 pieces
2 quarts water containing 1 bay leaf, 1 carrot cut in pieces, 1 stalk celery, 1 small onion cut in half, 2 sprigs parsley, 2 cloves, and 4 peppercorns
1 pound mulato chiles
4 ounces pasilla chiles
4 cups boiling water
½ to ¾ cup vegetable oil
½ large white onion, sliced
3 garlic cloves
½ pound vine-ripened tomatoes
⅛ teaspoon whole cloves
¼ teaspoon anise seeds
2 ounces sesame seeds
½ stick whole cinnamon
2 ounces whole shelled pine nuts
2 ounces whole shelled hazelnuts
2 ounces whole shelled walnuts
4 ounces pitted prunes
2 ounces raisins
1 small ripe plantain
1 piece toasted bread
1 corn tortilla, torn into small pieces
2 to 3 cups broth in which chicken was cooked
2 ounces brown sugar or *piloncillo* (available in Latin-American markets)
2 2½-ounce pieces or tablets Mexican chocolate
salt to taste

1. Boil the chicken pieces, uncovered, in the 2 quarts water containing the bay leaf, cut-up carrot, celery stalk, halved onion, parsley sprigs, cloves, and peppercorns. Cook for about 30 minutes. Reserve the chicken pieces and 2 to 3 cups of the broth in which the chicken was boiled. Strain the broth.
2. While the chicken is cooking, prepare the mole: Toast the chiles in a large dry sauté pan and turn with tongs to toast evenly until the chiles are pliable. Allow the chiles to cool enough to be handled. Remove the stems, veins, and seeds. Place the chiles in a bowl and pour the 4 cups boiling water over them. Let stand a minimum of 30 minutes.
3. Heat 2 tablespoons of the oil in a sauté pan and sauté the sliced onions for 4 to 5 minutes, or until translucent. Add the garlic and cook for 2 to 3 minutes more. Place in a blender.
4. Roast the tomatoes until charred. Peel and add to the blender.
5. Toast the spices and nuts in a dry pan until golden. Place in the blender.
6. In the sauté pan that was used for the onion and garlic, place the prunes, raisins, plantain, bread, and tortilla pieces. Add a little oil and sauté quickly. Add to the blender.
7. Strain the chiles. Place the chiles in the blender and blend all of the ingredients to form a paste.
8. Heat 3 tablespoons of the oil in a large, heavy pot. Sauté the paste for about 10 minutes. Add approximately 1 cup of the reserved chicken broth and simmer over a low fire.
9. Add the brown sugar or piloncillo, stir in the chocolate, and add salt to taste.
10. Continue to stir the mole over a low fire, adding approximately 2 more cups of chicken broth. Simmer for 20 minutes. Put the chicken pieces into the mole and simmer 10 minutes more (you should have a fairly thick sauce). Serve with plain tamales or white rice.

MOLE VERDE / GREEN MOLE

MAKES ABOUT 8 CUPS, OR 2 QUARTS

2 cups (about 1½ pounds) tomatillos, husked and washed
6 stalks cilantro, including leaves
6 red radish leaves, washed
4 romaine leaves, washed and cut in pieces
8 serrano chiles, stems and seeds removed, deveined, and coarsely chopped
3 cups chicken stock, plus enough to moisten tomatillo mixture
1½ cups pumpkin seeds
4 tablespoons vegetable oil
½ medium white onion, chopped
4 garlic cloves, finely chopped
salt, to taste

1. Bring 4 cups of water to a boil in a 2-quart saucepan. Boil the tomatillos for 5 minutes. Drain and allow tomatillos to cool slightly. Discard water. Blend them in a blender with the cilantro leaves, radish leaves, romaine lettuce, and serrano chiles. If necessary, add a little chicken stock to make the blades turn. Place in a small bowl and set aside.
2. First toast the pumpkin seeds in a hot/dry sauté pan. Then grind them in a spice grinder little by little. Transfer to the blender and blend with 1 cup of the chicken stock to form a paste. Set aside.
3. In a sauté pan heat the vegetable oil. Sauté the onions for 5 to 6 minutes, until translucent; then add the garlic and cook 2 to 3 minutes more.
4. Add the puree of tomatillos and cook for 4 to 5 minutes more, stirring occasionally with a wooden spoon.
5. Little by little, stir in the pumpkin-seed paste. Cook for 4 to 5 minutes. Continue to stir; do not boil the mixture.
6. Add the remaining 2 cups chicken stock and season to taste with salt. Reduce the flame to low and simmer for 20 to 30 minutes.

■ ■ ■ ENCHILADAS DE MOLE VERDE

SERVES 6

1 recipe Mole Verde, warmed
½ cup vegetable oil
12 white-corn tortillas
2 roasted ducks, meat removed from carcass and shredded
4 ounces queso fresco, grated
1 small white onion, sliced paper-thin
3 cups boiled rice

1. Warm the mole verde.
2. In the meantime, heat the vegetable oil in an 8- to 10-inch sauté pan. Fry the tortillas briefly in the oil, approximately 2 to 3 minutes on each side. Drain the tortillas on paper towels. They should be soft.
3. Place a spoonful of the duck and mole on each tortilla and fold in half. Place two filled tortillas on each plate and cover with a generous ladle of heated mole sauce.
4. Sprinkle with queso fresco and place under a heated broiler until the cheese melts.
5. Garnish with the thinly sliced onions and serve with boiled rice (½ cup per serving).

ADOBOS

Generally, the Spanish word *adobo* refers to a mixture of garlic, onion, pepper, and aromatic herbs, ingredients that have been used since Roman times to cover up the rank taste of meat, which could not be kept fresh until the invention of refrigeration. In Mexico an adobo is a type of marinade made with chiles, herbs, and sometimes citrus juices, which is used with poultry, meat, or fish. The addition of different types of powdered dried chiles is what distinguishes a Mexican adobo.

In the Yucatán Peninsula, adobos are called *recaudos* and their combinations of spices are sometimes flavored with the juice of bitter oranges. For every type of dish there is a specific recaudo, which is traditionally ground up in a molcajete. The flavor combinations in the recaudos are the secret of the delicious gastronomy of the Mexican southeast. Some of the spices they contain manifest a Middle Eastern influence, a result of the many immigrants from the Middle East who have settled in that part of the country. All of these recaudos should be rubbed on meat or poultry before roasting or grilling.

For an *adobo blanco* or *de puchero* (a white or stewpot adobo) grind into a wet paste: 1 tablespoon black peppercorns, 12 oregano leaves, 1 head raw garlic, 6 small whole cloves, 1 heaping teaspoon cumin, one heaping teaspoon coriander seeds, 3 or 4 sticks of cinnamon, the juice of half a bitter orange, and 1 teaspoon salt.

For an *adobo colorado,* or red adobo, to use for grilling: grind 10 to 12 cloves raw garlic, 15 oregano leaves, 1 teaspoon cumin, 1 teaspoon coriander seeds, 2 large whole cloves, 2 heaping tablespoons achiote, 1 tablespoon black peppercorns, 2 pieces whole allspice, the juice of half a bitter orange, and 1 teaspoon salt.

For stuffing a tamale *(recaudo de chilaquil):* 1 teaspoon black pepper, 6 or 7 cloves garlic, 5 oregano leaves, 10 epazote leaves, ½ teaspoon cumin, 1 tablespoon achiote, ½ teaspoon salt, and 3 tablespoons bitter orange juice.

For a salt-and-pepper recaudo to use on a turkey or a large piece of meat: 1 tablespoon black peppercorns, 4 whole cloves, 4 or 5 cloves raw garlic, 5 oregano leaves, 2 thick cinnamon sticks, 1 teaspoon coriander seeds, half an onion pureed, 4 sprigs parsley pureed. The spices are ground up together, and the onion and parsley are ground separately with a little water, then mixed with the rest of the spices; the resulting mixture is daubed all over the turkey before roasting.

For a special adobo to be used on duck: 4 or 5 cloves raw garlic, 4 or 5 cloves roasted garlic, 1 teaspoon black peppercorns, 2 cinnamon sticks, ¼ teaspoon cumin, 1 teaspoon achiote, 1 medium onion, the juice of half a bitter orange, or vinegar and salt to taste. A Yucatán-style duck is boiled until it has begun to soften, then covered with this mixture of spices and bitter orange juice or vinegar, then fried until it has begun to turn golden, and placed back in the oven with its juices until it is very soft.

The adobos or recaudos of the cuisine of southeastern Mexico can be found in the marketplaces there; they are sold in little cakes, and some of them have to be dried out for a while before being stored.

A FOREIGNER IN THE WORLD

Perhaps the feeling of belonging to the world and not to a single country is felt by everyone who has lived through a war, or maybe it's only me, but after I was forced to leave Spain as a young girl, I also abandoned any feeling of permanence in a country. However, during my long stay in Mexico, the people lavished on me the attention they give to people who treat them with respect. Mexicans are always eager to show their cultural riches to anyone living in their country; they are very kind to foreigners and especially to those who speak their language. As a Spanish woman who was hardworking and trustworthy, I met with extremely affable treatment.

While I lived in Mexico, I traveled to New York every year to see my mother. We spent whole days and nights talking without a pause, about our loves, our memories. I luxuriated in the wonderful feeling of still being a child that having a mother can give: The little girl inside me came alive when I was around her. My mother finally found a companion who loved her deeply, a man who was younger than she was; in the end, the poor woman had to watch him die. For my part, I found loves both happy and unhappy in Mexico, and a man with whom I had a long and I would say almost perfect relationship, in which we each lived our own lives yet had each other. He was also a foreigner in Mexico, from a country in South America.

Things were going well; I was working and giving work to the craftsmen who made fabrics and furniture for my interior-decorating business. At the Bazaar Sábado and La Posada I was selling Frank Lowenstein's jewelry. My sons were very Mexican. But, like all foreigners throughout the world, I was confronted with one pressing difficulty: the complicated matter of my papers, and of bureaucratic corruption. An agent of the Secretaría de Gobernación (the Mexican immigration service) learned I was about to receive the papers that would establish my legal right to stay in the country and decided it was a good opportunity for a little extortion. Frank Lowenstein paid a "fine" for me and I had to go into hiding on Paula's family ranch in the nearby town of Otumba. While my sons remained at home in the care of Paula, I went through a period of fear and despair, feeling that I would always be a foreigner in the world. My memories of the war years in Europe exacerbated my anxiety, which was calmed only by Paula's aunt, the lady of the house, who spent several days busily making me happy with all kinds of antojitos and other specialties of her kitchen.

Charles Howard was called upon to rescue me, and he arrived only to discover that everything had already been resolved. Since he was there, I took him for a walk in the maguey fields to show him a beautiful hacienda I could see from my window. We were strolling along, enjoying the day, when we saw a man on horseback wearing the elaborate outfit and enormous sombrero of a Mexican *charro,* or cowboy. After a series of formal greetings, we explained that we were foreigners who had been struck by the beauty of the hacienda and would like to see more of it. Without further ado, he took us to the hacienda, which he owned; we were astonished by its luxury and the collection of paintings on display, as well as by the elegance and warmth of our host, Señor Sánchez Navarro, who generously opened the doors of his house to us. The majority of the Mexicans we met, rich and poor alike, received us with open arms, but bureaucrats, in Mexico and the world over, can make one feel like a foreigner, even in one's own home.

MIXIOTES

No Sunday was complete without a walk through the marketplace. One day I noticed a woman whose stand was wedged into a tiny space; she had the classic look of the market women: An apron was tied around her plump body, her hair was in braids, and her white smile flashed when I responded to her cry of "Try my mixiotes! Try my mixiotes!"

These small pouches had aroused my curiosity; their aroma suggested that they contained mutton, chile, and herbs. The pouches were tied shut, like little beggar's purses, with a strand of the same stuff the filling was wrapped in. I tried one immediately. It was still very hot, and when the knot was untied, the pouch blossomed like a flower. Inside was a portion of meat in its reddish juices, sprinkled with herbs. The steam rose in a wave that filled the air with tantalizing aromas, and the meat seemed to dissolve in my mouth. The slight spiciness of the dish harmonized with the character of the meat. I was so busy experiencing the series of flavors in each mouthful that I finished the mixiote off without realizing it, and looked down to see only the remains of the juices on the wrapping. I went back several times to buy more mixiotes from that woman and to explore the mysteries of their preparation.

In Nahuatl, *mixiote* means the skin of young maguey leaves. The indigenous peoples of Mesoamerica, like many of the world's early peoples, cooked their foods by boiling them. The Aztecs also used steam to cook their tamales. Wise in the uses of the maguey and all its parts, they extracted from the young leaves a kind of transparent film, as thin and durable as Egyptian papyrus. They used it to wrap everything from the small fish of the lake to poultry and game. Seasoned with ground chiles and herbs—which functioned not only as a flavoring but also as a preservative—the mixture is steamed, and the juices of the meat, poultry, or fish mingle with the seasonings. No fat is added at all.

In those years—the mid-1970s—the woman who sold mixiotes and showed me how to make them said she now used parchment paper rather than the traditional maguey membrane because the maguey dies when the membrane is removed and it was fast becoming an endangered plant. The news media repeated the message over and over, and the use of maguey membranes was forbidden by law. I've always followed the instructions of the marketplace vendor of San Juan Teotihuacán and have never used maguey membrane to make mixiote in the traditional way; it is important to protect the environment and the beautiful magueys, which not only decorate the Mexican landscape but also yield an astonishing variety of products. I use parchment to wrap up the meat and its adobo.

To my surprise, however, vendors often show up at the door of the restaurant offering me thin sheets of maguey membrane; in the marketplaces of Mexico City and throughout central Mexico the membranes continue to be sold both as part of mixiotes that have already been prepared and in rolls to be used in making them. Magueys protect fertile land from wind erosion, and the indigenous cultures of Mexico put the maguey to innumerable uses. They must be protected at all costs; a Mexico without magueys is unthinkable.

MIXIOTES AT ROSA MEXICANO

Today, mixiotes are one of the dishes my guests beg for. I use the tenderest part of the lamb shank and wrap the meat on the bone in parchment paper. It is always a pleasure to untie the knot and see the paper open like a flower to reveal the delicious combination of meat and juices inside.

MIXIOTES DE CORDERO / LAMB SHANKS COATED WITH THREE CHILES, GARLIC, AND SPICES AND WRAPPED IN PARCHMENT PAPER AND STEAMED.

SERVES 6

For an even more spectacular dish which is perfect for a dinner party, make this recipe with a crown rack of lamb.

6 pasilla chiles
8 guajillo chiles
8 ancho chiles
4 garlic cloves
1 tablespoon ground cumin
1 tablespoon dried oregano
1 tablespoon dried thyme
6 whole cloves
1 bay leaf
5 black peppercorns
2 tablespoons white vinegar
1½ teaspoons salt
6 lamb shanks
1 12-ounce bottle of beer

---

6 12-inch squares of parchment paper
6 15-inch pieces of string
12 white-corn tortillas

1. Toast all the chiles in a hot/dry pan, turning with tongs until the chiles are evenly toasted and pliable. Remove the seeds and devein the chiles. Soak the chiles in abundant hot water for ½ hour. Set aside ¼ cup of the chile soaking water.

2. Combine the chiles, garlic, cumin, oregano, thyme, cloves, bay leaf, peppercorns, vinegar, salt, and 1/4 cup of the chile soaking water in a blender. Puree into a thick paste, adding more chile water if necessary.
3. Coat the lamb shanks with the paste and refrigerate, covered, overnight.

ASSEMBLY:

1. Place each shank in the center of a parchment square. Gather the corners of the parchment paper, making a loose package, and tie with kitchen string.
2. Bring the beer and 2 cups water to a boil in a large steamer over medium heat. Place the shanks on a rack above the liquid. Cover and steam, add water as needed. Cook for about 2 hours, until the meat falls from the bone (open one to check).
3. To serve, present the shanks in their packages and unfold the parchment at the table. Serve with hot fresh corn tortillas for making tacos.

Note: Chicken legs, rabbit, or any other meat can be substituted for the lamb shanks.

GRADUATION DAYS

When my sons graduated from the public school of San Juan Teotihuacán, I felt the same pride as all the other mothers around me, some of them wrapped in their rebozos, with tears in their eyes. Most of the Mexicans who come to my restaurant are the offspring of the upper classes, educated in private schools. When any of them expresses doubts about my identification with Mexico, I always give as an example my experience of living for so many years in Teotihuacán, and the fact that my sons attended a rural public elementary school. I chose to raise my children as Mexicans: How many foreigners can say as much? I lived in the country for so long and shared so much with the Mexican people. But now school was over and so was my six-year stay in the magical region of the pyramids, where I had become acquainted with the traces of the ancient peoples who once lived there.

LIFE IN SAN ÁNGEL

I liked the neighborhood of San Ángel and rented a nice, comfortable house with a garden for the boys on a cobblestone street called María Luisa. Toward the end of the nineteenth century, San Ángel was the place where some of Mexico City's wealthiest families built their country houses. It still retains some vestiges of the small town it was then. It has, like every town in Mexico, a central square known as a *zócalo,* narrow cobblestone streets, and a convent, and it once had great haciendas and ranches as well.

San Ángel is only a few steps from the Avenida Revolución; it lies very close to the Avenida Insurgentes as well, and is bordered by the southern part of the beltway known as the Periférico. For a while I went on working as the exclusive decorator of a very well-known company. In my Alfa Romeo, I made my way north on the city's long avenues to the Zona Rosa, where the Casa Galerías Chippendale was located. I liked my car, but unfortunately it spent more time in the shop than with me.

Around that time I discovered the sandwiches called *tortas compuestas,* which arrived with the lunch hour, to every employee's great delight. The purveyor of tortas was the same man who owned the newsstand on the corner; his wife brought them exactly at noon. After my first bite, I decided to have a torta for lunch every day. A torta compuesta is the perfect snack; a wide, round roll called a *telera* is sliced open horizontally and filled with refried beans, and a choice of ham, chicken, a veal cutlet, or even a chile relleno; then vegetables, cream, chiles, and fresh cheese are added. The bread is really only a golden crust that holds together what is practically a complete meal. At Rosa Mexicano I make tortas for parties. I've tried hard to achieve a bread with the same flavor and texture as the telera you find in Mexico, although the use of refined flour and chemical additives has made Mexican telera lose the flavor it used to have years ago.

PANADERÍAS

In those days I loved the smells that wafted from *panaderías* when the bread came out of the oven in the morning before breakfast and in the afternoon for the *merienda,* a smell so appealing it was hard to keep from stopping in to buy something. In the evenings, on my way home, I would stop at the Panadería La Espiga, where there was always a tumult of people—vendors of prepared foods and the panadería's customers—thronging around the entry. The shop's huge windows framed shelves lined with trays of bread in all shapes and sizes. Freshly baked bread was tossed straight from the oven into giant containers.

Initially, the system of selling bread in Mexican panaderías surprised me. The customer picks up a pair of tongs and a tray, then walks through the panadería, choosing different types of bread, sweet or savory, and placing them on the tray with the tongs. Then a very orderly line leads to a counter where an employee places the bread in a bag, savory breads at the bottom, and sweet breads on top. If the customer has chosen any filled pastry, it is wrapped individually in waxed paper before being placed in the bag.

In addition to telera bread and the rolls called bolillos, panaderías in cities and small towns sell a white bread they call Spanish bread; its surface is not as golden, and it comes in a variety of forms: round, long, or shaped like a bull's horn. Its flavor is slightly saltier and more acidic. But the varieties of sweet bread are innumerable, each made from a different recipe and with a name that usually describes its shape. Many of them are varieties of *bizcochos;* the prefix *biz-* means double or twice, and like the Italian biscotti that have become so popular in the United States, bizcochos are cooked once, then decorated and returned to the oven a second time. *Conchas* (shells) are round bizcochos marked with a swirl of frosting that looks like a seashell. Small, soft, sweet rolls that are dipped in sugar and smeared with jam are called *besos,* or kisses. Long, firm rolls are called "soldiers," and "brides" are rolls covered with white confectioners' sugar. The *chilindrina* is a small roll covered with dots of baked-on sugar that are separated by gaps (a *chilendrera* is someone with missing teeth). The names were necessary, they say, because in former years panaderías were organized differently; customers went directly to the

Special breads are made for the Day of the Dead. This kind is from Oaxaca, with some dabs of color and a lot of sugar.

counter and ordered the types of bread they wanted by name. And every baker took great pride in designing new forms for his or her breads.

Men riding bicycles while easily balancing enormous baskets of bread on their heads were a frequent sight in the Mexico City of that day, though accidents were common, of course. Automobile traffic was already very much on the rise, and from time to time you would see pieces of bread scattered across the street because a bread man had taken a tumble, basket and all. Still, the custom was popular because it was very convenient and pleasant to go to the door when the bread man came knocking and to choose your fresh bread right there.

THE CAKE WAR

Wheat, and with it the technique for baking bread, was brought to Mexico by the Spaniards; one of the many reasons the beginning of the colonial era is important in the history of Mexican gastronomy is that ovens were introduced then. The sweet rolls described above are Mexican bakers' interpretations of recipes they learned from the cooks—Spanish, French, and of other nationalities—who came to Mexico long before what was called the "Cake War."

As the story is commonly told, a French baker who lived in Mexico complained to his government because a group of young Mexican soldiers had started a brawl in his bakery and practically destroyed it, and the Mexican authorities had not offered him any compensation. Furious, the French baker turned to his ambassador and finally to the French government itself.

When powerful countries invade weak ones, it is sometimes difficult for the common people to understand why, since they are not fluent in the vocabulary of international economics and politics, and are not familiar with the loans and other circumstances that move the world. Individual citizens of every country are generally very far removed from the signing of international treaties, but they are the ones who finally will have to pay with their blood or their lives for debts they never acquired personally or benefited from even indirectly. Mexico was invaded on January 7, 1862, by European troops that occupied the port of Veracruz. As the Mexican people understood it, the invasion was the result of the debt that the government of Mexico had refused to pay the French baker, and so, ingenuously, they called it La Guerra de los Pasteles, "The Cake War."

Here is a synthesis of what I have been able to learn about the historical reality that followed. Mexico had just lived through a three-year civil conflict among conservatives, liberals, the military, and the Church, in which the liberals had finally won the upper hand. In the struggle, the country had acquired all kinds of debts: to the Catholic Church, which had been "despoiled" of enormous wealth, and to the British, French, and Spanish governments. And interest had, of course, swelled the original debts. The new government of Mexico managed to liberalize the laws, but its coffers were completely empty, so it decided to suspend payment of the debts. As a result, Mexico was invaded by troops under the leadership of a French general; the event is known in history as the "French Invasion," though the French arrived in the country with a pair of Austrian aristocrats who wanted to be emperor and empress of Mexico: Maximilian and his wife, Carlota. But those who try to conquer Mexico are always conquered themselves in the end. Today, in many places in Mexico, particularly in the state of Jalisco, you can find the descendants of the Frenchmen who came to take away some part of Mexico and are now themselves part of the Mexican nation. The same thing happened with the English and, of course, with many of the first Spanish conquistadors, among them Hernán Cortés himself.

CAKE- AND PASTRY-MAKING

The influence of European techniques on Mexican cake- and pastry-making is remarkable. On one of the colonial streets in the historic center of Mexico City is a bakery that is sui generis, El Molino. The building, which probably dates from the colonial era, has thick walls and spacious rooms; you stroll through the first floor of the bakery among sweet rolls, then move on to be tempted by cream-filled pastries on the second floor, and finally, on the third floor, you can admire a display of enormous cakes, sometimes as many as four or five layers high, covered with colorful frostings and decorated with flowers and sugar figures. These cakes are an essential component of any celebration of a new baby, a girl's all-important fifteenth birthday party *(quinceañera),* or a wedding.

MEXICO CITY: LIFE IN ANOTHER DIMENSION

To live in Mexico means, as a first step, to accept that time is no longer the same—and I'm not talking about punctuality or the hands of the clock. In Mexico, you live in another dimension. There is an art in every place and at every moment, an art that goes beyond museums and galleries and overflows at every street corner and in the ways people communicate with each other.

During my early days in Mexico City I had to accept a lot of things in order to feel that I belonged: that it isn't unusual for the electricity to go off (and that it quickly comes back), that the telephones don't work, that parties are very important to everyone, that in reality nothing happens, although everything is happening all the time. That there is always someone nearby who's ready to keep an eye on your car, and though it's usually someone with no official position, people leave their car, keys and all, and no one is surprised to come back and find their car intact and waiting. And that it rains because of Tlaloc, the rain god of the country's ancient inhabitants; when you want rain you have to ask Tlaloc. I can't forget the day an enormous stone figure of the god Tlaloc was brought to Mexico City to be placed at the entrance of the new Museum of Anthropology and History. People gathered and watched in silence as the enormous mass of stone was moved on a large rolling platform. The previous days had been intensely hot and dusty, but that day it rained and rained, and it was magic. You have to know how to live in Mexico.

IMAGES OF NATURE

Why is it that with such a large and varied country to live in, so many people are jammed into Mexico City? I imagine that there are well-documented answers to this question which explain the phenomenon of human concentration from various points of view: historical, economic, social, and political. To my mind, one of the city's most attractive factors is its climate. Winters are always moderate, almost imperceptible. When spring comes it is reflected not only in clear, bright days but also in the vibrant colors that come to life. In many areas of the city there are enormous jacaranda trees that fill with tiny lilac, purple, and blue flowers in spring, before their green leaves have sprouted. Jacarandas stay in flower for almost six months, filling people's hearts with joy. The spring winds blow softly and the jacarandas cover the sidewalks with a soft carpet of flowers. Azaleas, which are considered a native flower, bloom on all sides; bougainvilleas, which can also be of various colors and tones but are usually bright red, spill out over the walls.

The most lavish carpet of lilac-colored jacaranda flowers I ever saw was in the city of Guadalajara, a sizable, beautiful city that has somehow kept the feel of a small, provincial town. On one of its central avenues, the Avenida Juárez, there is a long line of jacarandas growing one next to the other. I was there at exactly the right moment to be amazed by the flowers that blanketed the entire avenue. It reminded me of the rocky peak of San Martín de Lodón, in Asturias, one slope of which is cloaked in bright yellow during the season when the chamomile flowers bloom. In the Mexican Guadalajara (there's also a city of the same name near Madrid), I thought the carpet of flowers I saw was growing out of the earth, as in Asturias; I was astonished to discover that the flowers don't grow from the ground but fall from the enormous trees. Beneath the thick layer of jacaranda flowers there was only asphalt. Trotting across the carpet of flowers were horse-drawn carts called *calandrias,* which take people on rides through the city. I jumped out of my car immediately and hailed a calandria.

On my frequent trips to Cuernavaca, I would see black birds flying in a circle near a certain section of the highway. I learned that they were *zopilotes* (a type of vulture), and when I saw one up close, with its large, naked, wrinkled gullet and voracious beak, I was quite horrified. But then someone explained how important they were to the ecology; they clean up the bodies of dead animals and keep insects and foul odors from proliferating. After that I could understand their usefulness and their presence in this world. I began to enjoy watching their relaxed flight, the way they rose and fell through the air; every time I passed by that point on the highway I would look for them in the sky. Poor things, I thought, they're so ugly but they fly so beautifully. And what a fate: to be the ones whose job it is to clean up life's debris. But the day came when I was traveling along the same road and didn't see them. I missed them for a long time and wondered where the zopilotes, which flew so slowly and performed such a necessary service, could have gone. For a while I thought they must be extinct, like so many other animals. Then, on another trip, this time to a city in the state of Veracruz, I saw them again, and was filled with unexpected jubilation. "How great that there are still zopilotes around!"

After those trips I always went back to my work and daily life in Mexico City. There are many places in Mexico that have a good climate, but in the former city of Tenochtitlán human activity and the marvelous climate combine to form a very appealing whole. The change of seasons is almost imperceptible, the temperature varies only a little, and then suddenly the rainy season comes.

THE RAINY SEASON

It cannot be denied that Mexico City, which is large and extremely populous, suffers from pollution, like many other cities in the world. Because it lies more than six thousand feet above sea level, its high altitude can have a slight negative effect on certain visitors. But this is offset by many piercingly clear days when the colors shine brilliantly. When I lived in Mexico City, it was the city with the largest number of green areas in the world; there were small and large parks everywhere. Nowadays, parks are vanishing little by little. You can look for a park that made an impression on you and simply not find it.

In Mexico, the rainy season occurs during the summer, and the heat is only moderate. When the rainy season comes to the city, the atmosphere changes completely. Generally, unless a hurricane is threatening the coastline, it rains in the afternoon, and then the city becomes tremendously chaotic, with traffic even more complicated. The jacarandas fill with tiny green shoots. The Paseo de la Reforma, which begins at the Caballito, lives up to its name and becomes a true *paseo* (place to stroll through) between enormous trees reaching from either side to form a kind of archway overhead; the leaves' infinite shades of green filter the sun's rays on hot afternoons and give some shelter from the fury of rainstorms. In the rainy season, Mexican markets change colors. First come the mangoes, especially those called mangoes de Manila, which are the most delicious kind. A little later, the mushrooms arrive.

Wild mushrooms were nothing new to me; in Spain and throughout Europe they are a much-appreciated delicacy. What surprised me was the way they were and are sold. When I lived in Mexico City, the tradition was to buy wild mushrooms at the San Juan market in the center of the city. The San Juan is a market with a long history; the quality of the fruits, vegetables, fish, and meat sold there is excellent, and you can find Spanish, Chinese, and Japanese cuisine, good French cheeses, and superb fish and seafood. The vendors are experienced and helpful. Without losing its Mexican atmosphere, the San Juan is an outstanding place to buy food, comparable to any other market in the world. Some time later I discovered the Jamaica market, which also sold wild mushrooms. Until the 1950s, the Jamaica market sold all the produce and flowers grown in Xochimilco. Although the farmers no longer arrive by canal, on boats loaded down with their products, the market's fame has persisted, along with its style.

When the rains let up and there's just the right degree of moisture in the air, the wild-mushroom sellers make their appearance. Humbly clothed men and women arrange small quantities of mushrooms by species and size on cotton sheets. I'll never forget one woman who had carefully sorted out her morels, from the tiniest to the largest, which were almost two inches long! In New York, mushrooms of a single species are all sold together, regardless of their size, so I was delighted by this perfect order. Mexicans use the smallest morels for casseroles and stews and save the larger ones to make what they call *panales rellenos* (stuffed honeycombs). The mushrooms are cleaned, then slit open along one side. They're usually filled with cheese, but I've had them stuffed with squash flowers. They're dipped in a little flour and beaten egg, then fried, and finally simmered in a thickish broth of dried chile or tomato.

The mushroom sellers are a very appealing sight, and the folk names that have been given to wild mushrooms are a real delight. There are *clavitos,* or little nails, and *señoritas;* a firm, red variety is called *enchilados* (covered in chile), and a variety called *yema* (egg yolk) is an intense yellow color; another variety is called *patas de pajarito* (little bird feet) or *coralitos* (little coral), and the mushrooms really do look like bird feet or branches of coral. A very round variety of mushroom is called *panzas,* or bellies. Mexican mushroom gatherers give mushrooms whatever names they dream up, names as funny as *oreja de palo* (stick's ear) or *cabeza de vaca* (cow's head) and even some names

From the woods to the table: When the rainy season ends, the mushroom hunters appear in the market with their bounty.

that are really vulgar, such as *pedo de lobo* (wolf's fart). Where wild mushrooms are eaten, whether in France, Spain, or England, there are always native descriptive names for them.

MUSHROOMS FOR HALLUCINATING, MUSHROOMS FOR SAVORING

Wild mushrooms have become increasingly popular in the United States since the sublime Asian mushroom known as the shiitake caught the fancy of U.S. gourmets. Today, many wild mushrooms grown in the states of Washington and Oregon are sold both fresh and dried.

In pre-Columbian Mexico, mushrooms were extremely important. In Nahuatl they were (and still are) called *nanactl,* which means meat. Oddly enough, mushrooms were the vegetables ancient Mexicans ate most frequently. Another syllable was added to the word *nanactl* to denote the place where the mushroom grew. According to a 1984 publication of the Mexican Society of Mycology, the ancient inhabitants divided the wild mushrooms they ate into five species, depending on whether the mushrooms were picked in forests, meadows, grassy areas, refuse heaps, or from tree trunks. They also classified them by their appearance; for example, the mushroom we know as a morel was called "honeycomb." Hallucinogenic mushrooms were called "intoxicating mushrooms." Hallucinogenic mushrooms, and Sabina, the indigenous woman from Oaxaca who knew their secrets, became famous among the youthful hippies of the seventies and among psychologists and students of the human mind. I knew several people who had experiences–some of them very unpleasant, others highly spiritual–with the shaman Sabina.

FAVORITE MEXICAN FLOWERS AND PLANTS

After my stay in the country town of San Martín de las Pirámides in Teotihuacán, Mexico City delighted me with its special style and natural beauty. In Teotihuacán I had been struck by the trees called ahuehuetes, with their roots that spread out and emerge aboveground. In Mexico City I saw another tree that was new to me: the *colorín.*

The maguey is just about to flower.

One day I happened to be passing in front of a shiny new fire station near the great marketplace of La Merced; I was in a good mood, happy to see how the city was being renovated. In front of the building was a group of trees with spreading branches and light-colored trunks but nothing green anywhere on them: They were covered with red flowers. I have never seen such a thing. The pointed petals of their flowers formed a kind of hand. When the season changes, these trees, like the jacaranda, cover the streets with their flowers, a slippery layer of red; tender green leaves in the shape of butterflies start springing from the colorín's branches soon after. One morning, my housekeeper appeared carrying a clay pot full of *tortitas de colorín,* or colorín cakes, floating in tomato sauce.

Mexicans love to shock other people with the foods they eat, and when they can get them, they make use of several kinds of flowers, including one that grows from the heart of the maguey. Still, despite their undeniable imagination, they almost always eat flowers in tortitas, coated in batter and submerged in a tomato sauce. Another type of flower, a bright yellow button with a smooth texture called *cabuche,* which grows from a cactus called *biznaga,* is eaten raw. Its color is magnificent in a nopal salad, and I use it as a garnish on the fish and seafood platter I serve at Rosa Mexicano. My guests compare its flavor to that of artichoke hearts or asparagus tips.

THE MANY HERBS OF MEXICO

Although people throughout the world use herbs that grow on the banks of rivers, streams, and creeks, the ancient Mexicans, whom I picture as constantly in quest of something new to eat, were particularly fond of them. There is a whole category of Mexican herbs called *quelites,* each variety of which is further distinguished by its own particular name. In every marketplace, there's always someone who specializes in selling them.

One variety of quelite, with small, round leaves and tender stems, is traditionally cooked in a green sauce with, if your pocketbook can stretch that far, chunks of pork; this very popular dish is known as *espinazo con verdolagas.* Another type of herb called *cenizo* (ash) has leaves that are an intense green on one side and a whitish green on the other. *Pepetza* is an aromatic grass that is added to *salsa verde de molcajete.* Of all these herbs, my favorite is *pápalo quelite,* which has thin, light-green leaves shaped like butterfly wings (*pápalo* means butterfly in Nahuatl) and an aroma that penetrates the brain and awakens all sorts of emotions. Just the memory of that scent makes me want to use some kind of aromatizer to fill my New York apartment.

It was the scent that first attracted me to pápalo quelite during one of my initial outings to the market of La Lagunilla. I asked the woman who was selling herbs where that intense smell was coming from. She didn't hesitate for a second; breaking a leaf of pápalo in two, she held it up to my nose. I took that small green leaf from her, and its penetrating scent made me wonder how it would be possible to cook with such an aromatic herb, what foods it could be combined with. In those days there were so many new things to respond to that I left the herb there and didn't think about it for a while.

I finally found the answer to my question during a visit to the city of Puebla, where it is practically obligatory to eat what are called *cemitas.* A savory bread made with coarsely ground flour, the cemita is round and soft inside, with a very crusty surface covered with sesame seeds. The bread is a local interpretation of the bread made by the Arabs and the Jews who lived in Puebla; its name must originally have been *semita,* or Semite, but the spelling varied over time. One of Puebla's regional specialties is a kind of sandwich made with cemita. The bread is sliced horizontally and hollowed out a little, then one surface is covered with cream and the client can choose among chicken, ham, leg of pork, and pickled pig's foot, which is then layered with cheese, strips of avocado, a marinated chipotle chile, and a few leaves of pápalo quelite. The herb is almost always eaten raw.

Recently, I made my own discovery. I was in the kitchen of a friend who was making a green ceviche and had a large amount of pápalo quelite on hand. From the ingredients that were available in her kitchen at that moment, I chose some olives, took out their pits, chopped them up, and mixed them with olive oil and pápalo. I couldn't stop eating the resulting mixture, which had a strong, fascinating flavor.

HERBS AT ROSA MEXICANO

I haven't put pápalo quelite on the menu yet because it only very recently became available in New York. In dishes that call for pápalo, I have substituted epazote, an herb with a pungent yet delicate flavor that, while not yet nearly as common as cilantro, is definitely moving up the scale of familiar flavors in the United States.

One day I decided my guests had to experience the delicate aroma of an extraordinary herb called hoja santa, or holy leaf, and sometimes also called *acuyo*. Cooks in Veracruz use this large, emerald-green leaf with an aniselike taste to give an extra dimension of flavor to their black beans, fish, and poultry. My supplier, Christina Arnold, brought me some, promising me that no one else in New York had it. After the precious hoja santa had finally reached my kitchen, I decided the best way to introduce it to my guests was in an ice cream. Later I made a variety of other dishes with it. Generally the hoja santa I use comes from Florida, but when the crop there is poor we order it from Hawaii. Just as hoja santa or acuyo is characteristic of the region of Veracruz, an herb called chaya is typical of the Yucatán Peninsula, but I'm still waiting for one of my suppliers to find a way of getting it for me.

One of the characteristics of Mexican cooking is color. When I think about it, there are few other cuisines that place so much emphasis on color, though a green sauce prepared with parsley and garlic makes a beautiful combination with red peppers in Spanish cooking, and paprika gives an element of color to Hungarian food. But both dishes were made possible by the European discovery of American chiles. Mexicans always seek out color, and at times they go to extremes. One such extreme is *chorizo verde,* or green sausage.

For a while I rented a cabin in a region called Ajusco, which was a country retreat then, though today it is a very densely populated area of Mexico City. Ajusco is part of the mountain range that lies on the southern rim of the valley of Mexico. Its climate is cooler than the city's and back then it was full of vegetation. From time to time my sons and I would spend a few days in that cabin, which perched on some pillars on the side of the mountain. We hiked across the surrounding area as far as the small town of the same name. There I met a man who was selling . . . green chorizo! He told me he was from Toluca, the capital city of the state of Mexico. I took the green sausages back to my kitchen, boiled them, and found that among the bits of meat, which were practically painted green, there were peanuts, pine nuts, and the taste of herbs.

CHORIZO VERDE AT ROSA MEXICANO

At the restaurant, we make our own chorizo, but I've never dared to make chorizo verde, perhaps because I'm afraid it might upset my guests to see meat that color. Nevertheless, a few of them have tried chorizo verde. During the early years of Rosa Mexicano, I tried to pay homage to the cooks who have promoted Mexican food. Of course, Diana Kennedy was among them; we were honored to have her visit and prepare some of her specialties for our guests. Among them was chorizo verde.

CHORIZO VERDE / GREEN CHORIZO

SERVES 6

This is a popular sausage from Toluca which I first had in the village of Ajusco. It was served at Rosa Mexicano during a guest chef appearance of Diana Kennedy with great success.

2 pounds pork cut into 1-inch pieces
¼ pound pork fat
¾ cup white vinegar
6 garlic cloves
1 teaspoon dried oregano
¼ teaspoon cumin seed
¼ teaspoon coriander seed
2 poblano chiles, veins and seeds removed
1 pasilla chile, toasted, seeded, and deveined, and ground into a powder
1 cup cilantro, roughly chopped
1 cup Italian parsley, roughly chopped
2 cups Swiss chard leaves, stems removed, roughly chopped
1 tablespoon salt

---

4 to 5 feet of narrow pork casing, rinsed under water and then soaked in 3 cups water with 1 tablespoon white vinegar
12 corn tortillas

1. Grind the pork and the fat in a meat grinder.
2. Blend ½ cup of the vinegar with the garlic, oregano, cumin, and coriander in a blender until the garlic and spices are finely ground. Add the rest of the vinegar, the poblano chiles, and the ground pasilla chile and blend until the chiles are finely ground. Gradually add the cilantro, parsley, and Swiss chard, and blend until smooth.
3. Mix the ground pork with the puree and the salt; mix well to evenly dis-

tribute the ingredients. Place in a bowl, cover, and refrigerate for at least 2 hours, ideally overnight.

4. Heat an 8-inch sauté pan. Fry a small patty of the sausage for 2 to 3 minutes on each side. Taste for seasoning, and add more salt if necessary.
5. Cut the sausage casings into approximately 2-foot lengths. Tie a knot in one of the ends. Place some of the sausage mixture in a pastry bag (not too much or it will be impossible to pipe) and pipe into sausage casings. Smooth out the filling in the casing to evenly distribute the meat; do not overstuff the casings or they will break. Twist into 4-inch lengths.
6. To cook: Prick the chorizo several times with a fork. Heat a large cast-iron skillet or a 10-inch sauté pan. Over medium heat, evenly brown the chorizo, approximately 8 to 10 minutes. Serve with warm tortillas to make tacos.

Only the genius of the omnivorous cooks of Mexico could have created a green chorizo. It is a delight for the eye and the palate.

CANTINAS

For me, the flavor of Mexico resides not only in its food but in the places where people come together, in the solutions each locale finds to the various problems that confront it, in the way each expresses itself. The cantinas and bars of Mexico have a very particular flavor. Every hotel and restaurant has its bar. There was a time when people would spend long hours in the bar of the Hotel María Cristina. The narrowness of the space made mingling easier for the various people who went there to enjoy the Mexican music of the day.

All kinds of people can be found in a Mexican bar, and their right to go to bars (a right which, not so long ago, was disputed) makes Mexican women feel liberated. Some bars offer snacks, which may include special dishes such as a broth made with dried shrimp and served in a demitasse cup, whose aromatic, spicy flavor incites you to have another cup. But everyone knows that the best snacks are in cantinas. Mexican cantinas serve a variety of spicy dishes that are really only the same stews or casseroles that characterize everyday home cooking: *chicharrón* (pork cracklings) or cow's feet in green sauce, pig's feet with vinaigrette or in salsa, pork in a sauce made with some variety of dried chiles, stewed beans, and so on.

The typical clientele of a cantina is not particularly varied; generally the customer is the average, working-class Mexican man, a type well known for his roguishness. Authentic Mexican cantinas are generally established next to a marketplace, in heavily commercialized zones, or in working-class neighborhoods. When I lived in Mexico, a certain type of cantina always had a sign on the door that said "No Women, Children, Policemen, or Dogs." The signs were taken down by law in the eighties, as a concession to feminists. Many women decided to exercise their newly won right to go to cantinas. The surprise was that cantinas had no bathrooms, only a urinal attached to one wall.

PULQUERÍAS

Another type of cantina that had the same kind of sign next to its swinging doors is the *pulquería*. The only drink sold there is pulque, accompanied by snacks. Pulquerías usually specialize in salsas that are eaten by themselves with tortillas and pulque. The most popular Mexican salsa is called *borracha,* or drunken salsa, and is made with dried chiles, oranges, pulque; the pulquerías serve it the same way they serve salsa verde, in enormous molcajetes.

Pulque is a thousand-year-old Mexican tradition. Extracted from the center of the maguey, it was the alcoholic drink invented by the ancient inhabitants of Mexico. During the pre-Hispanic era its consumption was severely restricted; only old men had the right to drink it. The restriction was supposedly intended to safeguard the population from alcoholism. When the Spaniards arrived, they discovered that controlling the production and sale of pulque was an excellent way to make money; the consumption of pulque was legalized and promoted, and great pulque-manufacturing haciendas were established, and their owners amassed huge fortunes and came to form a social class that people called "the pulque aristocracy."

During the 1950s and 1960s, pulque was still the most widely consumed alcoholic beverage in Mexico, but in the 1970s a vast advertising campaign helped beer become the preferred drink of Mexicans. There are still a few pulquerías around that offer a drink called *curado,* a mixture of white pulque and celery, nuts, strawberry, lemon, guava, pineapple, or oatmeal. I must confess that the first time I tasted pulque, I couldn't stand it. However, over time, as I tried it again, its acidic flavor and slightly thick texture have convinced me that it is a drink worth knowing more about, perhaps by seeking out the highest-quality pulque producer, and someday I hope to do that.

What I have really enjoyed are foods cooked with pulque. Mexican cooks have achieved delicious results by incorporating pulque into their recipes. Often, with mutton or poultry, pulque is used as a substitute for wine. On my frequent visits to Mexico, I've tasted both traditional and nouvelle cuisine dishes made with pulque, and the results have surprised me: Pulque adds a unique texture and flavor to the sauces in which meats or vegetables are cooked. Unfortunately, it's becoming harder and harder to find pulque in Mexico City; sometimes you have to leave the city to get it.

A great deal has been written about what some call the "culture of pulque." Several studies have demonstrated its nutritional value; according to the experts, it contains a generous amount of vitamin B12, and laboratory tests have demonstrated its antibacterial qualities. The names of pulquerías are also very significant: Mi Oficina (My Office), Recuerdos del Porvenir (Memories of the Future), Aquí Te Quiero Ver (I Want to See You Here), La Gran Mona (The Big Hangover), La Jícara Encantada (The Enchanted Jícara—a kind of gourd from which pulque is drunk), La Dama de las Camelias (The Lady of the Camellias, the title of a novel by Alexandre Dumas), El Nido de las Águilas (The Eagles' Nest). As these names show, pulquerías were mainly places for men who wanted to take refuge in a masculine world of their own. In the history of pulquerías, however, there were also places reserved exclusively for women. I remember the days when some pulquerías had a take-out window next to the door with a sign on it that said, "Pulque Served to Women Here."

BREAKFASTS

I've always loved a challenge, and new ones are continually presenting me with the opportunity to rise to them. When I stroll through Mexico City today, I point out to whoever is with me all the apartments, houses, and offices I designed during my days there. With the help of my friends, the craftsmen, I was able to create a special ambience for the office in that building. I don't know if the company's distinguished employees truly appreciated my work, but those offices were very lovely and functional. However, perhaps my most important achievement was to set up a kitchen that would serve lunch to the executives. In Mexico today it is common for the offices of highly placed government officials to have kitchens that serve breakfasts and lunches. Breakfast is an occasion for business meetings, gatherings of friends, and celebrations, and can sometimes last until 11:00 A.M. or noon.

A Mexican breakfast begins with fresh-squeezed orange or grapefruit juice and a platter of various kinds of fruit; then come eggs, which are either fried or scrambled with salsa mexicana (tomato, onion, jalapeño, and cilantro), or served as huevos rancheros (fried eggs on a lightly fried tortilla covered with pureed salsa mexicana). Some restaurants serve a dish from Yucatán called *huevos motuleños,* which includes fried plantains and many other things. Another egg dish I liked was served in the cafeteria called La Huerta at the Hotel Camino Real in Mexico City. In a small pot, made in the same shape as the much larger pots that are traditionally used for cooking beans, was a moderately thick bean puree on which a couple of eggs had been poached; a little jug of salsa with chile was served on the side. Ever since I first tasted it, I've always been on the lookout for this dish, which was called *huevos escalfados en fríjol,* but I've never seen them served anywhere else.

A Mexican breakfast can also include roasted meats, chorizo, tacos of every kind, and, always, refried beans. A classic Mexican breakfast dish is *chilaquiles,* which should be very spicy because it is considered a pick-me-up dish for people who drank too much the night before. Like many other Mexican dishes, chilaquiles can be prepared with a green tomatillo sauce or a red sauce made with tomatoes or dried chiles. Large strips of tortilla that have been lightly fried are stirred into a sauce which they absorb and which softens them. The mixture is then served with shredded chicken, cream, white cheese, and chopped onion. The cooks at Rosa Mexicano often make chilaquiles for themselves and they share them with me so I can enjoy the Mexican flavor.

Among the most popular places to have breakfast is Sanborns, which is now a large chain of restaurants, though when I lived in Mexico there were only a few of them. The most beautiful Sanborns is located in a historic building on a corner of Calle Madero in Mexico City's central zone. It is called the "House of Tiles" because its exterior is completely covered in beautiful blue-and-white Talavera tiles. In addition to its lovely restaurant, the building houses a bookstore, jewelry store, pharmacy, and other types of services as well. On the walls inside are murals by distinguished artists of the past and present. The waitresses wear a reinterpretation of the traditional dress of Michoacán, which was originally made with homespun fabrics. Another of my favorite Sanborns was the one on the Paseo de la Reforma, which boasts a large mural of watermelons by the great artist Rufino Tamayo. Among the many dishes served there, I particularly enjoyed *molletes:* a crusty bolillo, sliced horizontally and spread with refried beans, then covered with grated cheese and placed in the oven just long enough to melt the cheese. In Sanborns, molletes are served with a little jug of salsa.

Sanborns is actually only a kind of diner, although looking at the grandiose facade of the House of Tiles you might think you were at a four-star restaurant. The food served there is meant to please every taste, and Sanborns is a particular favorite among tourists. Another dish I liked was enchiladas served with melted cheese and called *enchiladas suizas,* or Swiss enchiladas. They have nothing to do with Switzerland, of course, but for anyone who is only just beginning to learn about the flavors of Mexico, they can be an appealing start. In the daily life of the residents of Mexico City, Sanborns was and still is a frequent choice for professional appointments, business meetings, even lovers' rendezvous.

For the more adventurous, there are spots like one located in a former bus stop, on a small square with a name it took me years to learn how to pronounce: Tlacoquemecatl. To describe it as rustic doesn't really go far enough. It's a place that exists on its own terms and for the needs of the locals; it still

These huge pots of *moles* and *molitos* are all empty by noon in the plaza of Tlacoquemecatl.

uses the same long tables and benches around which the bus drivers used to have their morning get-togethers. There are several of those tables with benches running along both sides, each of which can seat four or five. So eight or ten people will be placed together at a single table. I've often had to wedge myself in among a group of locals in order to get a seat.

Each waitress is in charge of a single table. After describing the day's dishes, she takes the order, goes to the cash register to deliver it, then takes money from her purse and pays for what the clients have requested. The same system is used in other traditional restaurants in Mexico City. Service is fast; most dishes are cooked in advance and kept warm. Orders for eggs or grilled meats are cooked on the spot. You can have huevos tirados or tortillas toasted on an anafre at your table. When someone orders toasted tortillas, the waitress throws some tortillas onto the anafre's metal grill. After they've been toasted on each side, they are practically black. Often customers simply grab the delicious, smoky-tasting tortillas off the anafre themselves and distribute them around the table.

The place also serves thick *bisteces* (thinly sliced steak) in pasilla chile sauce, pork with verde chile, and almost twenty other dishes, all for breakfast. They follow the tradition of opening for business at 6:00 A.M. and closing around 11:00 A.M., just as they did when their clientele was composed mainly of bus drivers. Today everyone who enjoys the authentic flavor of Mexican home cooking goes there. The food is served with bottled soft drinks or a kind of coffee called *café de olla*. Brown sugar—sold in Mexico in solid, cone-shaped cakes called *piloncillos*—and sometimes a stick or two of cinnamon are added to a clay pot filled with boiling water. When the piloncillos have dissolved, a little coarsely ground coffee is added; the mixture is boiled for so long that the coffee grounds virtually dissolve and the resulting watery, sweet coffee is served in clay mugs. When guests at Rosa Mexicano tell me they're planning a trip to Mexico City, I often recommend that they pay a visit to Tlacoquemecatl.

FRIJOLES REFRITOS / REFRIED BEANS

SERVES 6

3 tablespoons vegetable oil
½ medium white onion, finely chopped
1 garlic clove, finely chopped
3 cups black beans (preferably) or pinto beans, cooked and mashed
½ to ¾ cup bean cooking liquid
salt to taste

1. Heat the oil in a 12-inch sauté pan. Sauté the onion for 4 to 5 minutes over medium heat, add the garlic and cook for 2 to 3 minutes more or until the onions are translucent.
2. Add the black beans and sauté for 2 to 3 minutes, mashing the beans with a potato masher.
3. Add the cooking liquid from the beans and continue to cook until the liquid is absorbed by the beans.
4. To make Frijoles Martajados, the beans will be roughly mashed. Or mash to a smoother paste for Frijoles Refritos.

■ ■ ■ HUEVOS TIRADOS / FRIED BLACK BEANS WITH SCRAMBLED EGGS

1. Follow the recipe for Frijoles Refritos.
2. Push the beans to the edge of the pan and crack 2 to 3 eggs into the pan. Fry a little and then stir with the beans. Gather to the center of the pan. Shake the pan to make a roll out of the mass. The beans should have yellow spots from the eggs.

POACHED EGG IN BRIOCHE WITH POBLANO SAUCE

SERVES 6

I discovered this dish at a coffee shop in Mexico City. I always try to go there when I am in Mexico. I serve this dish to my friends for brunch, and everyone loves it—it is so *delicious.*

6 brioches
1 tablespoon white vinegar
1 tablespoon salt
6 extra-large eggs
Poblano Chile Sauce, heated (see page 85)

1. Cut off the tops of the brioches and, using a grapefruit knife or a melon baller, hollow out most of their centers.
2. In a saucepan, bring 1 quart of water to a boil with the vinegar and the salt. Reduce to a simmer and carefully crack the eggs into the water. Ideally, poach the eggs in egg cups to keep their shape. Poach for 3 to 4 minutes until the yolks are soft or have reached the desired consistency.
3. In the meantime, place the hollowed-out brioches and their tops on a baking tray and toast in a 375°F. oven for 5 to 6 minutes.
4. Carefully strain the eggs and place one in each brioche. Ladle approximately 4 ounces of the heated poblano sauce over the poached egg; the sauce will overflow and fill the plate. Place the top back on the brioche and serve immediately.

THE COASTLINE

The tropics have no particular appeal for me. Nevertheless, from time to time I went on a little jaunt to the seaside. I was particularly taken with the port town of Veracruz; the first time I was there I felt as if I were in Cuba. There was music on all sides, a kind of local music called *jarocha,* and people were lighthearted and joyous. Everyone gathers in the town's central square, or zócalo, where the Café la Parroquía is located. People meet there for breakfast, lunch, and dinner. The breakfast specialty is huevos tirados and *infladas,* small corn tortillas that puff up when cooked, very soft and delicate. When passersby stop in for a cup of coffee, which is served throughout the day, the waiters come to the table with two pitchers, one of coffee and the other of hot milk. The café is famous for its coffee urns, lovely silver vessels crowned with gilded eagles; they've been in use for more than a hundred years.

The atmosphere in the port of Veracruz is relaxed, and the food is excellent. La Bocana, a neighborhood located in Boca del Rio at the mouth of the river, boasts a long row of restaurants that specialize in fresh fish and seafood; you can spend hours and hours there enjoying many different dishes made with the bounty of the river and the sea. In La Bocana, I once had a coconut filled with delicately seasoned seafood mixed with coconut meat and covered with a thin crust of toasted cheese. The variety of textures and flavors, the tang of the seafood mingled with the aroma and freshness of the coconut, created a dish that was a delight both to behold and to eat.

In addition to *chilpachole,* the seafood stew made with masa dumplings, Veracruzanos were the first to achieve a successful gastronomical marriage of Mexican and Spanish cuisine. Two extraordinary local specialties are *huachinango a la veracruzana* (Veracruz-style red snapper) and *bacalao a la mexicana* (Mexican-style dried codfish). The locals are experts at making seafood cocktails; the best known is the *vuelve a la vida,* or return to life, named because the cocktail is reputed to make anyone whose energy level is flagging feel stronger. Veracruz is a state that seems to have everything, and its inhabitants, like all Mexicans, have accepted techniques and ingredients from around the world, incorporating them into their cuisine and transforming them into their own dishes.

Bottomless cups of coffee and as much milk as you want—that's how *café con leche* is served at La Parroquía. All around you is the hustle and bustle and music of the coastline along the Gulf of Mexico.

History has left many traces in the state of Veracruz, which is full of interesting things to see. You can find the remains of pre-Hispanic peoples there and the scars of a long series of invasions. In the faces of the local people, you can see African, Asian, and indigenous American traits. I am always seduced by the Anthropology Museum in Jalapa, the state capital. There you can see the similarity between the peoples who once lived in the Veracruz region and those of the Far East. It is an unforgettable experience to see the "little smiling faces," the clay figurines whose Asian features make me feel that the world is really small and united.

THE TASTE OF VERACRUZ

The state of Veracruz has many unusual flavors to offer to its visitors. A Veracruzana friend of mine, Raquel Torres (also a restaurateur), accepted my request to come to my apartment in New York and teach me the art of making Veracruz tamales. One day we were talking about regional specialties; she described in great detail a variety of unique dishes, and I mentioned some I knew from other regions. At a certain point in the conversation, she asked me, "What regions are we talking about, Josefina?" "The regions of Mexico, of course," I answered. "No!" Raquel explained, "I'm talking about the regions of Veracruz!" In Veracruz the food in the port is very different from that of the various towns in the interior.

A famous port town in the state of Veracruz is Alvarado, the perfect place to eat fish and seafood that is incredibly fresh and very different from what reached my grandmother's kitchen back in the mountains of Asturias. Away from the coast, the landscape of Veracruz changes, as do the faces of the people and the food. Jalapa has its own specialties; only a mile away is Coatepec, also with its own foods, and very close by is Xico, which specializes in a unique type of mole. Naolinco, a town whose artisans are great leatherworkers, produces the chipotle chile, a dried or smoked jalapeño. They use the chipotle to make a delicate mole; they also boil it in brown sugar and stuff it with cheese.

CHIPOTLES NAULINQUEÑOS / STUFFED CHIPOTLE CHILES FROM THE TOWN OF NAOLINCO

SERVES 6

6 chipotle chiles, dried, the largest and straightest possible

1 cup piloncillo, or dark brown sugar

¼ pound queso fresco, cut in thin strips approximately 3 inches long

3 egg whites

2 egg yolks

3 cups vegetable oil, for frying

½ cup flour, for dredging

6 white-corn tortillas

1. In a 1-quart saucepan, place the chipotle chiles with the piloncillo and 2 cups of water. Bring to a boil, reduce to simmer, and cook for 30 minutes. Strain and allow to cool. For milder chiles, repeat the process.
2. When cool, cut a small slit in the chiles and carefully remove the veins and seeds. Place 2 to 3 strips of cheese inside each chile.
3. To make the batter, whisk the egg whites until soft peaks form. Whisk the egg yolks and fold the whites into the yolks.
4. Heat the vegetable oil in a 2-quart saucepan. Holding each chile by the stem, dredge in the flour and carefully shake off any excess flour. Dip in the batter and carefully lower into the hot oil. Turn with tongs to brown evenly, and when golden brown, remove with a slotted spoon and drain on paper towels.
5. To serve, roll into the fresh hot tortillas.

MEMORIES OF ACAPULCO

There were days when I decided to take a short vacation and drove down to Acapulco, not to lie on the beach or swim in the sea, but just to go down to sea level for a while and rest up a little from my busy life in the heights of Mexico City. I liked to arrive at the Hotel de la Quebrada, take a room embraced by a curving balcony, open the windows, and sit down to read. For four or five days I would spend most of my time reading, and then I would visit some friends before going home. In the 1960s and 1970s Acapulco still had some of the charm of its best years. You could be certain of good weather, and the sea breeze blew in across the balcony of the old hotel. Though I have seen many beautiful beaches and, as I said, though I'm not exactly a lover of the tropics, undoubtedly the Acapulco that I knew then was the perfect refuge for reading and relaxing.

CEVICHE

The specialty of Acapulco is *ceviche de pescado;* it's made on the beach with freshly caught fish. Ceviche cannot be claimed as a Mexican creation; Peru and Colombia also insist on having invented it. But there's no dispute that the coast of America was where Europeans first learned of the Indian method of "cooking" fresh fish with the acidity of a citrus fruit. The "ceviche style" is currently used in many countries, especially those along the Pacific rim. A well-prepared ceviche includes just the right amount of lemon juice; the freshness of the tomato, onion, and chile provides a delicious, refreshing contrast to the soft smoothness of the fish.

CEVICHE DE HUACHINANGO / RED SNAPPER CEVICHE

SERVES 6

I believe ceviches originally came from the Oriental exchange with Mexico in the colonial days.

1½ to 2 pounds fillet of red snapper, skin trimmed and discarded
juice of 8 to 10 lemons, approximately 2 cups
½ cup water
3 small vine-ripened tomatoes
1 medium white onion, finely chopped
2 serrano chiles, seeded, and deveined, and very finely chopped
½ cup olive oil
1 tablespoon dry oregano
2 tablespoons fresh chopped cilantro
1 tablespoon salt
3 ripe Hass avocados
½ head romaine lettuce, washed and julienned

FOR GARNISH:

1 cup vegetable oil
4 corn tortillas, cut in quarters

1. Cut the red snapper into ½-inch squares. Marinate the fish in the lemon juice and water until the fish is opaque in color, 2 to 3 hours. Stir occasionally. To test "doneness," cut the piece of fish in half. It should be opaque or "cooked" through.
2. Strain the fish and quickly rinse with water.
3. Cut the tomatoes in half horizontally. Scoop out the insides with a spoon, leaving only the walls of the tomato. Cut out the core and dice the tomato.
4. Combine the fish with the onion, tomatoes, chiles, olive oil, oregano, cilantro, and salt in a glass bowl and stir until the fish is completely coated.
5. Holding an avocado in the palm of your hand, cut it in half lengthwise around the pit. Twist the top half of the avocado to separate the halves.

Carefully hit the pit with the edge of a sharp knife and twist to remove the seed. Slice it lengthwise in approximately 1/4-inch strips, then across to form a grid. Scoop the avocado out with a spoon next to the skin.

6. Mix the avocado with the fish and fill the avocado skins with the ceviche. Place on a bed of julienne romaine lettuce.
7. Heat the oil in a 1-quart fry pan. Fry the quartered tortillas until golden. Drain on paper towels.
8. Stick the tortilla chips in the ceviche; they should be pointing up to resemble the sails of a ship.

CEVICHE DE CALLOS DE HACHA / SCALLOP CEVICHE

SERVES 6

1 pound bay scallops, with the small attachments removed

3/4 cup lemon juice, freshly squeezed

1/4 cup water

4 tablespoons olive oil

1 jalapeño, finely chopped

1 tablespoon dried oregano

1/2 teaspoon salt or to taste

2 tablespoons chopped cilantro

1 small jar *cabuches* (small buds from the flower of a biznaga cactus) or substitute for cabuches 1 small jar artichoke hearts packed in water, diced

3 ripe avocados

FOR GARNISH:

1/2 head romaine lettuce, washed and julienned

4 corn tortillas, cut in quarters

1 cup vegetable oil

1. Marinate the scallops in the lemon juice and water for about an hour until opaque.
2. Strain the scallops and place in a bowl. Add the olive oil, jalapeño, oregano, salt, cilantro, and cabuches or artichoke hearts. Gently stir.
3. Holding an avocado in the palm of your hand, cut it in half lengthwise around the pit. Twist the top half of the avocado to separate the halves. Carefully hit the pit with the edge of a sharp knife and twist to remove the seed. Scoop the avocado with a small melon baller. Carefully incorporate the avocado into the ceviche. Save the skins.
4. Fill the avocado skins with ceviche. Place on the shredded lettuce and garnish with fried tortilla chips pointing up to resemble the sails of a ship.

THE GREAT BOOM IN TACOS AL CARBÓN

Mexicans are forever in search of new kinds of tacos to eat; their appetite is insatiable. Toward the end of the 1960s, a new kind of taco emerged in Mexico City, probably originating in the north of the country: *tacos al carbón* (charcoal-cooked tacos). The first establishment to sell tacos al carbón was called El Farolito in the neighborhood of La Condesa, an area with the feel of the 1920s and 1930s, on a corner of the Avenida Juanacatlán, which later changed its name to that of the famous writer and food lover Alfonso Reyes. Thin slices of meat are rapidly grilled over a charcoal fire, then chopped up and placed in handmade tortillas. Generally an order included two tacos and some grilled spring onions. Customers could also help themselves to red or green salsas from enormous molcajetes. El Farolito was a resounding success, and taquerías serving tacos al carbón spread across the city; there was even a chain that were more like restaurants than simple taquerías.

As in everything having to do with tacos, the variety of salsas was the key to success, but in this case what appealed to the customers was the concept of the smoky, charcoal-grilled meat and the slight sweetness of the grilled onions. New variations quickly appeared, including *tacos al pastor* (shepherd's tacos), which were initially sold in the same taquerías. Tacos al pastor are the Mexican version of the Middle Eastern, and particularly Lebanese, dish known as gyros. A large number of thin slices of pork are marinated in a sauce of garlic, onion, and powdered chile (used more for its color than for flavor), then squeezed onto a sharp steel stake that is crowned with an onion and a peeled pineapple. For several hours, the meat is rotated over a fire until it is fully roasted. The men who make tacos al pastor are not only masters at cutting meat but they also do a fairly impressive juggling act, which consists of skillfully cutting the meat along with a piece of pineapple from the top of the spit, then catching it all in a small tortilla, to which they add cilantro and chopped onion. The small taco is a sensational combination of saltiness, sweetness, acidity, spiciness, crunchiness, and smoothness. Soon tacos al carbón and tacos al pastor could be found on every street corner and all along the avenues, where the stands competed with one another.

My passion for tacos has never diminished but there was one occasion when it became a little traumatic. I was invited to a taquería with a very particular specialization. The place was very small, and the customers ate their tacos either sitting on benches or standing at a bar. The man making the tacos was hurriedly filling fresh tortillas with portions of . . . eyes. They could be sheep, pig, or cow eyes, all of them cooked and served with a quantity of chopped onion and cilantro and a spoonful of salsa on top. I couldn't eat those tacos and for several nights I had dreams about thousands of eyes that wouldn't stop staring at me. It shouldn't have surprised me to see people eating eyes; in Europe I knew people who enjoyed eating eyes, especially fish eyes!

A kind of juggling act is needed to make *tacos al pastor*.

BACK IN THE U.S.A.

Although life in Mexico was so intense, or perhaps because of that very intensity, the years passed almost without my realizing it, and I felt as young and strong and capable of anything as when I arrived. But my sons had grown up and were almost out of their teenage years. The time had come for us to leave. My elder boy received a scholarship to study at a university in California and decided to make his own way to Los Angeles; he wanted to see all there was to see along the way. My other son and I took a plane, but he got a ride all the way from Mexico City to the border. When he arrived in Los Angeles he was unshaven, wearing a heavy poncho, and carrying a colorful woven bag that contained a frosted-glass replica of a jade mask that is in Mexico City's Anthropology Museum.

He was delighted to tell me all about the adventures he had on his journey. He came across the border on foot; the border guards ignored him and he crossed from Mexico into the United States without once being asked for any identification. "I took a bus in San Isidro, then passed through San Diego and a lot of other places like that, as if I hadn't ever left Mexico," he commented. Later we realized he hadn't even had his passport with him; he had left it behind in Mexico. And even though the towns in California had Spanish names, everything was different.

Of course, it once wasn't different. A while ago, the *New York Times* published a map that shows how, little by little, Mexican territory, including what is now California, Arizona, New Mexico, and Texas, was conceded to or annexed by the United States. The Mexicans who live in the United States are a culture that has been part of this nation since it was founded. And that culture continued to have the same importance for me, whether I was south or north of a border that has existed for only a century and a half (not much time at all for a European like me).

In Los Angeles, at the end of the 1970s, I had to confront various realities. The country had changed; the era of plastic and everything disposable had arrived, and all of it seemed to me to be in bad taste or in no taste at all. At first I tried to continue working as a decorator, but it wasn't possible; the work was there but it simply wasn't my style. I took a job that I thought would help immigrant workers from Mexico. After taking a course and receiving a certificate from the University of California at Los Angeles, I was accepted as a court interpreter. I worked at a night court, where the majority of cases involved car accidents caused by drunk drivers. I noticed that the Spanish-speaking defendants were punished with fines and jail sentences, while English speakers paid a fine and had to take a special drivers' education class and enroll in Alcoholics Anonymous. When I asked the judge about the difference in sentencing, I learned that the center where the drivers' ed class was taught had no one who spoke Spanish. I got his permission to be trained to give those classes so that I could educate Spanish-speaking drivers. I also translated during trials in which Hispanic workers sought compensation from their employers for accidents in the workplace. It was an experience that revealed a lot about the U.S. justice system. The workers were usually compensated—something that probably would not have happened in Mexico—but not at the same level as U.S. workers. As an interpreter I was forbidden by law to have any contact with either the plaintiff or the defendant. Many times I left the courtroom with a broken heart, but there was nothing I could do.

The work paid well and left me enough free time to allow me to get to know L.A. The city was permeated with the spirit of Hollywood, or with that of a Hollywood set. I remember a very long and absolutely perfect avenue I once biked along. The asphalt was perfectly smooth, the sky was pure blue, and an endless row of palm trees divided the two lanes of traffic. Everything was so perfect that it disturbed me. I noticed how green the palm trees were and how uniform in size. When I touched them, I realized they were made of plastic. And the avenue ended in the white sand of a beach.

Meanwhile, my sons and I were starting to miss Mexican food. At first we had been happy eating corned beef, bagels and lox, potato latkes, and all the other New York–style foods that were available in L.A. Still, we were longing for Mexican flavors. So much so that we once let ourselves be drawn in by a restaurant that had a big sombrero and a garish Mexican serape on its sign. We knew it wasn't going to be anything like the real thing, but our desire for the taste of Mexico was so strong that we didn't stop to think. We asked for tacos and they served us what they called tacos, which consisted of hard "taco shells" (something we had never seen in Mexico), overflowing with Velveeta cheese and chopped lettuce, with a little ground beef inside. I was so disappointed I couldn't eat them; whatever that stuff on the plate was, it was nothing like the tacos we were missing. Maybe that was when an idea flashed into my mind: People in the United States should find out what real tacos are like. For a long time, the thought lay buried deep inside me, almost without my being conscious of it.

We still kept looking for Mexican food. One morning, at six or seven, I was coming home after my work at night court when I saw a long line of people in front of a grocery store. I'm curious by nature, and when I asked, I found out the store was selling tamales, very good tamales obviously, given the size of the line. I got on line and took some of the tamales home, but I couldn't manage to be there at six in the morning every day just so we could eat tamales. There is a street in Los Angeles called Olvera Street, known as a place for Mexican food and handicrafts (today it is a big tourist attraction). One day I met a woman there who, from a little improvised food stand, just like in Mexico, sold real tacos made with carnitas, soft fresh tortillas, and a cooked red sauce that was very good.

By then, my sons and I understood that Los Angeles was only the first step in envisioning what life in the United States would be like after our life in Mexico. And my opportunities for professional development were very limited. Two years later, the time came to return to New York, my hometown.

NEW YORK, NEW YORK, ONCE AGAIN

My mother was waiting for us, and fear and apprehension were dancing in my head. What would I do in this new New York? My first thought was to establish a place for myself; keeping busy always helps me when I have a lot of doubts and fears, and I bustled about, making the rounds of decorating stores and setting up my apartment. One morning my life turned over, in one instant; the saddest period I have ever lived through began. I buried my son on a hillside in a cemetery in Carmel, New York.

GOING ON . . .

My decorating style was out of step with the fashions of those years. In New York the largest apartments belonged to all sorts of artists and show people, many of them rock stars. I had no interest in their style, and it wasn't the moment for me to come to terms with the ambience of those people and that time. My one desire was to be hidden far from the world. What else did I know how to do? Cook! I could hide from the world among the fires of some distant kitchen. But first I would have to learn a new profession and obtain some kind of certification. I had to start all over again, or die. . . .

THE PROFESSIONAL DIPLOMA

Peter Kump had one of the best cooking schools in New York, and he offered a work-study program to students who wanted to take classes in exchange for working at the school. I made an appointment and met with him.

My appearance reflected my emotional state; the years had fallen hard on me. Peter Kump was hesitant; he told me the work was difficult, and that it was best for a student chef to be young and strong. He pulled out his last argument: "But you'll have to wash dishes."

"Mr. Kump," I told him in all sincerity, "you may not believe me, but washing dishes is what I like best, and I do it very well." His answer put the conversation on a less formal footing. "I do believe you, because I like to wash dishes, too," he confessed. Finally, without much conviction he accepted me as a student and, of course, I took over the chore of washing the dishes. I attended class with all the other students, and when the class was over I hurried to the sink. I've always liked washing dishes, since the days I spent in my grandmother's house, but at that point it was truly a release. The sound of running water filled my head, my hands ran over the surfaces, and my mind focused on getting into even the tiniest corner where the least bit of food might be hidden and scrubbing it clean. I finished the course and received my diploma. Peter Kump was always a little doubtful about me, but as the years went by he kept abreast of what I was doing. A few years before he died I received a letter from him that I have saved with particular care, in which he expressed his appreciation for my work. I feel very close to the Peter Kump School and whenever they invite me to give classes I go.

A LIGHT AT THE END OF THE TUNNEL

My money was running out; all of my savings were being used up by the rent on the apartment I had rented in Murray Hill, near my mother. A doctor was the one who finally gave me the advice: I needed to look for help. The burden was too heavy. A young psychologist was assigned to be my therapist. I had a hard time believing he was going to understand me, but I needed to get things off my chest. He listened and I talked and talked. During one of our sessions, I saw the poor man open his eyes wide when he heard what I was saying. "I want New Yorkers to taste real tacos," I had said. "I'm going to start a taquería." "How can you imagine such a thing?"

But my obsession was swelling like a storm. I bought a hibachi portable grill and turned to my small circle of friends. All of them offered to help me. The idea was to offer a tasting of tacos al carbón, with freshly made tortillas and salsa. The gatherings were small, but the fantasy of a taquería in New York such as the city had never seen had taken hold of my imagination. While my young therapist did his best to dissuade me (he thought it was not the right time for a woman in so much pain to meet with yet another disappointment), I hurried to carry out my plan. With a Mexican corn flour that was available in the U.S., I made tortillas. At the supermarket, I bought thin spareribs on the bone, the cheapest kind, and I found fresh tomatoes, green chiles, white onion, and cilantro in Chinatown. My friends invited their friends, and in the coldest winter I can remember I arrived with my little hibachi to grill meats on a balconies or fire escapes.

When I go back in my mind to those days in the winter of 1980–1981, I see myself as the survivor of a disaster. Again and again, the whole thing seemed useless. Everyone enjoyed the tacos, but there was no one who had the means to invest in starting a business. When I had as little strength as money left, the first ray of hope finally gleamed. A Dr. López called me up and asked me to make my tacos at a party he was giving. He was Mexican, originally from the state of Nuevo León; he took one bite and decided to invest.

My spirits were revived, and in a frantic race against time I set out to find the right place, which turned out to be a spot on Worth Street in downtown New York. Various contractors put in bids to do the work on the place. Frank Waisfeld's was the winning bid and in him I found a very special human being. All of our dealings with each other took place on a basis of talking things out, reaching a mutual understanding, and shaking hands on it—something completely unheard of in a world where red tape, signatures, and contracts are the norm. Frank Waisfeld introduced me to the architect Jan Diamond, who understood exactly what I wanted to do. I developed a great friendship with Frank that went beyond business, a relationship of mutual respect and confidence. I could talk about anything with him at any time, and his kindness and intelligence helped me not only to complete the decoration of the taquería but in many other ways as well. I admired his intelligence and his ability to understand. He had a brilliant mind and could keep calm in any kind of chaos. And he didn't just give me moral support; his prestige and good name opened many doors. Frank was my friend until he died. I miss him very much, and often ask myself, when I'm doubtful about something, What would Frank say? What advice would he give me?

LA FOGATA: A BONFIRE IN THE DARKNESS

La Fogata—The Bonfire—was lit in the heart of downtown New York, on Worth Street, not far from the state and federal courthouses, in 1982; it was the first such taquería in New York City. What I lived in the following months was something I hadn't even dared to dream. One strip of meat after another was flung on the grill. La Fogata had a warm, homey atmosphere, and our most faithful customers were lawyers, judges, and courthouse employees. Every day more people came. Many people who were involved in court cases came to eat tacos as well. We also delivered tacos to the offices of *The Wall Street Journal* and even to Beekman Downtown Hospital; we figured out how to wrap them so they would arrive steaming hot, just as if they were freshly made. When we opened in the morning, there would already be a long line of people waiting to get in. When we closed at 5:00 P.M., we sometimes had to turn people away.

In Mexico, tacos al carbón made with spareribs are served with the chopped meat in the tortilla and the bone on the side to suck on. New Yorkers don't particularly appreciate being served the bone. So, when the meat had been grilled, I put the bones to one side to use later in making flavorful broths and stocks. We also served tacos made with pork and marinated chicken, and, of course, the indispensable salsa mexicana. I had trained some young Mexican women to make tortillas according to the same recipe I used.

La Fogata was my New York City *taquería*.

Only a few months after La Fogata opened, we began, by popular demand, to serve dinner. The street, which went dark after the courts had closed for the day, was reanimated by La Fogata. I remember a client who came in one night yelling jubilantly, "It's a miracle! It's a miracle! I parked my car right next to the front door!" La Fogata lit up the street and began to melt the coldness inside me.

SPECIALTIES OF LA FOGATA

In addition to tacos, we also served a few varieties of Mexican sweet rolls, which I had made especially for us, and tamales. When we began serving dinner, I added *enchiladas de mole poblano* to the menu, which we made in the traditional way. One of the dishes my guests liked best was *coditos de cerdo en salsa de ajonjolí* (pig's knuckles in sesame sauce). Everyone liked the sesame sauce but not everyone could deal with the pig's knuckles, so some people ordered the dish without them, eating the sauce as if it were a soup.

I learned a lot about the eating habits of New Yorkers at La Fogata. In general, they're pretty adventurous, but there are some exceptions. Some people would come in, see tacos made with soft tortillas, and tell me that those weren't tacos; they knew that tacos were made with hard taco shells. When that happened, I always made the same suggestion, "Try it. If you don't like it, it's free." No one ever left a check unpaid. Another item on our menu was little tostada baskets made of fried tortilla and filled with refried beans or guacamole—that people took out and ate in the street as if they were eating a dish of ice cream. I no longer serve tostadas because they've become so popular they're available even in pseudo-taquerías.

Each order of tacos was served with three tacos, refried beans, and Mexican rice. It wasn't exactly the way tacos al carbón are served in Mexico, but I took advantage of the opportunity to offer the taste of Mexico in the refried beans and rice, and to give my customers a complete lunch.

MEXICAN RICE

Rice is a universal food that is known to have originated in India, where it has the greatest degree of genetic variety. There are many conjectures as to how rice came to America. Some say the Spaniards brought it, while others are certain it came directly from the Orient by the Nao China (the Chinese Ship), which was an extremely interesting conduit between the cultures of Mesoamerica, Europe, and the Far East. During the colonial era, the Nao China extended to Mexico's Pacific coast, carrying products from the Far East and creating a bridge for international exchange that connected various ancestral cultures.

THE NAO CHINA

The Nao China wasn't a ship at all but a route that boats would take from Acapulco to the Philippine Islands (which at that time belonged to Spain), exchanging merchandise and correspondence along the way. From 1565 to 1817 it was the only means of contact between Manila and the American continent. In Manila three trade routes came together: from Indochina (which in its turn exported products from Arabia, Persia, and India), from China, and from Japan. The same thing was happening on the Atlantic side with Europe.

Through the centuries of this intense exchange of goods, many foods were introduced into regions far from where they originated. The Chinese began eating chile, and the Mexicans discovered the pleasures and advantages of rice, which they adapted to their national taste in the classic Mexican rice that I served at La Fogata and continue to serve in Rosa Mexicano, as a traditional side dish. When I lived in Mexico, though, rice was always served between the soup and the main dish, and cooks took great pains to change its color and flavor. Rice was served white, red, green, and yellow like paella. To achieve the yellow color, Mexicans use a root they call *azafranillo* (little saffron), which, of course, doesn't have the same flavor as saffron, but has a distinct herblike taste and imparts the same yellow color. It's customary in the coastal regions of the Gulf to serve white rice with fried plantains along with black beans. Almost everywhere, Mexican rice contains peas and little cubes of carrot and sometimes potato.

ARROZ A LA MEXICANA / MEXICAN RICE

SERVES 6

1 cup short-grain rice
1½ pounds vine-ripened tomatoes
3 tablespoons vegetable oil
½ medium white onion, finely chopped
1 garlic clove, finely chopped
½ cup chicken stock
2 tablespoons salt

1. Place the rice in a bowl and soak in very hot water for 15 minutes. Rinse and strain well.
2. Roast, peel, and seed the tomatoes. Place in a blender and blend into a puree. This should yield approximately 1½ cups.
3. Heat the oil in a 2-quart saucepan. Sauté the onions quickly; add the garlic and stir.
4. Add the rice and stir with a wooden spoon to coat with the oil, onion, and garlic; separate the grains and slightly brown the rice. Pour out any excess oil.
5. Add the chicken stock, pureed tomatoes, and the salt. Bring to a boil, reduce to a simmer, and cook for 15 to 20 minutes or until all the liquid is absorbed and the grains of rice flake apart.

■ ■ ■ ARROZ VERDE / GREEN RICE MAKES 4 CUPS

2 cups Rajas de Chile Poblano (see page 118)
½ cup chicken stock
1 cup short-grain rice
3 tablespoons vegetable oil
½ medium white onion, finely chopped
1 garlic clove, finely chopped
1 tablespoon salt

1. Puree the rajas in the blender with the chicken stock.
2. Follow the recipe for Arroz a la Mexicana (see page 206), substituting the raja puree for the tomato puree.

FRIENDS FOREVER

At La Fogata I met young people I have watched grow up as the years go by, friends like Ruperto, who has worked with me ever since then. Ruperto is from Puebla, a place I've always particularly liked. We've had a terrific relationship from the very first moment. I would cook something in the kitchen of my apartment, and Ruperto would watch me and taste what I had made; then we would make it together. I felt as if I were in Mexico when I was with him; we talked about Mexico and I taught him to make sure that everything we cooked always had the flavor of Mexico. In fact, Ruperto was not a trained cook; I met him when he was making sandwiches at Madison Square Garden. At that point the taquería was still under construction; I invited him to come see me and he did. Since 1981, Ruperto and I have worked happily together.

WATER PUTS OUT THE BONFIRE

One day we showed up to open La Fogata and the whole place was inundated. Chairs and tables were floating in a flood of water that came up to our knees. The city pipelines that went under La Fogata had broken and the whole beautiful taquería had sunk like a ship. But apart from the accident, what really sank the place was bad legal advice given out of misplaced ambition. The lawyers wanted to get more than was fair out of the building's owner and we lost everything. But I was comforted by the thought that I had won a place in restaurant circles, had made a friend like Frank, and had a colleague like Ruperto.

CINCO DE MAYO

Only a few weeks later the owners of a supposedly Mexican restaurant in SoHo called Cinco de Mayo came to talk to me about the possibility of taking over their kitchen. Cinco de Mayo had confused every aspect of Mexican culture, from its very name to the way it was decorated. In Mexican communities in the United States, the Cinco de Mayo, or Fifth of May, is celebrated with such enthusiasm that people think it must be Mexico's independence day. Journalists have sometimes called to ask me what Mexicans traditionally eat on that day. But in fact the day only commemorates a battle with the French invaders which the Mexicans won. It happened in 1862, and its hero was General Ignacio Zaragoza, who was able to hold back the invading forces temporarily (though they did eventually take over the country). Furthermore, the restaurant was decorated with photos of Emiliano Zapata, who had absolutely nothing to do with the battle of the Cinco de Mayo. (It's as if a restaurant serving U.S. food were called "George Washington's" and was decorated with photos of Abraham Lincoln.) Zapata fought in the Mexican Revolution at the beginning of the twentieth century and his name has become an international symbol. His battle cry of "Land and Freedom!" was an expression of hope for the Mexican campesinos, particularly in the state of Morelos, who were oppressed by the big landowners. Emiliano Zapata is a fascinating figure in Mexican history, a symbol of our era, who fought not for power but for a better life for the campesinos of his region.

Cinco de Mayo pretended to serve Mexican food but it was far from authentic. I was excited about the chance to extend the menu I had served at La Fogata, and that was what I did. By then my list of suppliers had grown considerably and along with it the range of dishes I could offer. We served grilled meat, guacamole, arroz a la mexicana, refried beans, enchiladas de mole, chiles rellenos, and an ever-changing selection of daily specials. Guests began to arrive in numbers that multiplied each day. Ruperto and I worked side by side with a good team. It delighted me to see New Yorkers enjoying the authentic flavor of Mexico. The daily specials gave me the chance to venture farther afield with Mexican dishes that New Yorkers had not tried before. The tortillas were always freshly made, and I took special care with the flavor of every dish. I was living in a loft in SoHo, alone with my dog. Since I was involved in the restaurant business, no one in that neighborhood of artists knew who I was.

Though I missed making tacos, I enjoyed serving new Mexican dishes. I added *costillas de cerdo adobadas con chile* (pork ribs marinated in chile), shrimp brochettes, and *escabeche de pollo oriental,* a classic Yucatecan dish that seemed to me to have been strongly influenced by Spanish cooking. *Escabeche* refers to a way of pickling, a culinary technique Spaniards learned from the Arabs who occupied southern Spain for centuries.

The menu also included *puntas de filete* (sirloin tips), which were very popular when I was in Mexico. They were served everywhere and I enjoyed their simplicity and their very Mexican flavor. They can also be eaten in tacos. *Alambres de filete,* in which strips of meat are combined with the pulp of a poblano chile, onion, and fresh tomato, then grilled, were served with rice and refried beans.

For dessert, I served flan, which was very popular in Mexico, though it originated in Spain. I added a coffee-flavored sauce and touches of other flavors that had close links to America.

During my time at Cinco de Mayo I gave my guests a new perspective on what great Mexican cooking could be, offering a whole new range of flavors to their taste buds. Something I hadn't expected happened at that point, and it had a decisive effect on my life as a chef. Barbara Costikyan declared in *New York* magazine that authentic Mexican food had at last come to New York; she mentioned me by name and suddenly there I was in the public eye, and in *New York* magazine, no less! But my adventure at Cinco de Mayo ended quickly, once again because of someone else's overambition. The owners did not fulfill their agreement to share profits with me.

FLAN

SERVES 6

Flan is very plain and simple; the beauty of this dish is the sauce it is served with. I have included the recipe for Salsa de Café. You can also use any fruit to make a sauce.

FOR THE CARAMEL:

1½ cups sugar

FOR THE FLAN:

2 cups milk, heated
zest of 1 lemon
1 stick cinnamon
pinch of salt
5 eggs
1 cup sugar
Salsa de Café (recipe follows)

1. Heat the 1½ cups of sugar in a dry and completely clean saucepan over low heat. The sugar will dissolve and cook until a light caramel forms. Pour into a glass baking dish and carefully tilt to coat the bottom and sides of the dish.
2. Boil the milk with the lemon zest, cinnamon stick, and salt and stir to dissolve the 1 cup of sugar. Remove from the heat. Beat the eggs with the sugar in a medium-sized bowl. Whisk 1 cup of the hot milk into the egg-and-sugar mixture. Whisk the egg mixture into the rest of the milk. Whisk only enough to prevent the eggs from cooking; the mixture should not be too frothy. Skim any froth from the surface and discard.
3. Pour into the baking dish and set the dish within a larger roasting pan. Gently place in a 300° F. oven and pour enough water in the outer roasting pan to come halfway up the sides of the baking dish. Bake for about 1 hour, until the flan is set in the center.
4. Remove from the bain marie and allow to cool.

5. Run a knife around the edge of the flan. Invert a plate over the flan and carefully flip the plate and the baking dish. Remove the baking dish. Cut the flan into squares and serve each square with Salsa de Café.

■ ■ ■ SALSA DE CAFÉ / COFFEE CREAM SAUCE

MAKES APPROXIMATELY 6 CUPS

This dessert sauce is delicious with the flan or with the Mexican Chocolate Chile Mousse Cake on page 244.

2 cups milk
2 cups cream
6 ounces sugar
2 tablespoons instant coffee or espresso
6 egg yolks

1. Bring the milk, cream, sugar, and instant coffee to a boil in a 2-quart saucepan.
2. Whisk the egg yolks in a small bowl. Carefully whisk 1 cup of the hot milk mixture into the yolks to temper. Return to the saucepan.
3. Cook over low heat, stirring constantly with a wooden spoon. Cook until the mixture coats the back of the wooden spoon, approximately 5 to 6 minutes. Pour into a bowl and allow to cool.

Note: Fruit sauce can be made in the same way. Substitute fruit for the instant coffee.

THE ART OF HOSPITALITY

Good food will always attract people, but the formula for a good restaurant includes many other elements that will make them stay. From the day La Fogata first opened, I tried to entertain people the same way my mother and grandmother had. Each of those women, in her own way, had taught me the art of hospitality, from the organization of the staff to the way of making every person at every table feel cared for and respected, as if they were guests in my own home. This Josefina follows the example of Doña Josefa, my grandmother, and of my mother, who was also named Josefina. I must confess that sometimes my grandmother's way of looking at things would come over me: She would never have accepted the idea that her granddaughter could run a restaurant, which for her was something like being a housekeeper. But I finally convinced myself that I would be a good hostess, as she and my mother were, and as I've always tried to be.

FROM SOHO TO SUTTON PLACE: ROSA MEXICANO IS BORN

After more than fifteen years at Rosa Mexicano, I have to acknowledge more than ever my good luck at having been in the right place at the right time with the right people. New Yorkers were enthusiastic about the food and the atmosphere of Rosa Mexicano, and they like to try out new tastes. In this great city there is always someone who wants to try something new, and for anyone who is willing to work, the possibilities are limitless. I also have to acknowledge the luck I had in finding extraordinary people who supported and understood me so completely that they put down their money so that I could work and fulfill my desire to teach people about the flavors of Mexico.

Frank Waisfeld put his money on me. He knew the restaurant business, and went to a company that ran restaurants called Shelter Rupperts. He was the first to invest money to open a Mexican restaurant that I would run. Other investors and offers of money quickly presented themselves. But there were still obstacles to overcome, many of them in my head. La Fogata had been a question of survival for me as well as an expression of my love for Mexico. Cinco de Mayo was a very brief experience that made me feel quite secure about being able to succeed in the restaurant business. And I was still following my dream of enabling New Yorkers to enjoy authentic Mexican cooking. But the prospect of a restaurant where I would be the only person responsible for seeing to it that the money invested by my friends yielded a profit filled me with terror.

Doña Josefa must have been spinning in her grave, and I couldn't stop thinking about what she would have thought. But she wasn't me. And I knew that the mentality of the Spanish landowning classes was one of the primary causes of the bloody Spanish Civil War. Finally I got my grandmother's antiquated prejudices out of my head, but not before having some long and far-reaching dialogues with her ghost. Would I be able to make so many guests happy? My thoughts went back to the days at La Casa de las Brujas, when I would sometimes entertain about two hundred people at our weekly open house. If I could do it then, why couldn't I do it now in a restaurant? I turned to Ruperto and he reassured me.

My first real problem was finding a way of getting along with the five gentlemen who were my investors and who saw me as a rare bird indeed. I must admit that one stumbling block was the fact that I was a woman. And another problem can be added to these: I care a lot about quality, so I spend money on everything. It has been quite a struggle to reach a mutual understanding. After fifteen years, we've begun to have a more fluid dialogue.

ROSA MEXICANO: MEXICAN PINK

Quite a few people still think that my name is Rosa, and that the restaurant should therefore be called Rosa Mexicana, with a feminine *-a* at the end rather than a masculine *o,* since in Spanish an adjective has the same gender as the noun it modifies. But *rosa mexicano* is the name of a color, and in Spanish all colors are masculine. Mexican pink is an exciting combination of blue, red, and white. It is different from other pinks and very difficult to achieve outside of the particular luminosity of Mexico. It can only be compared to the shocking pink that was made fashionable by the designer Elsa Schiaparelli. The Mexican painter Rufino Tamayo achieved a true Mexican pink in many of his paintings.

For me it's a kind of occupational hazard: Color has been my passion and my eyes are trained to drink it in. When I'm in Mexico, the colors of the country fill me with emotion. During my life in Mexico, I often drove along highways on my way to visit a carpentry shop or a textile mill. I vividly remember the day I was driving to Toluca, which lies to the southwest of Mexico City. I saw in the distance a little village painted entirely in pink. It had just rained and the village was a glowing splash of pink against the surrounding green; the whole landscape was profoundly Mexican. When I saw it the idea went through my mind, Someday I'll start some kind of business and call it Rosa Mexicano. I didn't know then what kind of business it would be or where.

The location we decided on, at Sutton Place, had been occupied by a series of restaurants that had failed; there had never been a Mexican restaurant in that neighborhood before. I decorated it in my own style, positioning lights on the walls at strategic points, instead of covering them with decorations. I had and continue to have a continual struggle to get the color of the walls just right. The creation of spaces that would give customers a sense of privacy but be accessible to the staff was a balance I achieved by remembering the big old house in Asturias and everything I had done in my years of working as a professional designer.

THE AMATE PAPER GODS

The front entry to Rosa Mexicano has always been very important to me; in decorating it, I have tried to signal that this is a Mexican place without falling into the tackiness that is part of the general idea many people in the U.S. have of Mexico. My perception of Mexico is not limited to sombreros, serapes, and loud colors. The Mexico that I always try to convey, both in the look of the restaurant and in the food I serve, is a country of real elegance, and by elegance I mean proportion, balance, and the good manners that are found among well-educated families and in the forms of address used by most Mexicans. There is always a *"Por favor"* before any request, and *"Gracias"* is always heard in response to any answer. *"Buenos días," "Buenas tardes,"* or *"Buenas noches"* opens a conversation that can be brief or long. While this may strike some people as inconvenient, because long minutes are sometimes lost in formal salutations before the heart of the matter at hand is reached, most Mexicans–though to this rule, as to every other, there are exceptions–are people who care a great deal about good form and therefore are elegant by nature.

That elegance was what I tried to express in the design of my restaurant. During the early years, I placed a row of pines at the entrance, inspired by the trees among the canals of Xochimilco. But it was a continual battle to keep them there; someone was always trying to steal them. When we secured them with chains, the thieves broke the pots the trees were planted in. I spent a long time wondering how to solve the problem. I talked it over

with my dear friend, the sculptor Theresa Thompson, and we began thinking up new ideas. I thought about having her sculpt some pine trees, but neither of us was completely satisfied with the idea. Above my bed I had hung a series of figures of gods made of *amate* paper. These figures are supposedly used by Indian shamans either to curse or to bless. Theresa and I began toying with the idea of re-creating them. But the ones I had were depicted with shoes on, and I had learned that that meant they were to be used for cursing (of course, they're no longer hanging above my bed!). And I was having a hard time imagining how they would look in metal and in such a large size.

Amate paper is another part of Mexico's cultural wealth that is disappearing. Many of the ancient codices were printed on amate paper, an ancient tradition that is being lost because the trees from whose bark the paper is made are dying off. The method for making the paper consists of soaking the bark for a time until a series of strands remain. The craftsmen place the strands on a flat surface, then flatten and join them by beating them with rocks until they become a paper that retains the colors of the wood. Though it could be mistaken for parchment, it is softer and more flexible. The naive paintings that some campesinos paint on amate paper have become popular; they are one more of the artistic expressions that so frequently spring up among the humblest Mexicans, who often emerge as true artists.

On my next trip, I saw the same series of gods again in a store; these were made of metal and were larger than the originals. Meanwhile, Theresa was already at work, designing and taking measurements for a series of the right kind of gods, the barefoot kind. But some doubt still remained as to their color. I searched my library until I found a book that showed them, and I was struck by the soft, muted colors in which they were depicted; such colors seemed very un-Mexican to me and for a while I thought they must have resulted from some printer's error when the book was published. I had to know what color those gods really were.

I decided to go to the town of San Pablito Pahuatlán. I had been told that there were shamans there who could cure the sick and would give these gods as talismans to the local peasants to help them produce bountiful harvests. I also learned that the shamans of San Pablito were capable of wielding black magic and all the other kinds of magic, which work because of people's belief in them. The map I consulted showed that although San Pablito is located in the state of Puebla, it's easier to reach from the state of Hidalgo. The borders between the states in Mexico are different from those we have in most of the United States, where geography allows each state to be separated from the others by nearly straight lines. In Mexico the borders are irregular. What happened to San Pablito was that the town had once belonged to the state of Hidalgo, but a certain governor of Puebla wanted to straighten the border line of his state, and that made San Pablito part of Puebla. In any case, that's what I was told when I went looking for a logical explanation.

Manuel Souza, one of the people I work with and a good friend of mine, accompanied me on this fantastical journey. He drove slowly so I could admire the landscape. After a few hours, we began to go up and down hills and mountains, gliding smoothly over a straight road. Mist and moisture clouded the car's windows. Many stones had fallen off the hillsides onto the fragile asphalt. But I admired the mountains, which were covered with gigantic ferns whose foliage seemed to cascade down the slopes. From time to time we passed through a cloud that was resting on a mountaintop. We went through a small town whose streets were as wet as the highway. All the streets were paved with cobblestones, and they were more like stairways than streets, with few people walking along them, because there is always a bit of a drizzle in these mountaintop towns. But we hadn't yet reached San Pablito.

We continued along that road until we came to a bridge; on the other side there was only the slope of the mountain: no road. We opened the windows so the wind would blow away the mist that kept steaming them up. A group of people surrounded the car; their hands reached out to touch my hair, my face; my whole body seemed to awaken their curiosity. Our presence had created a stir, but there was no way to communicate with them. We heard their whispers, laughter, and comments, all in their own language, which we couldn't understand, and we were flustered; for a moment we couldn't speak. I quickly realized that they were not harming us in any way, and I accepted the moment as an almost spiritual experience, part of having arrived in this strange place and meeting people from a world that was so different. I began to speak and two little boys, twelve or fourteen years old, appeared on the scene; unlike their elders, they did speak Spanish.

First they tried to take me to see one of the shamans and I refused. Then, on what seemed to be the town's main street, I found the workshop of a craftsman. I discovered that the colors of the amate paper gods were indeed muted, and I understood that in this place which was so damp, so gray, and full of mist, brilliant colors weren't possible. The craftsman, who knew his business well, quickly understood me and agreed to make a series of gods for me out of amate paper in their original colors. There are many places like San Pablito scattered across Mexico. Its inhabitants are Otomís, another of the ancient peoples of Mesoamerica. The older people of the town still don't speak Spanish, the official language of Mexico, though the young people are now learning it, after five hundred years!

Soon after, the enormous paper gods were sent to me in New York. Theresa took her inspiration from them and in her hands hard metal became a perfect representation of the amate paper gods. With her own sensibility and art, she expressed their magic, and she worked long and hard to make their muted colors as close as possible to the ones that were sent from San Pablito. And now there they are, the amate paper gods, watching over the New Yorkers who pass by, blessing them and me, too. With the gods of chiles, tomatoes, beans, pomegranates, corn, and pineapples at the entrance instead of trees, I can finally stop worrying about thieves.

The beneficent gods of chiles, tomatoes, beans, pomegranates, corn, and pineapples protect and bless Rosa Mexicano and all of its guests.

THE HEART OF ROSA MEXICANO

Though I am very particular about details when it comes to decoration, I am also very conscious that a restaurant lives or dies by its food. The food is the heart of a restaurant, and nothing else is more important. A restaurant can be very beautiful, get a lot of attention, be very well located, use the finest ingredients, and have the most striking presentation, but everything will collapse if the food is not excellent. Combining an appealing ambience with good food in a city like New York is a unique challenge.

While the restaurant was being renovated and decorated, Ruperto and I planned out our menu in my kitchen at home. The repertory of dishes we had served up to that point was expanded once more. We had new ideas about how to present the food, and the idea of serving guacamole in a molcajete originated then. With the experience we had gained at Cinco de Mayo, I realized that we would need to serve a lot of guacamole at Rosa Mexicano, and there had to be a way of serving it fresh. As soon as avocado flesh comes into contact with the air, it tends to oxidize; its surface darkens, so for the best appearance and flavor, avocado should be prepared immediately before being eaten. In Mexico sauces are often served in the molcajete in which they were prepared, and I had the idea that guacamole could be prepared on the spot and served that way. It was especially important that the avocado be sliced open in front of the guests, who would then know they were eating a guacamole that was absolutely fresh.

MY PHILOSOPHY OF SERVICE

Service and attention to the customer were an area in which I tried to demonstrate my concept of hospitality. The basic concept underlying our service is that each guest should be greeted by a waiter who is cheerful and ready to give explanations about each dish or any other aspect of the restaurant. In addition, the dishes must be served promptly and at the right pace. No guest should have to face a long wait. People go to a restaurant to relax and eat, not to fight and demand service. The customer must be treated like a guest who is being received in someone's home. When a gathering takes place in a home, the hosts should welcome their guests warmly and with a smile to a perfectly clean space—and, of course, with the dignity of a host, not a servant.

I've taught the waiters the subtle line that separates the guest in a home and the customer in a restaurant. When customers come in from work, from the pressures of a very competitive and difficult city like New York, they want to relax and restore their strength. The waiter should be conscious that there are no social differences, but he or she must also be discreet and not overfamiliar with the "customer guest." The client must feel calm and comfortable as a result of the quality of the attention he or she is given. The waiter must also be a good salesman, and I give my waiters the training and resources for that. Our food is so different from what New Yorkers generally eat that the waiter has to know how to explain the ingredients and motivate the clientele to experience new flavors. Each one of the waiters and waitresses tastes all the dishes we serve and is trained to explain them. They are free to offer guests a taste of any sauce, herb, or dish that the customer is curious about. They are also free to offer courtesies of the house to frequent customers. Therefore, the waiters must know how to express themselves clearly and affably. They always feel that the respect they show the clientele is returned to them not only through the tips they receive but also in the respect with which the customers treat them in return.

Once a group of people who were waiting for their table in my restaurant called me over. "Mrs. Howard," they said, "we've been here several times, and seeing your system of organization we wondered if you had ever taken any classes from Edward Deming?" I knew nothing about Mr. Deming, but at the first chance I got I went to hear him lecture at Columbia University. The large auditorium was full of students and others eager to hear Deming explain his theories of business administration. I went back on other occasions, and like the rest of the audience I drank in his words and enjoyed the simple way in which he explained things. At the age of ninety-three he was a very lucid and easily understandable man. I have his books and I am always consulting them. Some have attributed Japan's many years of business success to the Deming method.

A SYMPHONY . . . IN PINK

When the doors of Rosa Mexicano open at 5:00 P.M., everything must be in perfect order, with no strange smells in the air or spots on the glasses. Then what I call a symphony begins. Everything must harmonize; the waiters and busboys each have their assigned tables, but everyone's ears must be open for any request from anywhere. From the beginning, I decided that there shouldn't be any music at Rosa Mexicano. I prefer that my guests focus their senses on the taste of the food and, if they want, on their own conversations. This has given Rosa Mexicano a very pleasant and often very happy atmosphere, as if there were music . . . My guests make the music with their own voices.

To keep everything working well, the staff must be treated fairly. We are constantly rotating hours, workdays, and stations in order to achieve a balance so that everyone will earn the same amount of money. The busboys are rotated as well. The busboys at Rosa Mexicano are very important because the preparation of guacamole is entrusted to them. It hasn't been easy, but I'm proud to say that most of the people on the team that works with me at Rosa Mexicano have been there for fifteen years.

NEW DISHES AT ROSA MEXICANO

Generally, it's hard to introduce new dishes with new ingredients into the organization of a kitchen that is operating continuously. But in our zeal to develop the taste of my guests for the flavors of Mexican food, Ruperto, the manager, and I overcome all obstacles. I'm always trying out new dishes at home, often after learning about them in a volume from my enormous library that specializes in Mexico—its architecture, literature, history, geography, and, of course, gastronomy. I also take inspiration from my frequent trips to Mexico. Ruperto, with a certain patronizing air, busies himself making the changes to the menu. Almost as an obligation, we both go back to Mexico as often as possible in order not to lose its flavor. Like me, he also visits the country for sentimental reasons.

Frequently, while I'm struggling to add a new dish to the menu, another one emerges during my constant work in the little kitchen in my apartment. When I finally do add a new dish, we first assemble the entire staff—from the kitchen personnel to the waiters and busboys—to taste it. We listen to their opinions and explain to them what they should tell the customers. The following are recipes for some of the recent additions to the menu.

SOPA DE AJO A LA MEXICANA / MEXICAN-STYLE GARLIC SOUP

SERVES 6

This is the Mexican version of a very simple and light Spanish soup. Do not be tempted to add anything *until you have tried it just like this!*

18 slices of baguette, cut 1/4 inch thick
8 to 10 garlic cloves
3/4 to 1 cup vegetable oil
6 cups hot chicken stock, homemade if possible
2 eggs, beaten
salt to taste
1/4 cup crumbled queso fresco

1. Slice the bread a few hours in advance and place the slices in a single layer on a platter or rack. Let them dry out, preferably overnight, turning once. They will absorb less oil when fried if dried slightly.
2. Peel the garlic cloves and crush them with the side of a French knife.
3. Heat 1/2 cup of the oil in an 8-inch sauté pan until very hot, but not smoking. Add the garlic and let it cook until golden, pressing on the cloves with the back of a spoon to release juices from the garlic. Be careful not to burn the oil or garlic. Remove the garlic with a slotted spoon and discard.
4. Very quickly fry the bread slices in the hot garlic-flavored oil until golden on both sides, then remove and drain on paper towels. Add more oil to the skillet as needed.
5. Transfer the oil into a saucepan and cool briefly. Carefully (it may splatter if the oil is still hot) add the hot stock and bring to a boil. Quickly whisk the beaten eggs into the soup. It should resemble egg-drop soup. Salt to taste.
6. Place three pieces of fried bread in the bottom of each bowl. Pour the hot soup over the bread. Sprinkle with queso fresco and serve immediately.

SOPA DE CALDO DE GUAJOLOTE / TURKEY AND TORTILLA SOUP

SERVES 6

When I was asked for a Thanksgiving recipe several years ago, I responded that Mexicans don't celebrate Thanksgiving. Turkey, however, is very Mexican, so I devised this soup and main dish combination—the perfect Thanksgiving dinner when served with rice or another starch.

2 large vine-ripened tomatoes
½ large white onion
1 garlic clove
2 serrano chiles, remove seeds and veins, coarsely chopped
2 teaspoons salt
2 tablespoons vegetable oil plus 2 cups vegetable oil, for frying
4 cups turkey stock (recipe follows)
salt and pepper to taste
6 white corn tortillas, cut into strips ¼ inch wide
3 ounces queso fresco, diced small

1. Roast the tomatoes and the onion over an open flame to char the skin. Remove most of the skin from the tomatoes. Coarsely chop the tomatoes and the onion.
2. Puree the tomatoes, onion, garlic, serrano chiles, and salt in a blender.
3. Heat the 2 tablespoons vegetable oil in a 2-quart saucepan. Add the tomato mixture and cook for approximately 10 minutes, stirring occasionally. Add the turkey stock and bring to a boil. Reduce to a simmer and cook for 20 to 30 minutes. Season with salt and pepper to taste.
4. In a 2-quart saucepan, heat the 2 cups vegetable oil. Fry the tortilla strips until golden in color and crisp. Drain on paper towels.
5. Ladle the soup into bowls. Garnish with queso fresco and fried tortillas.

TURKEY STOCK MAKES 6 CUPS

6 turkey drumsticks, preferably fresh and as small as possible; defrosted if frozen
2½ quarts water
2 cloves garlic
1 medium white onion (studded with 6 cloves)
8 black peppercorns
1 large bay leaf
⅛ teaspoon thyme
2 stalks celery, washed and cut into 2-inch pieces
2 carrots, peeled and cut into 2-inch pieces
salt to taste

Place all the ingredients in a large stockpot. Bring to a boil, reduce to simmer and cook for 1 hour. Remove drumsticks and use for making mixiote (see page 226). Strain and cool the stock. Refrigerate. Skim the surface. Reserve for Sopa de Caldo de Guajolote (see page 224).

Note: Drumsticks will finish cooking when used in the mixiote recipe that follows. Otherwise, continue cooking for 1 hour longer.

MIXIOTE DE GUAJOLOTE / TURKEY IN CHILE PASTE

SERVES 6

8 guajillo chiles, stems removed, seeded, and deveined
4 pasilla chiles, stems removed, seeded, and deveined
⅛ teaspoon marjoram
pinch of ground cumin
½ teaspoon dried, toasted oregano
8 whole cloves
1 bay leaf
⅛ teaspoon thyme
8 black peppercorns
4 garlic cloves, toasted in a dry pan
1 tablespoon white vinegar
2 teaspoons salt
6 turkey drumsticks, partially cooked (see page 225)
½ cup water in which chiles were soaking
6 16×16-inch square pieces parchment paper

1. Toast the guajillo and pasilla chiles in a dry/hot skillet, turning with tongs to toast evenly and until the chiles are pliable. Place the chiles in a bowl and cover with abundant hot water. Allow to soak for 15 minutes. Reserve ½ cup of the soaking water.
2. Grind the marjoram, cumin, oregano, cloves, bay leaf, thyme, and peppercorns in a spice or coffee grinder.
3. Drain the chiles and place in the blender along with the spice mixture, garlic, vinegar, salt, and the ½ cup of the chile soaking water; blend to make a paste.
4. Coat each drumstick with the paste and marinate for at least 1 hour, preferably overnight.
5. Place each drumstick in the center of a 16×16-inch square of parchment

paper. Bring the four corners together and tie with cooking string. Cook in a steamer for 1 hour.

6. To serve, place each bundle of parchment paper in the center of a plate, remove the string, and twist the parchment back and under.

OSTIONES DE SINALOA / MARINATED OYSTERS

SERVES 4

24 oysters
juice of 2 lemons
½ teaspoon salt
4 tablespoons olive oil
2 garlic cloves, minced
1 teaspoon ground black pepper
1 pickled jalapeño chile, julienned

1. Wash the oysters and scrub the shells. Open with an oyster shucker, being careful not to lose the liquid, and place the oysters in a bowl. Reserve the shells.
2. Mix the oysters with their juices, 4 or 5 tablespoons water, lemon juice, and salt. Bring 2 cups of salted water to a boil. Reserving marinade, place oysters in water and boil for 2 minutes; drain well and allow to cool.
3. Heat the olive oil in an 8-inch sauté pan. Sauté garlic for 2 to 3 minutes or until translucent. Add oysters and sauté for 1 to 2 minutes. Then add the marinade and season with salt and pepper. Cook for approximately 3 to 4 minutes, longer if the oysters are large. Allow to cool.
4. Place the oysters back in their shells and spoon over some of the cooking liquid. Garnish with fine julienne strips of jalapeño.

CREPAS CAMARONES CON SALSAS DE CHILE PASILLA / CREPES FILLED WITH SHRIMP IN A PASILLA CHILE SAUCE

SERVES 6

10 pasilla chiles
¼ large white onion, coarsely chopped
2 garlic cloves, finely chopped
1½ pounds vine-ripened tomatoes, roasted, peeled, and seeded
pinch of dried oregano
5 whole peppercorns
1 cup fish stock
6 tablespoons vegetable oil
1 teaspoon sugar
1½ teaspoons salt or to taste
¾ cup crème fraîche
2 pounds small shrimp, peeled and deveined
18 crepes (see page 49)
4 ounces manchego cheese, grated

1. Toast, devein, and seed the chiles. Soak in 6 cups hot water for at least ½ hour. Place the chiles with the onion, garlic, tomatoes, oregano, and whole peppercorns in a blender. Blend the mixture, adding enough fish stock so the blades will turn.
2. Heat 3 tablespoons of the vegetable oil in an 8-inch sauté pan and cook the chile mixture for 10 to 15 minutes over medium heat. Add the sugar, salt, and crème fraîche and reduce the heat. Cook the sauce for 3 minutes more.
3. Heat the remaining 3 tablespoons vegetable oil in an 8-inch sauté pan. Quickly sauté the shrimp until they are pink, 3 to 4 minutes. Add the cooked shrimp to the sauce. Stir to combine and set aside to cool.
4. Using a slotted spoon, remove the shrimp from the sauce and divide them

among the 18 crepes; place them across the center of each crepe. Roll the crepe around the filling.

5. Place three crepes on each plate, seam side down. Ladle the sauce over the crepes and sprinkle the cheese over the top.
6. Place under a hot broiler to melt the cheese and serve immediately.

CAMARONES GIGANTES CON ARROZ NEGRO / JUMBO BUTTERFLY SHRIMP WITH BLACK RICE

SERVES 6

36 large shrimp or 16 to 20 sweetwater prawns
6 tablespoons vegetable oil
6 tablespoons clarified butter
3 large garlic cloves, finely chopped
½ cup chopped parsley

1. Remove the shells from the shrimp, leaving the tails on. To butterfly, make a deep incision on the curved side of the shrimp and carefully remove the vein. Wash well, drain, and set aside.
2. Heat 3 tablespoons vegetable oil and 3 tablespoons butter in a 14-inch sauté pan. Sauté 18 shrimp at a time over high heat until they turn pink, 3 to 5 minutes. Add the chopped garlic and parsley, sauté for 1 minute, and remove from the heat. Repeat the process with the other shrimp.

■ ■ ■ SQUID BLACK RICE serves 6

This is based on a traditional recipe from Spain.

2 tablespoons vegetable oil
1 medium white onion, finely chopped
1 large garlic clove, finely chopped
3 cups rice
2 vine-ripened tomatoes (approximately 1 pound), roasted, peeled, cored, seeded, and finely chopped
6 cups chicken broth
2 tablespoons squid ink, dissolved in a little of the chicken broth (use more if necessary to make it blacker)
2 tablespoons finely chopped fresh parsley
pinch of thyme and oregano
1 bay leaf
salt and pepper to taste

1. Heat the oil in a 10-inch saucepan. Sauté the onion and garlic for 2 to 3 minutes. Add the rice and stir with a wooden spoon until lightly fried and toasted in color. Add the tomatoes, stir, and cook for 3 to 4 minutes.
2. Add the chicken broth and dissolved squid ink and stir well.
3. Stir in the seasonings and bring to a boil. Lower the heat to simmer, cover, and cook for 15 minutes or until tender.
4. To serve: Place the black rice in the center of each plate. Around the rice arrange 6 shrimp with the tails pointing up.

COCHINITA PIBIL

SERVES 6

1 tablespoon achiote (see Note)
½ teaspoon ground cumin
¼ tablespoon oregano
12 whole black peppercorns
4 whole allspice
4 garlic cloves
1 tablespoon salt
¼ cup bitter orange juice
5 pounds pork shoulder, trimmed, leaving some of the fat
1 package plantain or banana leaves (see Note)
12 corn tortillas

1. Place the spices, garlic, salt, and bitter orange juice in the blender. Blend to make a paste.
2. Rub the paste onto the pork and wrap the meat in the plantain or banana leaves. Place on a roasting pan and bake in a 350° F. oven for 5 hours. Turn the pork after 2½ hours.
3. Remove the pork from the plantain leaves and shred into large pieces. Tear one banana leaf into ¼-inch strips, which will be used to tie the packages of pork.
4. Fold a few pieces of the pork, approximately 6 ounces, in fresh banana leaves (not the ones used to cook the meat) and tie with a strip from the leaf.
5. Serve with hot tortillas to make tacos.

Note: Achiote and plantain or banana leaves are available at any specialty-food store or Caribbean market.

CHILES RELLENOS DE VERDURAS CON ARROZ ROSADO / POBLANO CHILES FILLED WITH VEGETABLES AND SERVED WITH RICE MADE WITH BEET JUICE

SERVES 6

6 large poblano chiles, roasted, peeled, and deveined

4 tablespoons vegetable oil

1 cup chopped white onion

2 garlic cloves, finely chopped

1 pound new or red bliss potatoes, peeled and cut into small dice

½ pound string beans, cut on the diagonal into ½-inch lengths

½ pound carrots, peeled and cut into small dice

½ pound zucchini, cut into small dice

¼ pound small peas (use frozen if fresh are not available)

3 ounces raisins, soaked in hot water

2 ounces toasted pine nuts

½ cup corn kernels cut from the cob (use frozen if fresh are not available)

1 cup queso fresco, cut into small dice

salt to taste

1. Roast chiles to char the skin. Place in a plastic bag to steam for 10 to 15 minutes. Peel the chiles, make an incision in each one, and carefully remove the seeds and veins. Be sure to keep the chiles intact. Set aside.
2. Heat the oil in a 3-quart saucepan. Sauté the onions for 3 to 4 minutes, add the garlic and sauté for 3 minutes more or until translucent. Add the potatoes, string beans, carrots, zucchini, peas, raisins, pine nuts, and corn. Sauté for 4 to 5 minutes, stirring occasionally to prevent the vegetables from sticking to the bottom of the pan.
3. Add enough water to just cover the vegetables; simmer until all ingredients are cooked and the liquid has evaporated, approximately 10 to 12 minutes.

Strain the vegetables if necessary. Remove from the heat, allow to cool, and stir in the diced cheese. Salt to taste.

4. Stuff the poblanos with the vegetable filling and place on an oiled baking sheet. Cover with foil and warm in the oven.

■ ■ ■ RICE MADE WITH BEET JUICE SERVES 6

2 cups long-grain rice
4 tablespoons vegetable oil
1 cup coarsely chopped onions
1 cup water
3 cups beet juice, made from peeled beets and run through a juicing machine
1 tablespoon sugar
1 tablespoon salt
2 tablespoons finely chopped parsley, for garnish

1. Soak the rice in very hot water for approximately 10 minutes. Stir occasionally and strain.
2. Heat oil in a shallow saucepan, sauté the onions for 2 to 3 minutes. Add the rice and stir until it becomes dry and slightly browned (some will stick to the bottom). Stir in the water and beet juice; simmer, partly covered, for 10 minutes, stirring occasionally. Add the sugar and salt and loosen any "stuck" rice from the bottom of the pan. Simmer for another 10 minutes or until the liquid has evaporated and rice is fully cooked.
3. To serve, spread rice on the plates (oval preferably). Place the stuffed poblano in the center of the rice. Sprinkle chopped parsley around the outside edge of the rice.

PLÁTANOS RELLENOS DE PICADILLO / PLANTAINS FILLED WITH GROUND BEEF

SERVES 4

This dish is from the state of Tabasco, which is a major producer of plantains.

4 ripe, almost black plantains, peeled, ends cut off to make them even in size, and cut into pieces approximately 2 inches long

Using an apple corer, carefully cut a hole through the center of each plantain section.

FOR THE BEEF OR PORK PICADILLO:

4 tablespoons vegetable oil
1 medium white onion, chopped
1 garlic clove, finely chopped
2½ pounds vine-ripened tomatoes, roasted, peeled, cored, seeds removed, and coarsely chopped
pinch of oregano
pinch of thyme
1 bay leaf
salt and freshly ground pepper to taste
½ pound coarsely ground beef sirloin or coarsely ground pork shoulder
2 heaping tablespoons raisins, soaked in water
10 pitted olives, cut in quarters

1. Heat the 4 tablespoons oil in a sauté pan and sauté the onion for 4 to 5 minutes; add the garlic and cook for approximately 2 to 3 minutes until the onions are translucent. Do not brown. Raise the flame and add the tomatoes and spices. Sauté for 10 minutes. Add the meat and break up any clumps with a wooden spoon. Stir in the drained raisins and olives. Sauté for 10 minutes more. Remove the mixture from the heat and allow to cool.

2. After cooling, fill the plantains with the beef or pork picadillo or other fillings (see Note).

FOR THE BATTER:

6 egg whites

5 egg yolks

3 cups vegetable oil

1. Whisk the egg whites until soft peaks form. Whisk the egg yolks and fold the whites into the yolks.
2. Heat the 3 cups oil in a 2-quart saucepan. Dip the plantains into the batter, allow the excess to drip off, and gently lower into the hot oil. Turn carefully in the oil to brown on all sides. When the plantains are browned on all sides, remove from the oil with a slotted spoon and drain on paper towels.
3. Serve with Tomato Broth (see page 118).

Note: Other recommended fillings for the plantains are (a) 6 ounces of queso fresco and (b) 2 cups of black bean puree with 4 ounces of queso fresco cut into 2-inch sticks.

TOSTADAS DE PESCADO / FISH TOSTADAS

SERVES 6

Tostadas can be made with any leftovers. Serve with one of the salsas in the chapter on salsas and chiles.

3 tablespoons plus ½ cup vegetable oil
12 ounces hake, grouper, red snapper, or other lean white fish
salt and pepper to taste
6 6-to-8-inch white corn tortillas
2 teaspoons chopped pickled jalapeño chiles plus 1 teaspoon of liquid from the jar
1 medium onion, finely chopped
1 medium vine-ripened tomato, roasted, peeled, seeded, and cut into ½-inch dice
¼ cup olive oil
2 tablespoons fresh lemon juice
2 tablespoons chopped cilantro plus extra for garnish
1 teaspoon salt
½ teaspoon freshly ground black pepper
⅓ cup crème fraîche
½ head romaine lettuce, finely shredded
2 ripe Hass avocados, cut into ½-inch dice

1. Heat the 3 tablespoons vegetable oil in a 10-inch sauté pan. Season the fish with salt and pepper. Cook the fish for 3 to 4 minutes on each side or until it is fully cooked.
2. In an 8-inch sauté pan, heat the ½ cup vegetable oil over moderately high heat. Fry the tortillas one at a time, turning gently several times with tongs, for 3 to 4 minutes, until golden and crispy. Drain on paper towels and allow to cool to room temperature.

3. Chop the jalapeño extremely fine until it is almost a paste. Set aside.
4. Flake the fish into a large bowl. Add the onion and toss gently. Gently stir in the jalapeño paste, jalapeño juice, tomato, olive oil, lemon juice, and cilantro. Season with salt and pepper and set aside.
5. Spread each tortilla with a heaping teaspoon of crème fraîche. Sprinkle the lettuce on top. Place a spoon of the fish mixture to cover the tortilla evenly. Place the avocado cubes and some chopped cilantro on top of the fish. Dollop the remaining crème fraîche in the middle of each tostada.

POLLO ALMENDRADO / CHICKEN WITH ALMOND SAUCE

SERVES 6

6 medium vine-ripened tomatoes
5 tablespoons unsalted butter
1 medium white onion, chopped
2 garlic cloves, chopped
3 cups blanched, sliced or slivered almonds
1 cup heavy cream
12 chicken breasts, 7 to 8 ounces each, skinned and boned
salt and freshly ground black pepper to taste

1. Roast the tomatoes over a flame or under a hot broiler until the skin is charred. Peel, remove seeds, and chop coarsely.
2. Add 1 tablespoon of the butter and sauté the onion and garlic over medium heat until translucent. Add the tomatoes and cook for about 5 minutes. Add the almonds, reserving 1/4 cup for garnish. Cook for 5 minutes more. Remove from the heat and cool slightly.
3. Puree the mixture in a blender. Strain, pressing on the solids with the back of a spoon to force as much through the sieve as possible, and scrape the back of the sieve with a rubber spatula. Discard the remaining solids in the sieve.
4. Toast the reserved almonds in a skillet or in a 375° F. oven for 8 minutes until golden. Set aside.
5. In a clean skillet, melt 2 tablespoons of the butter and add the almond puree. Cook over medium heat until it simmers, stirring constantly. Add the cream and bring back to a simmer.
6. Season the chicken lightly with salt and pepper. Heat the remaining 2 tablespoons butter in a 12-inch sauté pan or cast-iron skillet and sauté the chicken very slowly until golden and cooked through. Using tongs, turn the breasts after 8 to 10 minutes. The total cooking time is 15 to 20 minutes. Transfer the chicken to a platter and keep warm.
7. Pour the sauce over the chicken. Garnish with toasted almonds and serve immediately.

SOMETHING SWEET

Sugarcane reached Mexico with the Spaniards, but long before that Mexicans were acquainted with a kind of honey they extracted from the maguey and with bees' honey, which they used to sweeten their drinks, and which they added to masa, to fruit, and to their nieves, or sorbets. Today, Mexicans in general have a very sweet tooth; since the colonial period a whole culture of Mexican candy has been created, using fruit, almonds, and nuts. The imaginations of Mexican cooks have overflowed. Certain regions are famous for their candies; Puebla is well known for one kind, *camotes,* made from sweetened, pureed sweet potatoes, flavored with fruit, then rolled up in wax paper to form a tube tied at each end. The Poblanos also make a kind of cookie smothered with a very sweet frosting that they call a *tortita,* which is sometimes flavored with coconut. Many Mexican candies are a kind of local handicraft; in Yucatán, a lemon is hollowed out and the peel is filled with a paste made of sugar, milk, and coconut; the peel is also covered with sugar. *Manzanitas* are a sweet made from coconut or almond paste, perfumed with cinnamon or vanilla. In general, Mexican sweets are local versions of French and Spanish imports, but they always have their own Mexican stamp.

Vanilla, which is native to Mexico, has given its aroma to the whole world.

In the tropics, even fruits—like this papaya—exude sexuality.

These rice-paper wafers have only the delicate taste of their color.

A box of very Mexican sweets.

The candies of the very gastronomical state of Michoacán are also famous; a variety of fruits are mixed with a lot of sugar to create thin sheets of jelly called *ates de frutas,* which are served as a dessert accompanied with cheese in the Spanish manner. There is an enormous variety of delicious fruit available throughout the year in Mexico, where fruit is eaten more than any other food. It is served during breakfast, and at lunch fresh fruit is sometimes served before dessert; it's served then because although the ripe fruit is very sweet it is always less sweet than the dessert.

AND SPEAKING OF CHOCOLATE . . .

In Spain it's a common custom to give children a slice of bread with a piece of chocolate on top. Many generations of Spaniards have happy memories of eating bread and chocolate after school, and it is also enjoyed by children in a number of other European countries.

Though a person from Switzerland or Belgium might find it incredible that chocolate did not originate in his own country, and there are some scholars who still don't want to accept it as fact, there is a great deal of evidence that chocolate and the basic recipe for drinking chocolate is of Mesoamerican and particularly Mexican origin. One hypothesis derives the word *chocolate* from the Maya word *chokol,* which means hot and can also mean liquid or drink. A second, more roundabout, etymological theory, derives the word from the Nahuatl *xococ,* which means bitter, or *xocolia,* which means an acidic taste, and *atil,* which means water. Whether the word was originally Nahuatl or Maya, the name of the fermented drink known as *xocolatl* has been adapted in many languages. In French it's *chocolat,* in Italian *sioccolata,* and in virtually every other language the word for chocolate derives from the indigenous Mesoamerican word.

Cacao, the essential ingredient of chocolate, was cultivated during the early years of the Spanish Colonial era in Oaxaca, Chiapas, and the region of Tabasco called Soconusco. Long before the Spaniards arrived, the indigenous peoples of Mesoamerica placed a high value on cacao seeds. Mexico City's Anthropology Museum displays some cacao seeds made of clay, which are thought to be forgeries of what was then the currency, for cacao also functioned as a kind of money. We know, for example, that a slave could be bought for a hundred cacao seeds. Hernán Cortés must have been thrilled by the idea of a currency that could be planted and harvested, and it's easy to understand why; after the King of Spain first learned of cacao in 1528, its cultivation was extended to every region with a tropical climate within reach, from Brazil, to Trinidad and Haiti, to certain African nations. For more than a century, the Spanish empire had an absolute monopoly on cacao.

The original recipe for chocolate was to mix cacao paste with water and sweeten it with honey; that, they say, is how Emperor Moctezuma drank it. Bernal Díaz del Castillo writes, "From time to time cups of fine gold were brought in to him full of a certain drink made of cacao and they said it was to have access to women . . ." (This may be why Europeans believed for centuries that chocolate was an aphrodisiac.) Today, the basic recipe can be made at home; spices such as cardamom, cloves, cinnamon, or nutmeg can also be added, or even nuts, almonds, or any other kind of seed or nut, if it is finely chopped.

Legend has it that another ingredient was sometimes added to this chocolate beverage: vanilla. When the Mexicas established the city of Tenochtitlán and began to develop a social organization and a large military to defend themselves, and later to attack and invade, they used men known as *pochtecas* as part of a unique strategy for enlarging their empire.

The pochteca was a merchant who was the first scout for Mexica invasions; he bore no arms and was not accompanied by an army, only by men carrying merchandise to sell. The pochteca investigated the resources of every group in the region and reported his findings back to the emperor. With the information thus obtained, the Mexica empire would decide whether an invasion would be worthwhile. Once, the story goes, one of the empire's most important generals began advancing toward the coast to invade a group of Totonacas who lived in what is now part of the state of Veracruz. After they had overrun the town, one of his missions was to catch seventeen virgins to take to the emperor. But the Indians ran away into the jungle and the Aztec general ran after them, desperate to catch the virgins. A tantalizing aroma distracted him from his mission; he searched for its source and found an orchid, part of the vanilla plant. Later, kneeling before his emperor, he begged forgiveness for not having caught the virgins and, instead, presented the flower and its fruit, the vanilla bean. The palace cooks decided that the best way to use this flavor was in the chocolate beverage they often made, and so chocolate flavored with vanilla was created.

In ancient Mexico and still today, chocolate is above all a drink; it is used in certain types of mole, though not in all of them. In the food of Catalonia, southern Italy, and southwestern France, chocolate is used in sauces that are served with fish, rabbit, poultry, and meat. But chocolate is also an ingredient in fine desserts across the world. Linnaeus, the famous eighteenth-century botanist who classified and gave scientific names to the world's plants, gave cacao the scientific name of *Theobroma,* meaning food of the gods. But for the inhabitants of Mesoamerica, the fruit of the cacao tree was the symbolic equivalent of the human heart and the chocolate drink made from it was the equivalent of blood.

CHOCOLATE AT ROSA MEXICANO

The books I read always stimulate my imagination, and I decided that it would be a good idea to start working on serving chocolate to my guests in a way they would not have tasted it before, in combination with chile. First I decided that the best way to get people to try such an unusual combination would be to use it in a very popular cake like the French genoise, a chocolate cake with chocolate filling and frosting. I'm not a particularly skilled pastry chef, so I turned to an expert, Michel Gilardi. My young friend could not understand what I was trying to do. We had to make the chile work as a kind of stimulant to the palate; its heat had to give tone to but not interfere with the taste of the chocolate, and it also had to blend in with the cream and all of the cake's other ingredients. We tried pasilla, ancho, and chipotle chiles, but all of them were too strongly flavored and clashed with the other ingredients. Finally I found what I needed: chile de árbol. It had just the tone and heat necessary to bring our genoise to life. The Mexican Chocolate Chile Mousse Cake is one of Rosa Mexicano's biggest hits. The touch of chile excites the mouth, while a coffee-flavored sauce contrasts with the deep darkness of the chocolate. After the variety of dishes my guests have eaten, this grand finale rounds out their meal.

PASTEL DE CHOCOLATE CON CHILE / MEXICAN CHOCOLATE CHILE MOUSSE CAKE

SERVES 12

Of all native American ingredients, chocolate, made from cacao seeds that have been ground or roasted, is the best known throughout the world; it may come as a surprise to learn that chile peppers are the most widely used. In the sixteenth century, Mexicans welcomed Europeans with a cup of chocolate spiked with chile peppers. Four hundred years later we combine them, along with other indigenous Mexican ingredients like vanilla and Kahlúa, to create a very modern dessert.

FOR THE CHOCOLATE GENOISE:

1 cup plus 3 tablespoons cake flour

⅓ cup cocoa powder

6 large eggs

1 cup sugar

2 tablespoons butter, melted and cooled

1. Preheat the oven to 375°F.
2. Grease the inside of a 9- or 10-inch cake pan with butter. Line with a parchment circle to fit the pan, brush again with butter, and dust with flour. Shake out the excess flour.
3. Measure out the ingredients. Sift the flour and cocoa into a bowl.
4. Beat the eggs and sugar in a bowl over a pot of simmering water. Whisk for 3 to 5 minutes until the mixture is warm to the touch and frothy.
5. Transfer into the bowl of a mixer. Beat with the whisk attachment for 6 to 8 minutes on high until pale yellow, thick, and almost tripled in volume.
6. Gently fold the sifted cocoa and flour into the egg mixture in three stages. Fold in the butter just to combine. Do not overmix or the mixture will deflate and loose its volume.
7. Pour into the prepared pan and place in the oven. Bake for 30 to 35 minutes until a toothpick comes out clean when tested. Remove from the oven and allow to cool on a wire rack.

8. Unmold onto a cake board and, using a serrated knife, cut the cake horizontally into 3 even layers.

FOR THE KAHLÚA SYRUP:

1/4 cup sugar
1/2 cup water
3 tablespoons Kahlúa

In a small saucepan bring the sugar and water to a boil. Cool and stir in the Kahlúa.

FOR THE CHOCOLATE CHILE MOUSSE:

2 cups heavy cream, whipped to soft peaks
1 package or 1 tablespoon gelatin
2 tablespoons cold water
2/3 cup heavy cream, boiled
9 ounces semisweet baking chocolate, finely chopped
1/4 cup sugar
approximately 1/2 teaspoon chile de árbol powder

1. Whip 2 cups heavy cream and refrigerate.
2. In a small measuring cup, sprinkle the gelatin over the water and allow to sit for 5 minutes. Set a cup in a pan of simmering water to melt the gelatin (or in a microwave for 30 seconds).
3. In a separate bowl, pour 2/3 cup hot cream over the chocolate pieces to melt. Whisk in the chile de árbol powder (see Note) and gelatin until well incorporated.
4. When cool to the touch and beginning to set, fold a cup of whipped cream into the chocolate mixture to lighten the chocolate. Fold in the rest of the cream and mix just to combine. Work quickly or the mousse will set.

Note: Toast 20 to 25 chiles de árbol according to the instructions on page 284. Remove and discard the seeds, veins, and stems. Finely grind the chiles in a spice grinder. Sift the chiles through a fine strainer to obtain a very fine powder.

FOR THE GANACHE:

1 cup heavy cream

4½ tablespoons unsalted butter, cut into small pieces

9 ounces semisweet baking chocolate, finely chopped

Bring the cream and butter to a boil. Pour the mixture over the chocolate pieces to melt. Gently stir until smooth and allow to cool until tepid. Reserve.

FILLING AND DECORATING THE CAKE:

1. Set the bottom layer of the cake on a cardboard cake round. Brush with ⅓ of the Kahlúa syrup. Spread ½ of the chocolate chile mousse on the cake.
2. Carefully place the second layer and align with the bottom layer. Repeat the procedure with the syrup and the mousse.
3. Add the final layer of the cake and brush with the remaining syrup.
4. Carefully wrap the cake in plastic wrap or foil. Freeze the cake to set. The cake at this stage can be stored for 5 days in the refrigerator or 2 months in the freezer.
5. Unwrap and place on a cake turntable or the counter. Evenly spread the top and sides of the cake with a thin layer of ganache. This is to mask the cake and even out the edges. Refrigerate to set.
6. Warm the remaining ganache in a bowl over a pot of simmering water or in the microwave. Place the masked cake on a wire rack on a larger plate or baking tray. Pour the warm ganache over the cake and spread with a spatula making sure the entire cake is covered. Refrigerate to set.
7. Serve with Salsa de Café (see page 211).

OTHER DESSERTS AT ROSA MEXICANO

Ancient and contemporary Mexicans, especially the common people, accompany their tamales with a very ancient masa-based drink: *atole.* Atole is usually a thick drink to which fruits or nuts are added. It comes in all flavors, but if it is made with chocolate, it is called *champurrado.* For a long time I wondered how to serve atole to my guests in New York. I knew they wouldn't like it hot, or thick, or want to drink it as a beverage. A moment arrived when desserts served in a soup dish and made with fresh fruits, fruit juice, and ice cream became fashionable in New York; they were called fruit soups. It occurred to me that I could make a lighter version of atole, with a puree of strawberries, served cold. I sprinkled some of my stock of dried, powdered hoja santa on top to give the dish a touch of green and a slight anise flavor. It is still on the menu. On the dessert menu at Rosa Mexicano we also have ice creams flavored with Mexican herbs, flan, and plantains filled with pineapple and coconut and flambéed with rum.

ATOLE DE FRESA / STRAWBERRY DESSERT SOUP

MAKES 6 CUPS

2 pints ripe strawberries (reserve 6 whole strawberries for garnish)
1¼ cups sugar
6 ounces masa harina
2 cups water
2 cups milk
1 stick cinnamon
4 to 5 mint leaves, dried and finely chopped, like a powder (or hoja santa powder, if available)

1. Remove the hulls from the strawberries and wash. Cut into thin slices, place in a bowl, and mix with ½ cup of the sugar. Allow to sit for 1 hour or preferably overnight. Stir occasionally. Puree strawberries in a blender and set aside.
2. Stir the masa harina into the water to dissolve; strain through a sieve. In a 2-quart saucepan, heat the masa mixture, milk, and cinnamon stick. Cook over medium heat and stir continuously with a wooden spoon. When the atole thickens after approximately 3 to 4 minutes, reduce the heat to low

and add ¾ cup of the sugar and the puree of strawberries. Continue to cook for 5 minutes, stirring continuously. Add additional milk if necessary; the atole should have a slightly thick but pourable consistency. Strain into a serving bowl.

3. Pour into cups. Serve as a dessert soup garnished with powdered mint and half a strawberry fanned out.

Note: Blackberries, prunes, or any tropical fruit can be substituted for the strawberries.

CHAMPURRADO / CHOCOLATE MASA DRINK

MAKES 6 CUPS

6 ounces masa harina
2 cups water
2 cups milk
1 cinnamon stick
¾ cup sugar
½ cup semisweet chocolate, cut into small pieces
2 ounces chocolate, shaved with a vegetable peeler

Follow step 2 of the recipe for Atole de Fresa (see page 247), with the exception of the strawberries. Rather than using the strawberry puree, stir the chocolate into the masa mixture and thin with milk or water if the mixture becomes too thick. Pour into cups and serve as a dessert soup. Garnish with chocolate shavings.

HELADO DE HOJA SANTA / HOJA SANTA ICE CREAM

MAKES ABOUT 1½ QUARTS

Hoja santa is an herb from Mexico traditionally used in savory preparations. It's hard to find, but you can look for it in Latin markets. One day I attempted to make something sweet with it and was enormously successful.

3 cups hoja santa, chopped
1½ cups heavy cream
½ cup milk
1 cup granulated sugar
8 egg yolks
¼ cup powdered sugar

1. Boil hoja santa with ½ cup of the heavy cream, the milk, and the granulated sugar for 10 to 15 minutes. Allow to cool slightly. Liquefy in the blender and strain through a fine sieve. Add the remaining 1 cup of cream and liquefy again.
2. Beat the egg yolks with the powdered sugar until mixture is thick. Cook over a double boiler on medium heat for 5 minutes.
3. Combine the hoja santa and egg yolks, put mixture in an ice cream maker, and proceed according to manufacturer's directions.

WHAT'S TO DRINK?

I always try to have a fruit drink on the menu, and also, in the classic Mexican tradition, the drink made from hibiscus flowers called *agua de jamaica.* It's difficult to know exactly how this drink–which is extremely popular in many regions of Mexico–originated; this question arises with many foods that have taken such deep roots in the traditions and habits of certain cultures that the people consider them their own. At Mexican celebrations, agua de jamaica is served, as well as another drink called *agua de chia,* which I have also served my guests. Chia was one of the basic seeds used by the Aztecs. It is an extraordinary aid to digestion because of its high fiber content. In the state of Chiapas there is a river that used to be called Chiapan (though today it is called Rió Grande de Chiapa or Grijalva). Some authors believe that Chiapas derives from chiapan (the river of chia), though, of course, the river does not carry the chia seed. What is clear is that chia seeds are grown in warm places like Veracruz, San Luis Potosí, Nayarit, Oaxaca, and, of course, Chiapas.

Aguas frescas **made with pineapple, rose hips, lemon, and whatever else you like.**

Chroniclers of ancient Mexico such as Fray Bernardino de Sahagún and Francisco Clavijero make mention of chia; they describe how the Indians made an atole with chia, and also ground the chia to a powder (which they called *pinole*) and used it to make candy. An oil extracted from chia seeds was used to make lacquer.

When chia seeds are placed in water and soaked for a short time each seed forms a small exterior layer that is slightly gelatinous, so that when it reaches the mouth it has none of the hard grittiness that would normally be associated with a seed. It's traditional to add a small quantity of chia seeds to lemonade as a special touch. At Mexican fiestas, drinks made with hibiscus flowers, chia seeds, and fruits are always present in enormous glass barrels; their color is part of the party.

AGUAS FRESCAS / FRUIT-FLAVORED WATERS

EACH RECIPE SERVES 8

■ ■ ■ TAMARIND

1½ pounds tamarind pods (available in most Latin and Caribbean markets)
2 quarts water
1½ cups bar sugar or to taste

Soak the tamarind pods overnight in water to cover. Squeeze the pulp. Strain through a very fine mesh strainer. Mix with water, sugar, and lots of ice.

■ ■ ■ JAMAICA

2 cups Jamaica (available as sorrel in West Indian markets)
2½ quarts water
1 cup bar sugar

Boil the flowers in 2 cups water until a very dark wine color, about 10 minutes. Strain and squeeze all the water into a container. Add the sugar, the rest of the water, and plenty of ice.

TEQUILA AND THE MOVIES

For years now, tequila has been so popular that even the Japanese, the Dutch, and other countries have made their own versions of it—none too successfully, I might add. When I first tasted tequila during my early years in Mexico, it was a harsh drink that stung the throat and had strongly masculine connotations, the drink of the "macho man." Recently I learned a new way of serving tequila: a green serrano chile cut in half is placed across the top of a shot glass of tequila. This is called "tequila macho."

During the first years I lived in New York, one of my favorite pastimes was going to the movies. Like many other young women, I was influenced by Bette Davis, Joan Crawford, Hedy Lamarr . . . I smoked the way they did, walked the way they did, dreamed of being like them or like the characters they played. But when it came to male characters and landscapes my best moments were spent on Forty-eighth Street, when a movie theater showed the classics of Mexican cinema. I thrilled to the images of the Mexican landscape, the clouds that crossed over mountains and plains, the figures and attitudes of actors like Pedro Armendariz, who was superb at playing big macho guys who knew how to bear the pain caused them by the love of a woman, and who played landowners or peasants with the same great dignity. I remember the beauty of the Mexican actress Dolores del Río, and I was delighted by María Félix and Jorge Negrete; but more than anything my imagination was captivated by the landscape of that unknown country. When the movie was over, an actor who was very well known in Mexico was always brought out and introduced to the audience. My mother knew them all because she interviewed them on her radio program. There, imperceptibly, my curiosity about Mexico was born.

Various generations of Mexicans and Latin Americans watched their male movie stars—and even some of the women—arriving at small-town cantinas or big-city bars and demanding tequila. Whether they were serenading a beloved woman or suffering from her disdain, the actors would drink huge quantities of tequila, directly from the bottle. There is a whole series of Mexican songs in which tequila is mentioned as a means of celebration and as a means of enduring pain, and there is a whole ritual associated with drinking tequila. It is served either in a small glass called a *caballito* (little horse), or another type of glass that is wider, but also short, called a *veladora,* or candleholder, because the same cup is used for the candles that are lit in front of saints. A little salt is placed on the back of the left hand, near the index finger, while the right hand holds half a lemon. The rules can vary; some say you drink the tequila, then lick the salt and suck on the lemon, others say the lemon and salt come first. However it's drunk, tequila is an excellent aperitif; it stimulates the appetite but is relatively neutral and very dry, and prepares the taste buds to enjoy any kind of meal, especially a Mexican one.

Tequila also stands out as an ingredient in preparing food and cocktails; its unique personality can enliven foods and drinks of various kinds, and, as with wine, each different type of tequila—*blanco* (white), *anejo* (aged), *reposado* (rested), or *joven* (young)—has its specific uses in cooking and bartending.

A BRIEF HISTORY OF TEQUILA

In every culture and at every time, man has sought out some form of alcoholic beverage. The Aztecs had their pulque, made from the fermented juice of the maguey (the indigenous name for a plant known to botanists as the agave or century plant). Under the government of the Spanish viceroys, the mestizos (of mixed Spanish and indigenous blood) and criollos (of pure Spanish blood, but born in America)—who had seen how profitable the production of pulque could be—probably tried to refine the process in order to obtain distilled drinks such as mezcal. The maguey was stripped of its leaves until there was nothing left but its heart (called the *cabeza* or *piña*), which was ground up. The juice was left to ferment, then distilled by evaporation, in other words, boiled in a clay pot until a liquid with a high alcoholic content was obtained. Mezcal was and is still made in various regions of the country.

In fact, the generic name for any beverage made from distilled maguey juice is *mezcal,* and tequila is therefore a subspecies of mezcal—a more highly distilled drink made from a particular type of maguey called "Tequilana Weber," a variety of blue agave grown primarily in the state of Jalisco. There are several interpretations of the meaning and etymology of the word *tequila.* Some say it comes from the Nahuatl words *tequitl,* meaning work, and *tlan,* place. Others say its Nahuatl name refers to the boiling of the maguey. In any case, Tequila is now the name of a town that dates back to pre-Hispanic times, inhabited by members of the Tequila tribe, which claims to have discovered how to grind up the heart of the blue agave, ferment its juice, and then distill it in a very rudimentary fashion by evaporation in a clay pot.

In 1651 the Spanish doctor Jerónimo Hernández said that rubbing tequila onto the joints was a treatment for stiffness. In 1758 José Antonio Cuervo was, by order of the corregidor, or governor, of what was then called Nueva Galicia (today Jalisco), given large tracts of land exactly where the "blue agave" grows. In 1795 José Ma Guadalupe Cuervo received the first concession for producing tequila from the King of Spain.

At first, families had the distilleries in their homes, competing among themselves for the best quality. Nowadays, with the worldwide recognition of the denomination of origin, large and small companies, most of them originally family businesses, continue to fight for a share of the national and international market with products of increasing quality, all of them made entirely of blue agave, which are sold at prices comparable to those of the most expensive whiskeys or cognacs.

TEQUILA WITH SANGRITA

In addition to salt and lemon, a swig of sangrita can be used to wash down a shot of tequila. When I was setting up the bar at Rosa Mexicano, I wanted everything related to tequila to be as authentic as possible, so I used Diana Kennedy's recipe for sangrita. In Mexico a concoction called *granadina,* supposedly made with pomegranate juice, is sold in stores, but I make fresh pomegranate juice for sangrita.

SANGRITA / TEQUILA CHASER

MAKES 1¼ QUARTS

2 cups fresh pomegranate juice
2 cups bitter orange juice (available in Caribbean markets or fine specialty stores)
½ cup freshly squeezed orange juice
½ cup freshly squeezed lemon juice
2 teaspoons salt
pinch of cayenne pepper powder

Mix all the ingredients together, strain, and chill. When cold, serve in shot glasses.

MARGARITAS

Margaritas have started to become popular in the eastern United States; they've been great favorites throughout the southern and western parts of the country for a while now and are said to have been invented by a bartender along the Mexican border. Drinking margaritas is part of the fun for tourists who go to Mexico. It's the perfect cocktail for starting a good meal, especially when it's made well. The margaritas we serve at Rosa Mexicano are made in the usual fashion. But the Rosa margaritas, which have become one of the things the restaurant is known for, happened spontaneously when it occurred to me to use the same fresh pomegranate juice we make for sangrita. Our pink margaritas are served straight from the machine that freezes them into a delicate frappé.

POMEGRANATE JUICE MARGARITAS

What distinguishes this cocktail is its pink hue and the piquancy added by the pomegranate juice.

FOR 1 MARGARITA:

2 ounces white tequila
½ ounce Triple Sec
1 ounce fresh lime juice
1 tablespoon fresh pomegranate juice
Ice

Mix all the ingredients in a blender until smooth and frothy.

CHAMPAGNE AND ENCHILADAS

Many people enjoy margaritas so much that they want to drink them with their meal. This is a mistake, I think, because margaritas are quite acidic and therefore are ideal for preparing the palate and the stomach for a meal, but not for accompanying one. Most Mexicans drink beer with meals, while others have a soft drink; the bubbles and sugars the soft drinks contain function as digestive aids. Experts have explained to me that our organism uses up a lot of energy digesting food, so that many people need something sweet after a good meal to compensate the body for the energies it has expended in the hard work of digestion. Alcoholic drinks of any kind produce sugar, that is, calories. Of course, if drinking and eating are done in moderation, they complement each other in satisfying our physical and emotional needs.

I've discovered that a good Mexican meal can begin with a margarita, but when the food is served, it goes very well with something bubbly. Champagne is an excellent companion to a mole, an adobo, rajas, enchiladas, or other specialties. Sangría, a popular wine cocktail that originated in Spain, can also be a good accompaniment to a Mexican meal. I would recommend enjoying a good tequila after the meal as a digestive.

SANGRÍA

MAKES ONE 60-OUNCE PITCHER

juice of 8 oranges (approximately 2 cups)
juice of 2 lemons
¾ cup sugar
1 x 750 ml bottle Rioja wine, such as Marqués de Cáceres/Faustino
2 to 3 ounces Grand Marnier
thin slices of orange and lemon

Stir ingredients in a pitcher, adding a small amount of ice. Serve in iced goblets with fruit slices.

A FEW LAST BITES

In my experience as a chef, I've had the opportunity to get to know several colleagues who were in love with foreign cuisines. I know some who have become impassioned with Chinese culture and are true experts in the great cuisine of that country. I've known others who were fascinated by Japanese, Indian, French, or Thai cooking. Just as I travel to Mexico, they travel to the countries that have cast a spell over them; they delve into the cultures and always explain with great passion the dishes of the various cuisines. For my part I must confess that my education about Mexican cooking never ends; every time I travel to Mexico I find something new for my eyes, my emotions, and my taste buds. As a last bite at the end of this story, I'll tell you about some of these recent experiences.

THE TORTITAS DE HABAS OF CUETZALAN

When I go to Mexico, I forget about time and distance and even whatever it is that I've gone to look for; I'm carried along only by the desire to find something, and what's interesting is that most of the time I do find something: an extraordinary landscape, a sweet little village, people who tell me a story or say something that stays in my mind as a life lesson, and, sometimes, a surprise for my mouth. I've often driven down Mexican highways with the feeling of seeking, but never with any certainty about what I would find. . . .

Cuetzalan is a small, almost hidden town in the state of Puebla. To get there, you have to go up steep slopes and along trails until you reach what is practically the peak of a mountain. The little zócalo seems more like a scenic overlook than a town square. Most of the streets you walk along are staircases, the climate is humid, and the air is a little misty; you walk through clouds that have settled on the mountaintop.

After checking into the town's "finest hotel," I spent most of my time taking pictures of this place, where the traces of many cultures persist. Ancient indigenous culture is represented in a pyramid that is architecturally very similar to El Tajín in Veracruz, but smaller. The houses, with their red-tiled roofs, seem straight out of a Spanish village. Most of the women wear wide

Cuetzalan, the mountain village where time has stopped.

white cotton skirts tied at the waist with a belt embroidered with red thread. Cuetzalan is one of those Mexican villages that stay in your mind: On this remote mountaintop, time and history have stopped.

After a while, I get hungry. The most striking characteristic of the hotel is its dampness, and I don't like the food there. I ask a passerby, who first recommends the hotel, then tells me, "If you want to eat the kind of food we eat here, go downtown; there are a lot of places there but the best is Doña Lupe's." I found a series of little spots with chairs and tables in no particular order and I asked for Señora Lupe. There were moles and several types of stewed dishes, but I wanted to taste the *tortitas de habas* (broad bean fritters)

I had seen sold in the village. I'm not exactly sure how they were made, but the softness lying under their crispy surface comes as a surprise; they're cooked on a comal and preserve the taste of the charcoal smoke. I couldn't stop eating them, and just the thought of Cuetzalan and its tortitas de habas makes my mouth water. . . .

SURPRISES IN ZACAPUAXTLA, PUEBLA

There was a period when I resisted the idea of going to Mexico. I didn't want to go back because I was afraid it would awaken memories of my son and make the wound of his loss bleed again. But I had to go in order to keep alive in my mind the flavor of Mexico, its color, and particular style. Rosa Mexicano must always have the most authentic flavors possible. When I finally did go back, I was seduced by the country all over again, and everyone was kind; going back to the old places and memories turned out to be a soothing balm. I took some time to travel around a little.

One day I was going down the Veracruz highway when a sign appeared pointing the way to Zacapuaxtla in the state of Puebla. Zacapuaxtla is the hometown of my colleague Ruperto Cantor, the head chef at Rosa Mexicano. Everything Ruperto had told me didn't begin to prepare me for what I found. The "Cumbres de Maltrata" highway, which we drove down quickly, reaches the main street of the small town. It was a sunny day and I could sense an atmosphere of happiness; the stone houses are decorated with balconies supported by wooden posts. We walked among them and I was struck by the neatness of the place, everything in perfect order and the buildings all symmetrical and roofed with red tiles. For a moment I thought I was in a Spanish village, perhaps in Asturias. Walking across the town we reached the plaza, and without looking for it we stumbled on a door with a sign that said "Carpentry Workshop." The next surprise was finding an enormous furniture factory that made extremely beautiful pieces for export to France. I noticed that all the people who were working there, and all those who were walking through the streets, had a very unusual physiognomy: they were taller and more robust than the majority of Mexicans, with light-colored hair and eyes and all the characteristics of a Celtic people. When I left that town, I had the feeling I had been in a magical place, a Mexican village that was also a memory of the Spain I once knew.

ADVENTURES IN MICHOACÁN

The state of Michoacán is in the west of the Mexican Republic and like many other places it has kept its pre-Hispanic name. Some believe its name comes from Nahuatl and means "place of the fishes." But Michoacán was primarily the kingdom of the Tarascos, and its name is more probably a derivation of the Tarasca word *michmacuan,* which means "to be close to the water." The names of the towns are striking, too; there is one called Tzintzuntzán, where beautiful ceramic handicrafts are made that have a very particular beige color and are always decorated with images of fishing. In another spot named Paracho, the best guitars in Mexico are made. In some regions of Michoacán all types of fruits and vegetables are cultivated.

When I first went to Mexico, the best restaurants all served a fish called *blanco de Pátzcuaro* or Pátzcuaro whitefish, one of the delicacies for which Michoacán's Lake Pátzcuaro was famous. The image of fishermen in long wooden canoes on that lake with their nets unfolded like the wings of butterflies was famous throughout the world. In the center of the lake is a tiny island called Janitzio, and that image made it so famous and so valued by Mexicans that one day they decided to import a new kind of fish into the lake to save it from a plague of water lilies. The new species was unable to get rid of the water lilies but did manage to almost exterminate the "Pátzcuaro whitefish."

In Michoacán there are many delicious things to eat, from enchiladas made with dried chile to a broth called *caldo michi,* made with fish freshly caught from the lake. It was traditionally prepared on country outings to the lakeside; the freshly caught fish was cooked in a chile broth along with a variety of vegetables. *Uchepos, pollo de plaza,* and *corundas* are typical of the region. In Michoacán and throughout Mexico, the influence of other countries is always present in the cooking, the architecture, and even in the names of certain towns. For example, there is a town in Michoacán called Nueva Italia (New Italy). The last time I visited Morelia,

Michoacán's capital—in addition to being dazzled by the beautiful city, which was the site of the first university in the Americas, and whose parks and little plazas with a severe and at times Franciscan look reminded me of Florence—I learned of an interesting way to discover the local cuisine. After 6:00 P.M., the priests of the parish of La Inmaculada have arranged for the best local dishes and antojitos to be sold in front of the church. They choose vendors who offer not only good taste and quality but also good hygiene. The vendors set up their traditional carts or their buckets of tamales around the steps leading to the front porch of the church. The diners sit on the porch, on folding chairs and tables that have been put there for them. Inexpensive books of tickets are used to pay the food vendors. People go from cart to cart, choosing their meals, and a group of young men is in charge of bringing soft drinks or aguas frescas to the tables. It struck me as an excellent way to allow visitors and residents of the city alike to have access to the best of the local cooking.

VILLAHERMOSA, TABASCO

While I lived in Mexico, I traveled on its highways and visited various places that caught my imagination, but since I spent most of my time working and taking care of my sons and doing all the other things that force us to mark off a limited territory in which to spend our daily life I didn't venture out over great distances. Tabasco is a state far to the south of Mexico City that shares a border with Guatemala. It is a very hot, jungly place. Tabasco has two meanings in Nahuatl: "flooded land" and "place that has a master." More than anything, it's a very wet place. My last visit to Villahermosa, the capital, was very short, but I was able to visit its spectacular park, which conserves many endangered species of animals. I couldn't stop admiring the beautiful jaguars with such soft, smooth fur that you long to run your hands through it. Just walking through the park's gardens can take almost an entire day, if you can stand the heat.

But I was in Tabasco for gastronomical reasons. I went straight to a restaurant on the banks of the Grijalva River, and was quickly served a plate of *piguas*—freshly boiled, without any seasoning. Piguas are a kind of langous-

A very lively *pigua* stares at the camera in the marketplace at Villahermosa, in Tabasco.

tine cultivated in the shallows of the Grijalva. I love the white, firm, and juicy flesh, which has a slight sweetness and saltiness at the same time; each mouthful better than the last, as if an aquatic god had gone to great effort to please our taste buds.

In the Villahermosa market, I saw the favorite fish of the Tabasqueños, called the *pejelagarto* (lizardfish) because it has the head of a lizard and a fish's body. It's sold with a stick in its mouth to hold it by when it is grilled. But all the other fish in the fish section of the market were practically still alive and frolicking. And there were the beautiful, live piguas, which seemed to go straight to the camera when I photographed them.

During that same visit, I also tried salt beef with chaya; how much I wish I could serve my guests that delicious herb from southeastern Mexico! I serve one of Tabasco's regional specialties in Rosa Mexicano: stuffed plantains. With a special tool designed for coring apples, I take out the seeds of the plantain and stuff it with picadillo. Then the plantains are lightly fried and served with tomato sauce.

CIUDAD DEL CARMEN

Driving along the coast of Villahermosa toward Campeche, I reached Ciudad del Carmen. It isn't exactly a tourist destination, though it offers a lot to those who are interested in history and anthropology. It is currently the port from which workers embark for the oil platforms in the Gulf of Mexico. On the road from there to Campeche, in the port of Champotón, I tasted some miniature shrimp that were about the size of a thumbnail. I felt a bit guilty about eating them because they were sold to me with the warning that it's practically against the law. They are truly a gastronomical curiosity because you wonder how they can possibly be cleaned, tiny as they are. To clean them, the cook takes a bunch of them in the palm of one hand and rubs with the other hand until the shells come off. You can eat up to a dozen of these shrimp in a single mouthful, and their flavor is very delicate.

THE GREATNESS OF CAMPECHE

Perhaps it happens in many places in the world, but in Campeche I found a place where every nook and cranny had a story to tell. The name of this walled city overlooking the sea means "land of snakes and ticks" in Maya and it is located on the Yucatán peninsula. During the sixteenth, seventeenth, and eighteenth centuries, Campeche was a Spanish fortress under constant attack by English, Dutch, and French pirates, including the famous Sir Francis Drake, who all wanted to loot the gold that was stored there before it was shipped to Spain. The Spaniards built walls and bulwarks to defend it, some of which are now museums. When I went to Campeche, the city had just undergone major renovations; even the original colors of its big old houses

The beautiful and tasty wings of the manta ray, on display in the Campeche marketplace.

These groupers emerged from the sea around Campeche.

have been restored, and it is very pleasant to walk along its streets, where my eyes fell on something beautiful at every step.

Seafood is definitely the thing to eat in Campeche. On a huge platter, langoustines, crabs, and an enormous variety of shrimps, small and large, are arrayed in perfect rows. Campechanos boast that their gastronomy is even finer than that of Yucatán. The delicacy of a fish pâté in a restaurant called La Pigua was a revelation, and the joyful nature of the Campechano people was a delight. But my favorite experience was the visit to the marketplace. As in Tabasco, you're surprised to see the fish and shellfish wriggling on the cement counters of the fish shops. There are never more than a few of them there at a time, and when I asked why they don't put them on ice and why they have so few, the answer was stunning: "They're so fresh they don't need ice, and we have so few because when these have been sold we just go get some more from the ocean, which is right over there." They also sell the legs of a kind of crab called *cangrejo moro,* already cooked; the flesh is slightly sweeter than that of ordinary crab, and only the legs of this particular species are eaten. Something I had never seen before were the manta rays, enormous, fan-shaped pieces of meat, similar to skate. "How is that eaten?" I asked. "It's stewed, just like codfish," was the answer.

From Zacatecas to Jérez: some delicious chorizo *tortas de Malpaso.*

When I returned to the city I kept asking about manta ray and finally I was able to taste it in black butter with capers. Real skill is required to fillet the manta ray; it looks like a fan because of the regular grooves that are left in the flesh once the bones are removed. First, chop up a good quantity of capers, then melt a generous amount of butter in a frying pan until it begins to change color, place the manta ray in the butter and cook it over low heat for a few minutes, then turn it over and add the capers. Cover the frying pan, and in a few more minutes the butter will be black, the capers almost invisible, and the fish ready to eat. The aroma of the capers was a real surprise combined with the softness of the fish and the crust of butter; all you need is a bit of bread with it, to leave the plate shining clean. This recipe is basically French, but I improve and Mexicanize it by adding very finely chopped Serrano chiles.

ZACATECAS TO THE NORTH

The north of Mexico begins with Zacatecas, a city whose atmosphere took me back in time because the shape of its streets made me think of Spain. Peaceful and well kept, this small city has become popular with tourists. It was built over the shafts of what were once rich gold and silver mines, and the streets are connected by stair-stepped alleyways. One of the convents houses an enormous collection of masks from all over Mexico which are used in carnivals or celebrations of historic events.

From a culinary point of view, Zacatecas was the place where I finally made my peace with cumin. For a long time, I had an aversion to that spice; it is used in "Southwestern" restaurants to such an exaggerated degree that I refused to include it in our dishes at Rosa Mexicano. Cumin is used in the food of central and southern Mexico, but in almost imperceptible quantities. In Zacatecas, I enjoyed the way cumin was used, in stewed beans, for example, in such moderation that it was a pleasure to taste. I started using cumin again after my visit there.

MEXICO CITY AND ITS HISTORIC CENTER

Mexico City can startle even the most seasoned traveler nowadays, especially in the downtown streets that are, with good reason, called the historic center. You seem to be moving through a world that has already passed into history, yet remains completely alive.

I've always regretted the fact that Mexicans don't promote their cultural events in the United States; they don't let North Americans who are interested know about the fascinating exhibits taking place in Mexico—collections of furniture, paintings, and the decorative arts of sixteenth-, seventeenth-, and eighteenth-century Mexico. It seems a pity to me that Mexicans don't do more to promote their treasures from every era. Despite all the ransacking and looting to which it has been subjected, Mexico has extraordinary pieces from pre-Hispanic times, the colonial era, and all the other periods that left their traces on the city, at once so old and so young.

In the renovated historic center, in an elegant mansion from the beginning of the twentieth century, is a restaurant called El Cardenal, where my conviction of the interest Mexicans have in their food was reaffirmed. Without wanting to, I overheard the conversation of a group of four casually dressed gentlemen who were talking about business. When the waiter came to ask for their order, their attitude and their conversation changed completely. They concentrated on the dishes listed in the menu, and asked about the quantities of chile and the herbs and spices used in a way that showed they were familiar with the recipes. When the waiter left, they went back to their business discussion but, when their food arrived, their talk centered on it once more. I was glad to observe this particular scene because I felt that as long as there are Mexicans who are interested in eating well, Mexican cuisine will continue to develop and its borders will widen to include the whole world.

WITH THIS ONE, I'LL SAY GOOD-BYE . . .

At fiestas, popular restaurants, local hangouts, bars, and cantinas throughout Mexico, there are often trios of singers who stroll the room, offering to sing whatever the merrymakers gathered for the evening would like to hear. If the atmosphere is congenial and the drinks are flowing, the singers generally run through a very wide repertory, and everyone sings along for hours on end until someone says, "Y con esta me despido!"—"With this one, I'll say good-bye." And with that the fiesta or the night on the town comes to an end. This happens in the kind of places where a wide mix of people go, to eat, yes, but mainly to have fun drinking and singing. In my restaurant, I've steered clear of this type of atmosphere because my primary interest is in having my guests enjoy fine traditional Mexican cuisine. For me, it has become a continual battle against the myths that surround Mexico, its culture, its culinary traditions, and everything Hispanic in general.

I'm saddened and surprised by the way historians of gastronomy almost never take Mexico's contributions into account. They also forget that we can't speak of a great international cuisine without remembering that both the European and the American culinary traditions were mutually enriched by their contact with each other, and the fusion of their flavors and ingredients.

My beloved guests, after having regaled themselves on oysters, pompano, trout, rack of lamb, quail, pheasant, rabbit, or duck, often come over and ask me if such things exist in Mexico. Yes, all those things exist in Mexico, and in my restaurant they are cooked in a Mexican way and with Mexican flavors that I reproduce. In Mexico City's Anthropology Museum I learned that the Muscovy duck is native to Lake Texcoco, on whose banks one of the country's many indigenous cultures flourished.

I sometimes think it may have been Hollywood movies that presented Mexico in such a negative light and that have given so many people such a horrible image of it. Or perhaps it's simply human nature that there will always be problems between neighboring countries. But it is my conviction and faith that there is nothing that brings us together better, as individuals, than a good meal. I devote my days and my energy to giving people that opportunity.

My battle to offer the best in Mexican food goes on, even though it breaks my heart that those who criticize Mexico do so without understanding it and sometimes without even being acquainted with it. But I can't finish this book without thanking each and every one of the men and women who fill Rosa Mexicano night after night, every day of the year—thank you, thank you, a thousand times thank you.

The End

A BRIEF DICTIONARY OF CHILES

BY ARTURO LOMELI

Most chiles are known in the United States by their Spanish names. The translations that sometimes appear in parentheses in this list are there only to give an idea of the literal meanings of chile names, which are often quite delightful. For example, one variety is known in this country as a cascabel chile; cascabel *means bell, and when you shake this small, round chile you can hear its seeds rattling inside.*

Chiles vary in flavor and appearance according to the places they grow, and often local growers or vendors give names of their own to their chiles. It is therefore sometimes very difficult to know exactly what kind of chile you have before you. We hope that this dictionary, with its accompanying photographs, will be of some help in identifying them.

ANAHEIM CHILE

ANAHEIM A variety of chile grown and consumed on a mass scale in California. It is large, green or red, relatively hot, and used in many different ways, particularly in such dishes as chiles rellenos.

ANCHO CHILES

ANCHO (WIDE CHILE) A dried chile, called poblano when it is fresh and green. Numerous varieties and subvarieties are known in various states of Mexico, especially in the central and southeastern regions. Dark red, usually not very hot and a little sweet, it is a culinary classic used across Mexico, an indispensable ingredient in many kinds of adobos and moles.

ANCHO ESMERALDA A type of ancho chile.

ANCHO FLOR DE PABELLÓN A type of ancho chile.

ANCHO VERDEÑO A type of ancho chile.

CHINO (CHINESE CHILE) A variety of ancho chile; when fresh it is a poblano and when dry it is very dark red, almost black. Its skin is more wrinkled than the common ancho. It is sold in the markets of central Mexico: San Luis Potosí, Zacatecas, Guanajuato, and Aguascalientes. Significantly hotter than the ancho chile, it is used to make hotter versions of dishes, moles, or sauces that usually call for ancho chiles.

MORELIA A dried chile, a variety of ancho chile (which is called poblano when it is fresh), but slightly darker in color. Its flavor is also slightly different from the ancho's, more aromatic and a bit less sweet. It is grown only in the city of Queréndaro in the state of Michoacán. The culinary specialties of Michoacán, such as enchiladas or pollo de la plaza, must be made entirely with Morelia chiles. They are also used for chiles rellenos, sauces, and adobos. They are in season only during the months of July and August.

MULATO ROQUE Variety of ancho chile.

SAN LUIS A type of dried ancho chile, grown in San Luis Potosí.

ÁRBOL, CHILES DE

CHILE DE ÁRBOL (TREE CHILE) Grows on a shrub belonging to the same species as the piquín; it resembles the serrano, though a bit wider and generally hotter. When dried it turns brownish red. It is very hot, and in dried form is often used to make a sauce with fried garlic. Many salsas de molcajete are also prepared with this chile.

AJÍ AMARILLO or **CUSQUEÑO (YELLOW** or **CUZCO CHILE)** Grown primarily in Peru and Brazil and almost unknown in Mexico. Similar to a chile de árbol, it can be yellow or green. It is the most popular chile in Peru, where it is used in such classic dishes as ceviche caucán, cuye chactado, and anticuchos. As hot as the habanero.

BRAVO Name often used for dried chile de árbol, or for piquín.

COLA DE RATA (RATTAIL CHILE) A variety of chile de árbol.

PUCA-UCHU Grown primarily in Peru, Bolivia, and Central America, where it is very popular. In Peru, especially, it is used for a variety of salsas, in particular ají molido and salsa de ají. It is green, lemon-yellow, and red, and somewhat resembles the Mexican chile de árbol.

PUYA A chile de árbol, though generally a little longer. Found primarily in the state of San Luis Potosí.

YAHUALICA DE ÁRBOL A dried chile, a variety of the chile de árbol which is native to Yahualica.

BOLA OR BOLITA CHILES

BOLA or **BOLITA (BALL** or **LITTLE-BALL CHILE)** An oval chile, eaten fresh. About 1 inch long and 2/3 inch wide. Dark red and very hot, it is grown in the Mexican cities of San Luis Potosí, Coahuila, and Durango.

BOLUDO A fresh chile, round and very similar to the bolita, but larger. Dark red and very hot. Grown in the Mexican cities of Durango and San Luis Potosí.

CASCABEL (BELL CHILE) A dried chile. When fresh, it can be a bolita, dark red and very hot. A classic chile, it is used primarily in sauces, stews, and adobos.

CEREZA (CHERRY CHILE) A variety of the bola or the cascabel chile. Outside Mexico, it is used more as an ornamental plant than as a food.

COBÁN The name used in Guatemala for the cascabel chile.

FRESNO So named because it is grown in Fresno, California. A variety of cascabel.

CATARINA CHILE

CATARINA or **CATARINITA (CATHERINE** or **LITTLE CATHERINE CHILE)** A dried chile with an elongated form, green when fresh and reddish brown when dried. Hot. Originally grown in Aguascalientes, it is used for sauces and adobos.

CHIPOTLE AND MORITA CHILES

CHIPOTLE A dried chile, light or dark sepia. In fact, this is the well-known jalapeño, in smoked form. It is very hot and aromatic, and was used by the Aztecs. Today, it is pickled or used in adobos and in many salsas; it can even be stuffed with cheese to make chiles rellenos.

CHILAILE A dried chile, elongated, oval and reddish brown. Grown in Veracruz and México states. It is also called a mora or morita and is a type of small jalapeño.

HUAUCHINANGO Name used in Oaxaca for chipotle chile.

MECO A dried chile which, strictly speaking, isn't a chipotle, because it isn't smoked. It is a dried, unsmoked jalapeño chile, light brown, hot, and used for salsas, adobos, and pickling.

MORITA, MORA, or **MORA ROJA** A dried chile, slightly oval in shape, with a reddish stem, also sometimes called chilaile. Like a kind of small chipotle, with wrinkled skin, very hot, somewhat aromatic. Used for a variety of sauces and adobos. When fresh, it is a small jalapeño.

VERACRUZ A dried chile, it is a chipotle that has not been smoked, that is, a slightly larger type of jalapeño. Light brown in color, hot and aromatic.

CHIPOTLE NAVIDEÑO

CHIPOTLE NAVIDEÑO or **PASILLA DE OAXACA (CHRISTMAS CHIPOTLE)** A dried chile from Oaxaca, dark reddish sepia, which, when fresh, resembles a small poblano. It is prized for its delicate flavor and is also used for chiles rellenos.

CRIOLLO Name used for several varieties that were developed as hybrids; this chile is similar to the chiltepín or the piquín, though larger, and is also known as the uvilla grande. It is very hot and is also used as an ornamental plant.

UVILLA GRANDE (BIG GRAPE CHILE) Another name for the criollo chile.

COSTEÑO CHILE

COSTEÑO (COASTAL CHILE) A dried chile, red, larger than the chile de árbol. It is primarily grown in Oaxaca, Veracruz, and along Mexico's Costa Chica.

GUAJILLO CHILES

GUAJILLO, GUAJÍO (LITTLE-GOURD CHILE) A dried chile, related to the pasilla though quite different from it, 2 to 4 inches in length and reddish sepia in color. It comes in many different sizes and widths. Generally, the smaller ones are hotter and the larger ones have almost no heat at all and are used primarily to add flavor and color. The differences among the various types of guajillo are due to the different places they are grown. They are cultivated across Mexico. When fresh, they can be green, yellow, or red. A classic ingredient in many Mexican dishes.

AMARILLO, CHICOSTLE A dried chile similar to a small guajillo but lighter in color. Grown in Oaxaca and used in the cuisine of that region.

CALORO Name by which güero chiles are known in San Luis Potosí and a few states in central Mexico. It is conical in shape, and about 2 inches long; its lime-green color turns red as it ripens. When dried, it is a variety of guajillo. Quite hot.

CHILHUACLE A dried chile, probably the chile de agua when fresh. Dark sepia, almost black, and medium hot. A classic chile in the cuisine of Oaxaca, it is, among other things, an indispensable ingredient in mole negro. Actually a variety of guajillo.

MIRASOL A fresh, oval-shaped chile, spicy, grown in Jalisco. It is a variety of guajillo, also called puya. It gets its name from the fact that the plant it grows on always turns toward the sun.

SAN FELIPE A variety of guajillo, small in size, hot, dark brown.

TRAVIESO (MISCHIEVOUS CHILE) A variety of guajillo, given its name because of its scalding hotness.

GÜERO CHILES

GÜERO (LIGHT-SKINNED CHILE) Name used for a variety of fresh chiles, usually cone-shaped and fleshy, lemon-yellow or sometimes lime-green, that, when ripe, become a reddish orange. They are grown in various states of Mexico, especially in Veracruz and the southeast and central regions. Some varieties are hot and others are mild; some are quite aromatic. Used in regional dishes or pickled. When large, they are also used for chiles rellenos.

CALORO Name by which güero chiles are known in San Luis Potosí and a few states in central Mexico. The caloro chile is conical in shape, and about 2 inches long; its lime-green color turns red as it ripens. When dried, it is a variety of guajillo. Quite hot.

CARIBE (CARIBBEAN CHILE) A fresh chile, cone-shaped and about 1½ to 2 inches in length. Normally yellow or lime-green, it tends to turn orange as it ripens. Hot and slightly aromatic. It is a variety of güero chile, usually pickled or used in salsas. It is grown in Aguascalientes and other parts of northern Mexico.

CRISTALINO or **CRISTAL (CRYSTAL CHILE)** Fresh chile a little smaller than the poblano, also called caloro and güero.

FLORAL A yellow chile similar to the Hungarian or caloro chile, grown in the southern United States.

HÚNGARO (HUNGARIAN CHILE) Name used in San Luis Potosí and other Mexican states for the chile also known as caloro, which is a variety of güero.

IXCATIC A type of güero chile, yellow-green in color. Grown in southeastern Mexico and Chiapas.

SANTA FE GRANDE A variety of caribe or güero chile grown in the southern United States.

TROMPITA (LITTLE-NOSE CHILE) A variety of güero chile, but spherical in shape, and green or lemon-yellow in color. It resembles certain Italian pepperonis. As it ripens it becomes red, and when dried it could be a cascabel. Pleasantly hot and mildly aromatic, it is grown in the states of central and northwestern Mexico and in San Luis Potosí.

HABANERO CHILES

HABANERO, HABAÑERO (HAVANA CHILE) A fresh chile which, despite its name, originated in Yucatán and southeastern Mexico. It is pear-shaped, about 1 inch long and ½ inch wide. It is green or lemon-yellow and turns orange when it ripens. Habanero chiles are the great passion of anyone who likes hot food because they are undoubtedly the hottest variety of chile known. Their characteristic flavor is unmistakable. They are finely chopped or cut into very thin strips, then mixed with a little lemon juice and salt to become the obligatory condiment for the cooking of southeastern Mexico. They are very hot and aromatic and are rarely used in stews because cooking them would destroy their flavor. Botanists call them Chinese capsicum.

CHINCHI-UCHU Could be considered the cousin of the Mexican habanero. Grown in Peru and Bolivia, it also resembles the manzano chile or a small tomato. It is used to make *sanchocado,* a kind of stew, and its flavor is said to be exquisite.

JALAPEÑO CHILES

JALAPEÑO (JALAPA CHILE) Fresh and very fleshy chile from 1½ to 2½ inches long; it is dark green in color, or red when it has ripened. Hot and slightly aromatic. When dried it turns a sepia color, and when dried and smoked it becomes the famous chipotle. It is generally pickled, either whole or in strips. It is indispensable for making chiles en vinagre with onion, garlic, carrots, and flavorful herbs. It can also be used for chiles rellenos.

CUARESMEÑO (LENT CHILE) Another name for jalapeño.

ESPINALTECO or **PINALTECO** Another name for jalapeño.

JAROCHO A smaller variety of jalapeño.

PAPALOAPÁN A variety of jalapeño.

PELUDO (SHAGGY CHILE) A variety of small jalapeño.

RAYADA A variety of jalapeño, frequently used to make chipotle.

LARGO CHILES

LARGO (LONG CHILE) Fresh chile, lemon-yellow or lime-green in color, very narrow and up to 4½ inches long. It is usually pickled and served as a characteristic garnish for various fishes and codfish a la mexicana. It has little flesh and is only moderately hot.

CARRICILLO A largo or güero chile.

LOCO (CRAZY CHILE) Name used for any variety resulting from a mutation, graft, or some kind of hybridization. For example, in San Martín Texmelucán, in the state of Puebla, chilacas are sometimes found that are shorter than usual and somewhat deformed, with strange wrinkles in their skin and a much hotter taste.

TONALCHILLI See *carricillo* (above).

MANZANO CHILES

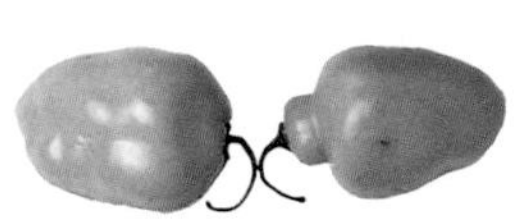

MANZANO Fresh chile, spherical in shape, which resembles an apple and can have a diameter of up to 1½ inches. It is very fleshy and spicy, with attractive, glossy colors (green, yellow, orange, and red). Generally eaten in a salsa with onion and various other condiments. The seeds, which are black, are always discarded.

CABALLO (HORSE CHILE) A type of ricoto or manzano.

CANARIO (CANARY CHILE) A type of ricoto or manzano.

CHAMBURATO A type of ricoto or manzano.

GRINGO or **HUANUCHI** A type of ricoto or manzano.

LADINO See manzano or ricoto.

PERÓN Name for rocoto or manzano chiles in the Mexican state of Chiapas.

PETENERO (PETÉN CHILE) Name for ricoto or manzano chile in Honduras.

RICOTO or **ROCOTO** A spherical green or yellow chile, a bit like the trompa chile. Grown in the Mexican states of Pátzcuaro and Michoacán. Also called caballo, garrapato, canario (in Oaxaca), jalapeño, or perón (in Chiapas). Some also call it manzano. In Peru they call it raise-the-dead or gringo huanuchi because "it kills the gringo." Clearly a very hot chile.

ROCOTILLO A smallish chile, very irregular in shape, found primarily in Costa Rica and Texas. In Peru it is known as rosas-uchu because its irregular form looks like a flower. In Mexico it is boiled with beans, grilled with meat, or used as an ingredient in salads.

MULATO CHILES

MULATO (MULATTO CHILE) A dried chile (when fresh, it is a type of poblano). Almost black and quite hot, though not very penetrating and slightly sweet, it differs from the ancho chile in that it is darker in color and less aromatic. A classic ingredient in many Mexican dishes.

CHOCOLATE, CHILE DE (CHOCOLATE CHILE) A variety of dark or mulato chile grown in Tesquincla, Chiapas.

SAN MARTÍN A dried chile, a variety of mulato, generally large and dark. Used in all kinds of adobos, salsas, and chiles rellenos.

PASILLA CHILES

PASILLA A dry chile, very dark and long; it is known as chilaca when fresh. It is very hot, and many different varieties are known (it can also be called achocolatado). The essential ingredient in salsa borracha and in numerous moles and adobos.

ACHOCOLATADO ("CHOCOLATED" CHILE) Another term for pasilla chile.

NEGRO Name used for pasilla chile on the coast of Baja California.

PIQUÍN CHILES

PIQUÍN, CHILTEPÍN, or **PULGA** This is the smallest of the chiles, and its many varieties are grown across Mexico and throughout the world. When fresh it is a green that turns red as it ripens. When dried, it is reddish brown. Undoubtedly one of the hottest chiles. When fresh, it is slightly aromatic. Fresh or dried, it is used for a multitude of salsas, among them the famous Tabasco; ground into a powder, it is a condiment used across the globe.

AMASH A variety of the piquín chile of Tabasco; the Tabasco chile, grown in Louisiana for the famous Tabasco sauce, undoubtedly originated from this variety.

AMOMO A piquín chile.

BRAVO Name often used for dried chile de árbol, or for piquín.

CHILILLO (LITTLE CHILE) A variety of piquín found in Yucatán. In the Valley of Mexico, the same name is used for a grassy plant whose leaves have a spicy taste.

CHILTEPÍN, CHILTIPÍN, CHILTEPIQUÍN Other names for piquín.

DIENTE DE TLACOACHE (TLACOACHE'S-TOOTH CHILE) Name for piquín chile in Tamaulipas.

ENANO (DWARF CHILE) A piquín chile.

GACHUPÍN Name for piquín chile in Veracruz.

GUINDILLA Name for piquín chile in Spain.

MONTE, CHILE DE (MOUNTAIN CHILE) Name for a variety of piquín in Yucatán and parts of northern Mexico.

MOSQUITO A piquín chile.

ONZA (OUNCE CHILE) Small and reddish, a larger variety of piquín or of dried serrano chile.

PERRO, CHILE DE (DOG'S CHILE) A piquín chile.

PILIENTO A piquín chile.

PULGA (FLEA CHILE) A piquín chile.

QUIMICHE Name used in Oaxaca for a variety of piquín chile.

SIETE CALDOS (SEVEN-BROTHS CHILE) A variety of piquín chile from the region of Soconuco, Chiapas; undoubtedly given its name because it is the indispensable seasoning in broths, pozoles, and menudo.

TABASCO A variety of piquín which owes its name to Mr. McIlhenny, who invented the famous Tabasco sauce, of which these chiles are the principal ingredient. They are grown in Louisiana.

TICHUSNI Name for piquín chile in Oaxaca.

POBLANO CHILES

POBLANO (PUEBLA CHILE) A long, thick, fresh chile. When dried it is called ancho, mulato, or chino. Poblanos come in a great diversity of sizes, and can be anywhere from 1½ to 6 inches long. They are dark green, sometimes almost black. Some varieties are very hot and others are almost sweet. The pimiento or sweet pepper must have evolved from this variety. The hotter ones are said to be recognizable because their stem is more twisted and they are lighter in color, though in fact there is no real way to tell. They are made into many different types of chiles rellenos, and are also served as rajas in many different ways. A classic chile, eaten everywhere in Mexico.

AGUA, CHILE DE (WATER CHILE) More or less cone-shaped, with a form similar to a small poblano, though this chile is lime-green. Used mainly in Oaxaca, for salsas and stews.

CAPÓN A poblano chile made into a chile relleno or stuffed chile. Capón means castrated; the name derives from the fact that the chile's veins are removed.

CHORRO A poblano chile.

ESMERALDA A variety of poblano chile.

JOTO Name used in Aguascalientes for poblano chile; "joto" is a pejorative term for homosexual.

MIAHUATECO A poblano chile.

PASILLA VERDE Name used in Colima, Mexico, for a variety of poblano.

VALENCIANO (VALENCIA CHILE) Fresh chile, similar in shape to the poblano; it is wide, cylindrical, and red. Grown in the United States and in San Luis Potosí.

VERDEÑO A variety of poblano chile, somewhat lighter green in color.

RICOTO OR ROCOTO CHILES

RICOTO or **ROCOTO** A spherical green or yellow chile, a bit like the trompa chile. Grown in the Mexican states of Pátzcuaro and Michoacán. Also called caballo, garrapato, canario (in Oaxaca), jalapeño, or perón (in Chiapas). Some also call it manzano. In Peru they call it raise-the-dead: clearly a very hot chile.

SERRANO CHILES

SERRANO (MOUNTAIN CHILE) A fresh chile, intensely green, 1 to 2 inches long, and fleshy, which turns red as it ripens. It is also sold dried, when its color is reddish brown. In both cases it is generally very hot, though in recent years consumers have frequently complained that they're not as hot anymore. This is undoubtedly due to the fact that the serrano is one of the varieties in greatest demand, and it is therefore harvested too quickly, which prevents it from ripening sufficiently. It is used to give flavor and heat to many Mexican dishes and is of course the indispensable ingredient in salsa verde and salsa a la mexicana. It is also pickled. The serrano and the jalapeño are the two varieties most commonly available in cans.

ALTAMIRA A variety of serrano chile.

COTAXTLA A variety of serrano chile.

CUAUHTÉMOC A variety of serrano chile, named after the last ruler of the Aztec empire.

PANUCO A variety of serrano chile.

PICO DE PÁJARO (BIRD'S-BEAK CHILE) Similar to a dry serrano chile, colored an almost orange-red, and very hot, it is used in salsas and adobos.

TAMPIQUEÑO (TAMPICA CHILE) A variety of serrano chile.

VERDE (GREEN CHILE) Another name for serrano.

OTHER CHILES

BANANA A yellow, somewhat sweet chile, quite hot, also called Hungarian chile. Grown in the United States.

BELL PEPPER Also a kind of chile, though not usually thought of as one in the United States; known as pimiento in Mexico.

CAYENNE This was a name used for many chiles which the conquistadors thought were a type of pepper. Today, the name is used for a long and very hot variety that would otherwise be called chile de árbol, guajillo, or mirasol. Many varieties of cayenne are used across the world, almost always to make the powdered chile known as cayenne or red pepper.

CHILACA A name that designates several varieties, in both central and northern Mexico. The varieties known as chilaca in central Mexico can be up to 7 inches long and are dark green, like the poblano. They are medium-hot. When dried, they become the famous pasilla chile. In northern Mexico, they are shorter and broader, lime-green in color, and not very hot; when dried they are similar to a large guajillo and are used more to give color to dishes than as a spice.

CHILCOXLE Dried chile from Oaxaca, light sepia in color. Used in Oaxacan cuisine. Very hot.

CHILE SEEDS Dried chile seeds are often used to make dishes even hotter. They are toasted, then ground up before being added. Other people use them as birdseed, since the birds particularly like them.

CHILE VEINS Dried chile veins are used to improve the flavor of salsas, adobos, or moles, or to make them hotter. The veins are lightly toasted, then ground up with the rest of the ingredients.

CUBANELLA A sweet chile, like Hungarian chile, it is prized by Italians and Slavs, and is used in making pepperonata.

NUEVO (NEW CHILE) Name for the most recently harvested dried chiles, of any variety.

PEPPERONCINI A fresh chile, green or lemon-yellow, and relatively sweet. Frequently used in Italy in salads and with pickled vegetables.

PETER or **PENIS** A relatively uncommon variety grown primarily in Texas and named for its resemblance to the male sex organ. There are red and yellow varieties, and it is medium-hot.

PICO DE PALOMA (DOVE'S-BEAK CHILE) A fresh chile, conical in shape, 1 to 1½ inches long and ¾ inch in diameter. Dark red, and hot, it is used almost exclusively in the state of Chiapas.

PIMIENTOS, MORRONES, SWEET PEPPERS, or **BELL PEPPERS** Large fresh chiles with glossy skin that are green, red, or yellow in color. Though originally from Mexico, like all chiles, these varieties were taken to Spain and cultivated there; they were initially used as ornamental plants in the region of Castile because of their vivid colors. They are dried and powdered to make what is called *pimentón* in Spain and paprika in Hungary. These sweet "peppers" are the best-known type of chile in Europe. They are rarely used in Mexican cuisine, though Mexican chefs do sometimes add them to international dishes, such as paellas or stuffed peppers, or use them as a decorative garnish. They can be grilled, made into rajas, or canned in brine.

TOMATO A variety of sweet pepper, not at all hot.

TZINCUAYO A long, dry, reddish chile from Michoacán.

A FEW COOKING TIPS

CHOPPING CHILES For all recipes requiring raw jalapeño, serrano, or poblano chiles, the finer they are minced the more evenly the heat will be distributed throughout the recipe.

ROASTING CHILES Fresh chiles (poblanos and jalapeños): Roast chiles in an open flame and rotate with tongs to char the entire surface of the chile. Place the charred chile in a bowl and cover with plastic wrap. Allow to steam for 10 to 15 minutes. Remove the blackened skin by placing the chile under running water. Remove the veins and the seeds.

TOASTING CHILES Dried chiles (pasilla, guajillo, and cascabel): Heat a comal, a cast-iron skillet, or a heavy-duty sauté pan. Toast the chiles in the hot/dry pan and turn with tongs to toast evenly. Allow to cool, remove seeds and veins.

CHIPOTLE PASTE Blend the contents of 1 can of chipotle to make a paste. This paste is used for *tingas de poblana* and can be used to flavor soups or sauces. It stores well in a sealed container in the refrigerator for up to 1 month.

TOMATOES Medium or large vine-ripened tomatoes are available throughout the year and are preferred in all the recipes in this book.

ROASTING TOMATOES Roast tomatoes over an open flame to blacken the skin. Turn with tongs to char the entire tomato. Allow to cool slightly. Remove the blackened skin, cut the tomato in half and remove the seeds.

INDEX

*Page numbers in **bold** type refer to recipes.*